CONNECTED CAUSES

HF
5415
W957
2011

Also available from Lyceum Books, Inc.

Advisory Editor: Thomas M. Meenaghan, *New York University*

Strategic Leadership and Management in Nonprofit Organizations: Theory and Practice
by Martha Golensky

Improving Performance in Service Organizations: How to Implement a Lean Transformation
by Joyce A. Miller, Tatiana Bogatova, and Bruce Carnohan

Pracademics and Community Change: A True Story of Nonprofit Development and Social Entrepreneurship
by Odell Cleveland and Bob Wineburg

Navigating Human Service Organizations, 2nd Edition
by Margaret Gibelman and Rich Furman

Advocacy Practice for Social Justice
by Richard Hoefer

Caught in the Storm: Navigating Policy and Practice in the Welfare Reform Era
by Miguel Ferguson, Heather Neuroth-Gatlin, and Stacey Borasky

The Dynamics of Family Policy: Analysis and Advocacy
by Alice K. Butterfield, Cynthia J. Rocha, and William H. Butterfield

Using Statistical Methods in Social Work Practice with SPSS
by Soleman H. Abu-Bader

Advanced and Multivariate Statistical Methods for Social Science Research, with a Complete SPSS Guide
by Soleman H. Abu-Bader

Generalist Practice in Larger Settings: Knowledge and Skill Concepts, 2nd Edition
by Thomas M. Meenaghan, W. Eugene Gibbons, and John G. McNutt

CONNECTED CAUSES
ONLINE MARKETING STRATEGIES FOR NONPROFIT ORGANIZATIONS

Walter Wymer
University of Lethbridge

Stacy Landreth Grau
Texas Christian University

BOOKS, INC.

Chicago, Illinois

© 2011 Lyceum Books, Inc.

Published by

LYCEUM BOOKS, INC.
5758 S. Blackstone Ave.
Chicago, Illinois 60637
773+643-1903 (Fax)
773+643-1902 (Phone)
lyceum@lyceumbooks.com
www.lyceumbooks.com

All rights reserved under International and Pan-American Copyright Conventions. No part of the publication may be reproduced, stored in a retrieval system, copied, or transmitted in any form or by any means without written permission from the publisher.

6 5 4 3 2 1   11 12 13 14

ISBN 978-1-933478-63-0

Printed in the United States of America.

Library of Congress Cataloging-in-Publication Data

Wymer, Walter W.
   Connected causes : online marketing strategies for nonprofit organizations / Walter Wymer, Stacy Landreth Grau.
     p. cm.
   Includes bibliographical references and index.
   ISBN 978-1-933478-63-0 (pbk. : alk. paper)
   1. Nonprofit organizations—Marketing. 2. Internet marketing. I. Grau, Stacy Landreth. II. Title.
   HF5415.W957   2011
   658.8'72—dc22

                                       2010031902

For Donna, Steven, and Kelli
—Walter Wymer

This book is dedicated to my husband, George, and daughters, Eleanor and Madelyn—my very patient family.
—Stacy Landreth Grau

About the Authors

Walter Wymer is professor of marketing at the University of Lethbridge in Alberta, Canada. His academic work has continually helped develop the field of nonprofit marketing. Professor Wymer has authored several books and scholarly articles and has given presentations at numerous academic conferences. He is the former editor of the *Journal of Nonprofit & Public Sector Marketing*, and he is currently associate editor for the *European Journal of Marketing*. He can be reached at walter.wymer@uleth.ca.

Stacy Landreth Grau is associate professor of professional practice in marketing at the Neeley School of Business, Texas Christian University. Her research areas include cause-related marketing, corporate social responsibility initiatives, nonprofit branding, and social media and social innovation. She serves on several academic editorial review boards and professional organizations. Her work can be found at www.stacylandrethgrau.com. She can be reached at s.grau@tcu.edu.

Contents

CHAPTER 1
INTRODUCTION — 1
  The Importance of Online Volunteer Recruitment Efforts — 1
  Online Marketing for Nonprofit Organizations — 2
  The Importance of Online Marketing for Nonprofit Organizations — 2
  The Need for Additional Communication Pathways — 3
  The Need for Additional Resource Attraction Pathways — 4
  Online Marketing Offsets Declining Effectiveness of Traditional
    Direct-Marketing Fund-Raising — 6
  Online Tools Become Standardized by the Nonprofit Community — 7
  Organization of This Book — 8

CHAPTER 2
THE NONPROFIT BRAND IN A DIGITAL WORLD — 14
  The American Heart Association and Go Red for Women — 14
  Taking the First Step — 16
  What Is a Brand? — 17
  The Importance of Branding for Nonprofits — 18
  The Making of Strong Nonprofit Brands in Digital Space — 19
  Communicating Your Brand — 24
  Starting from Scratch: The Brand Audit — 27
  The Ultimate Digital Branding Effort: The Obama Campaign — 32
  Lessons Learned — 38
  Further Reading — 38

CHAPTER 3
**WEB SITE DESIGN AND FUNCTIONALITY FOR
EFFECTIVE COMMUNICATION** — 40
  Do Something Aims to Engage Teens and Tweens — 40
  More Than a Pretty Face: The Importance of Design — 41
  All Visitors Are Not Created Equal: The Visitor Engagement Cycle — 43

The Big Picture: Fundamental Questions About Your Web Site	45
Getting Started: Planning Your Web Site	46
The Web Site Assessment Tool	48
The Functionality of Nonprofit Organization Web Sites	57
Usability Tests: Doing It Yourself	69
Web Site Analysis Worksheet	73
Lessons Learned	74
Further Reading and Recommended Sites	75

CHAPTER 4
SOCIAL MEDIA CONTENT STRATEGY — 77

Livestrong—The Lance Armstrong Foundation	77
What Is Social Media?	78
The Importance of a Strategy	80
Start with a Plan	80
Objectives	81
Audiences	82
Internal Buy In	83
Tactics and Tools	85
The Importance of Content Strategy	87
Lessons Learned	89

CHAPTER 5
SOCIAL MEDIA AND DIGITAL TECHNOLOGY TOOLS FOR STAKEHOLDER ENGAGEMENT — 91

Texting to Save Haiti	91
Blogs and Wikis	92
Microblogs	96
Social Networks	99
Photo Sharing	104
Video Creation and Sharing	106
Podcasting and Audio Sharing	109
Virtual Worlds	111
Mobile and Smartphone Technology	112
Applications and Widgets	113
Productivity Tools	117
Aggregators, Social Bookmarks, and Review Sites	117
Social-Media Measurement	119
Lessons Learned	122
Further Reading	122

CHAPTER 6
ONLINE FUND-RAISING   125

Breast Cancer Fund	125
Advantages of Online Fund-raising	126
Disadvantages of Online Fund-raising	127
Micro-donations	128
Major Donations	128
Developing Online Communities	129
Attracting New Donors	130
E-mail Campaigns	132
Viral Fund-raising	134
Online Advertising	135
Online Events	136
Fund-raising Campaign Promotions	138
Other Tools	139
Privacy and Ethical Issues	140
Monitoring Your Organization's Image and Reputation	141
Lessons Learned	142
Further Reading	142

CHAPTER 7
VOLUNTEER RECRUITMENT   145

Importance of Online Volunteer Recruitment Efforts	145
The Importance of Volunteers	146
Types of Volunteering	146
Volunteer Roles	147
Motivations for Volunteering	149
Facilitation	150
Attitudes	150
Benefits of Volunteering	150
Volunteer Recruitment Tactics	151
Supplementing Recruitment Efforts with Online Support	153
Practical Tips for Effective Web Site Use	155
Lessons Learned	158
Further Reading	158

CHAPTER 8
ONLINE ADVOCACY AND ACTIVISM   160

Online Activism Improves Transparency in U.K. Government	160
The Growth of Online Advocacy	161
An Integrated Strategy Works Best	162

Ethics in Online Activism — 162
A Review of Tools for Online Activism — 168
Developing Relationships — 163
Lessons Learned — 173
Further Reading — 173

CHAPTER 9
PUBLIC RELATIONS IN A DIGITAL WORLD — 175

Samaritan's Feet Gets Mileage from a Sticky Idea — 175
Public Relations and the Importance of Relationships — 176
The Role of Stakeholders — 177
Developing Stakeholder Insights — 178
Media Relations — 180
Crisis Communication — 185
Community Relations — 186
A Note about Credibility — 187
Lessons Learned — 189
Further Reading — 190

CHAPTER 10
DIGITAL INSIGHTS AND RESEARCH — 191

Red Cross Listens after Hurricane Katrina — 191
The Importance of Research and Evaluation — 192
The Research Process — 193
Digital Insights: Social-Media Monitoring — 196
Put on Your Listening Ears: Developing a Listening System — 197
The Importance of a Good Evaluation System — 203
Getting People to Your Web Site — 205
Lessons Learned — 206
Further Reading — 210

Appendix: Social Media Glossary of Terms — 213

INDEX — 217

CHAPTER 1

Introduction

"Online outreach should be the domain of whoever undertakes activities relating to communications, donor relations, volunteers, and clients/customers. Your Web master or other technical staff should follow the lead of program staff (including the volunteer manager) and marketing staff when it comes to online activities, not the other way around."
—Jayne Cravens, Coyote Communications

CHAPTER OVERVIEW

In this chapter, we will introduce the reader to online nonprofit marketing. We will describe several emerging areas of importance and various applications that offer nonprofit managers the ability to more effectively communicate their organizations' messages to their supporters. The reader will better understand how the general public is using the Internet for information-gathering and social-networking. Finally, we will present the organization and major topics of this book.

THE IMPORTANCE OF ONLINE VOLUNTEER RECRUITMENT EFFORTS

The following nonprofit organizations joined forces in creating the I Love Mountains campaign:[1] Appalachian Voices, Coal River Mountain Watch, Keeper of the Mountains Foundation, Kentuckians for the Commonwealth, Ohio Valley Environmental Coalition, Save Our Cumberland Mountains, and Southern Appalachian Mountain Stewards.

The purpose of the campaign is to stop mountaintop removal (MTR) coal-mining in the Eastern U.S. Appalachian Mountain region. Supporters can sign a pledge and track the impact of their pledge on a map, download Willie Nelson's rendition of the song "Blowin' in the Wind," and watch a video about mountaintop removal coal-mining on YouTube. They can also view the National Memorial for the Mountains on Google Earth. Each flag they see from Google Earth's satellite image of the memorial represents a mountain that has been destroyed.

The campaign's Web site (www.ilovemountains.org) provides information on MTR and its costs to communities and the environment. On the Web site, visitors can find how to contact their congressional representative about MTR, donate to the campaign, send an e-mail about their support of the cause to a friend, view pictures of the environmental devastation caused by this type of mining, read press releases or blogs, and connect to an RSS feed to get current information from the advocacy coalition.

ONLINE MARKETING FOR NONPROFIT ORGANIZATIONS

By online nonprofit marketing, we are referring to use of online applications to further a nonprofit organization's marketing objectives. In a very practical sense, marketing for nonprofit organizations typically concerns itself with public relations, donor relations, and volunteer relations. But nonprofit marketing also includes branding activities, fund-raising activities, special events, and volunteer recruitment. It includes promoting the organization, its mission, issues it is involved with, and its activities, including branding. Branding refers to promotional activities intended to strengthen the organization's familiarity and favorability in the public's mind. Nonprofit online marketing also entails research and intelligence-gathering about everything from donor motivations to social-network connections[2]; coalition-building activities among nonprofit partners working together toward a common goal; and supporter relations, for example, when an activist organization motivates individuals who care about the issue to take action or to recruit others.

The marketing activities described above are not new. Nonprofit organizations have been performing these marketing activities for years, but doing so online is a relatively recent development. As such, nonprofits are adding online capabilities to complement their traditional, offline activities.

Even as nonprofit organizations learn how to better use existing online applications, new applications continue to emerge. It can be confusing. Terms like Web 2.0, social networking, Facebook, YouTube, Twitter, Flickr, and blogs get added to our lexicon regularly. How much about these topics should a nonprofit manager know? The purpose of this book is to help nonprofit managers learn how to more effectively use online tools to further their marketing objectives.

THE IMPORTANCE OF ONLINE MARKETING FOR NONPROFIT ORGANIZATIONS

The Internet provides new communication pathways and other opportunities for nonprofit organizations. It allows nonprofits to communicate with more people than was possible using traditional communication mediums, especially when taking limited resources into account. Online applications are not replacing the legacy communication channels (e.g., traditional, offline marketing tactics, such as direct mail and special events), but it is creating an opportunity for more effective marketing. E-mail, for example, has become a revolutionary tool for opening up new ways to communicate with donors and colleagues, alerting activists, and distributing information.[3]

With the use of inexpensive online applications, nonprofit organizations can recruit new members, accept credit card donations/payments, host online discussions, conduct surveys, send invitations, and provide a wealth of information to the public on the nonprofit's focal issue. Furthermore, the use of online applications allows the organizations to reach many more people than it could if it only relied on traditional offline methods.

There is nothing magical about using online tools. But developing a Web site and placing a "Donate Now" button on the front page does not guarantee increased donations. Online nonprofit marketing must be done thoughtfully, and its tactics must be integrated into the organization's total marketing activities program to achieve the desired results. We have written this book to help nonprofit managers understand how to more effectively use available online applications.

THE NEED FOR ADDITIONAL COMMUNICATION PATHWAYS

Traditionally, nonprofits communicated to their supporters in meetings or events through direct mail and telephone calls. Communicating to supporters in periodic meetings or events was good but insufficient—the organization cannot communicate with supporters frequently enough to maintain relationships and to keep supporters informed and motivated using only these tactics. Printing and postage costs for newsletters and direct mail are expensive. Furthermore, this is one-way communication and does not provide a convenient means for supporters to provide their own feedback. Telephone calls allow for two-way communication, but while a telephone call is a great means of contacting a specific individual, it is not suitable for communicating with a large number of supporters. Telemarketing carries with it its own set of challenges—many people dislike receiving such phone calls at home, and an increasing amount of people are migrating from traditional telephone service to mobile phones. One out of every six American homes has only mobile phone service, and an additional 13 percent of homes primarily use mobile service even though they also have traditional land lines.[4]

Online applications are providing new pathways for communicating with supporters. In a 2005 study, 79 percent of nonprofit organizations surveyed reported an increased use of e-mail, and 62 percent reported an increased use of Web postings. About 80 percent of organizations said that e-mail use was one of their most important online tools.[5]

The Internet provides the nonprofit organization with additional communication capabilities, but as nonprofits continue to learn how to most effectively use these online tools, some of their efforts are not being implemented successfully. One study of charity supporters reported that individuals required two types of information before making a donation: (1) the organization's mission, goals, objectives, and work; and (2) how the organization used its donations. The study examined a sample of nonprofit Web sites, finding that 43 percent of the Web sites provided information on the organization's mission, goals, objectives, and work. Only 4 percent of Web sites provided information on how the organization used its supporters' donations.[6] This only highlights the point that online marketing tools must still rely on a smart strategy to be effective.[7]

The economic downturn created by the financial system convulsion in the final quarter of 2008 has impacted nonprofits around the world.[8] It is interesting to note that nonprofit organizations that engaged their supporters through multiple communication channels were affected less severely. Some positive news is that, even during the economic downturn, nonprofit organizations' Web site traffic continues to increase, and their e-mail lists of supporters continues to grow. Whereas online engagement tactics (e.g., Web site traffic and registration, e-mail lists, online fund-raising, online communication, and advocacy) increased in 2008, traditional direct-mail engagement and fund-raising declined, especially in the last quarter. Nonprofits that engage their supporters online are doing better.[9]

THE NEED FOR ADDITIONAL RESOURCE ATTRACTION PATHWAYS

Just as online tools open up new pathways for communicating with supporters, they open up new pathways for attracting resources. The two work together. While new communication pathways allow the organization to reach more people, they also allow the organization to communicate regularly with supporters, developing strong bonds. This facilitates fund-raising.

Opening up new pathways to attract resources is especially important during periods of economic stress. Many nonprofit organizations suffered deficits during the 2001 recession. It took them several years to bring funding levels back up. This was especially true for organizations that relied heavily on traditional direct-mail fund-raising methods and government grants.[10]

The current recession created by reckless speculative behavior among major investment banks[11] has created similar funding shortfalls for nonprofit organizations. A June 2009, study by GuideStar[12] reported that:

- more than half of nonprofits have experienced declining funding,
- 36 percent of grant makers gave less funding to nonprofits,
- those nonprofits that have been forced to reduce their budgets have done so by reducing services and freezing staff salaries, and
- 8 percent of nonprofits are at immediate risk of termination.

The Nonprofit Finance Fund surveyed 986 nonprofit organizations, examining the impact of the recession.[13] They found that only about 16 percent of nonprofits expected to be able to cover their operating expenses for 2009. They found that 52 percent of organizations anticipated a long-term or permanent negative impact from the recession. Social welfare organizations, which provide a safety net for the most vulnerable populations, are experiencing a steep rise in demand for their services. Unfortunately, it appears that many will not exist in the future to continue providing these services. Others are retrenching their operations, attempting to cope with declining resources, even while demand is increasing. For example, Boys and Girls Clubs of Newark had to close one of its five locations—reducing the number of its programs from 47 to 30—and dismiss 28 percent of its paid staff.

As mentioned previously, the use of online communication channels continues to grow. Unfortunately, nonprofits are still only beginning to develop online resource attraction pathways. Online donations account for a small proportion of total funding for most nonprofits, limiting the ability of online fundraising to more fully insulate nonprofits from funding dips during economic downturns.

It is interesting to note that there were some warning signs ahead of the downturn. For example, nonprofit management expert and blogger, Christopher

---

Chapter Insight: The Howard Dean Presidential Campaign

Political parties and other nonprofit organizations were amazed at the success of the Howard Dean presidential campaign in 2004. No political or activist group had ever used the Internet before with such success. Thousands of people got involved in the Dean campaign who previously had never been involved or taken in an interest in politics. The Dean campaign registered 630,000 citizens for electronic updates and 180,000 people for group meetings and raised $18 million online in nine months, with a $68 average donation. Vinay Bhagat, the founder of Convio, an Internet-solutions provider to nonprofit organizations, suggests the following was learned from the Dean campaign:

- The Internet can be used as a strategic marketing tool, not simply an IT tool.
- The Internet can be used as a tool for developing relationships for supporters (i.e., donors and other individuals) who want to get involved.
- Micro campaigns can be used to raise small amounts from a large number of people.
- The strongest supporters can be asked to give more and are best activated as volunteer fund-raisers.

Penn, as early as March 2008, was recommending strategies for nonprofits to employ to weather the pending economic downturn. He recommended that nonprofit managers tightly control expenses, make sure investments were safe, and accelerate annual fund-raising campaigns. Of special note, Penn recommended that nonprofit managers more actively market themselves using the Internet. Specifically, he advised nonprofit managers to make greater use of the Internet for public relations purposes (the topic of chapter 9) and to focus on attracting micro-donations using online marketing tactics (covered in chapter 6).[14]

ONLINE MARKETING OFFSETS DECLINING EFFECTIVENESS OF TRADITIONAL DIRECT-MARKETING FUND-RAISING

The evidence suggests that traditional fund-raising tactics, such as direct mail and telemarketing, are becoming less effective over time.[15] The population's responsiveness to these communication channels is declining as more people adopt mobile phone and online communication channels, and this trend is expected to continue.[16] Simply put, it appears that many donors are moving online. For example, total U.S. donor contributions declined in 2008 for the first time since 1987. However, online contributions rose from $6.9 billion in 2006 to more than $15 billion in 2008.[17] Surprisingly, even donors who give larger amounts are adopting online channels. A 2008 study reported that 51 percent of wealthy donors said they preferred to give online.[18]

The following points lead to a conclusion that online fund-raising will continue to increase in importance:[19]

- The Baby Boomer generation is declining at a 5 percent annual rate and making room for Generation X and Y, who are conditioned to use online and mobile communication channels.
- Online channels allow nonprofits to ask a large number of people for small donations, a tactic that was not cost-effective with traditional direct-marketing methods.
- Traditional direct-marketing tactics are becoming more expensive and less effective.
- Online channels allow nonprofits to communicate across geographic boundaries. International affairs charities are experiencing rapid growth in contributions.
- About 75 percent of people research their nonprofit organizations online prior to donating.
- The expanding use of social media and networking is allowing supporters to become fund-raisers. This trend also enables more effective micro-donation campaigns.

ONLINE TOOLS BECOME STANDARDIZED BY THE NONPROFIT COMMUNITY

In the mid-1990s, nonprofit organizations scrambled to develop a basic, static Web site in order not to be left behind in the Internet revolution. Later, nonprofit organizations became more sophisticated in using e-mail lists for communicating with supporters. Many nonprofits added a means for interested persons to subscribe to e-newsletters.

There have been many advances since then. As the I Love Mountains campaign presented in the opening vignette shows, online tools can allow nonprofits to collaborate for greater impact; to educate, to persuade, to connect, to motivate, and to activate supporters. Interested individuals can go to a Web site—for example, Smiletrain.org—and learn about the organization's mission, see before-and-after pictures of children whose lives have been profoundly changed, access accountability information about the organization, learn how their donations will be used, and make donations. As the public gradually adopts new Internet and communication applications, and as more and more nonprofit organizations take advantage of online tools, the public's expectations for what a nonprofit's Web site ought to offer has increased. There is a tacit higher standard for how a nonprofit organization should use online applications.

In terms of the successful use of online marketing tools, large nonprofits, on average, appear to be outperforming smaller organizations, especially in the area of online fund-raising. This has been attributed to larger nonprofit organizations' stronger brands, their greater resources, and their higher levels of sophistication in online marketing. It appears that nonprofit organizations that are better at using online marketing tools will be better able to attract support and weather difficult times.[20]

Individuals have come to expect nonprofit organizations to have comprehensive information on an issue, the ability to help supporters take action, and the ability to engage supporters—all in an online environment. Nonprofit organizations that only have a static Web site with old content look amateurish by comparison. Nonprofits that are not making effective use of the online tools that are available are putting themselves at a disadvantage.

Are many nonprofits, large and small, making limited use of online applications because they lack resources or because they lack an interest in using these tools? Jayne Cravens, who writes about and consults with nonprofit organizations on communication and supporter engagement tactics, has examined this question. She has attended numerous conferences and observed differences among nonprofit managers who embrace online marketing tactics and those who do not. Nonprofits that embrace the use of online marketing tools use the Internet as a part of their core activities. In addition to Web sites and e-mail, these nonprofits engage people using online discussion groups, blogs, podcasting, video-conferencing, and online social networks. Nonprofit personnel responsible for fund-raising, public relations, volunteer management, and program management all use online tools as a normal part of their work. Cravens says there are also thousands of nonprofits that are limited to having e-mail addresses for staff and a Web site that is controlled by one or two IT staffers. She has found that the divide between organizations that embrace online marketing tools and those that do not is not the result of resource differences, but of managerial attitudes. Managers in nonprofits that embrace the use of online tools believe in openness and transparency. They want supporters to be highly involved; managers seek out their feedback and listen to what they have to say. Managers in nonprofits that fail to embrace online tools, Cravens found, cannot imagine ceding any decisions to volunteers and other supporters. They are not really interested in engaging them or seeking out their feedback. The digital divide is the result of different management styles: one is traditional, hierarchical, and wary of technology; the other is progressive, inclusive, and tech-savvy.[21]

At this point, we would like to emphasize a few points:

- As time goes on, the proportion of the population that uses information technology tools to communicate and search for information will increase.
- Online tools provide an excellent opportunity for nonprofits to disseminate information about their causes.
- Online tools provide an excellent opportunity for nonprofits to engage supporters.
- Nonprofit organizations that fail to effectively use online marketing tools will be at a disadvantage.
- Online marketing tactics work best when effectively integrated with offline marketing tactics.
- Traditional direct-marketing methods (primarily telemarketing and direct mail) will continue to decline in effectiveness.
- Online fund-raising tactics will continue to evolve and increase in effectiveness.
- Effective use of online marketing tools requires planning, thoughtful implementation, and an overall integrated marketing strategy.

ORGANIZATION OF THIS BOOK

We will highlight the contents and structure of this book by providing an introduction to the major topics of each chapter below.

Chapter 2: Nonprofit Branding

Nonprofit branding refers to those marketing activities implemented in order to increase public familiarity and favorability of the nonprofit organization.

Many activities will have multiple purposes. For example, when a nonprofit disseminates information about an issue as part of a public education program, that program is also serving a branding function. By promoting an issue, the public gains a greater awareness that the organization exists and what it represents.

There are three levels of brand development for a nonprofit organization. First, there is brand awareness. Brand awareness refers to the level of public familiarity of the nonprofit organization. Once brand awareness has been firmly established, the organization can progress to brand preference, the next level of brand development. Usually more than one nonprofit organization is working on a specific issue. Brand preference refers to the likelihood that an individual seeking to support an issue will prefer to do this through one organization over another. The highest level of brand development is known as brand insistence. Brand insistence refers to a situation in which an individual will only support one organization when supporting a specific cause.

The brand represents the meaning of the organization in the public's mind. The public will integrate what it sees and hears about an organization to arrive at an understanding of what the organization represents. The more frequently the public is exposed to information about the organization, the more solidly defined the organization becomes in the public's mind. Repeated, prolonged exposure to information about the organization increases the brand familiarity (how familiar the public is with the nonprofit).

For example, Greenpeace (www.greenpeace.org) has a relatively high level of brand familiarity. Most people have heard of Greenpeace from what they have seen in news reports on television. The average person thinks of Greenpeace as a confrontational activist organization that opposes certain fishing practices, like whaling. The meaning of the Greenpeace brand, for much of the public, has been framed by the news coverage they have seen over the years. However, challenging destructive fishing practices is only a part of the Greenpeace mission. Other issues of central importance to Greenpeace are: (1) promoting renewable energy to stem the negative effects of climate change, (2) creating a global network of marine reserves, (3) protecting ancient forests, (4) peace, (5) nuclear disarmament, (6) reducing the use of harmful chemicals, (7) opposing genetically engineered organisms, (8) protecting biodiversity, and (9) encouraging socially responsible farming.[22] From a marketing perspective, the Greenpeace brand has been distorted because its meaning has been framed by the news media and not Greenpeace's communications. The public would have a richer and more accurate understanding of the organization if Greenpeace actively promoted its own brand.

Chapter 3: Web Site Design and Functionality

A nonprofit organization's Web site is a central component of the organization's online marketing strategy. It is the location to which the organization works diligently to attract visitors in order to provide them with information about the organization and its cause. The organization's Web site is the repository of information on the nonprofit's issues of concern. Most people will visit the Web site before making the decision to donate to the organization for the first time.

Chapter 3 deals first with Web site design issues and then functionality. Design refers to how the layout, format, and content of the Web site communicates the core distinctiveness of the nonprofit to Web site visitors. Is the Web site easy to navigate? Does it anticipate the information needs of visitors? Does the Web site inform visitors about the organization and the importance of its issues? Functionality refers to what the Web site can do. The Web site's design and functional capabilities work together to enable the Web site to serve as an effective platform for online marketing activities.

Chapter 4 and Chapter 5: Social Media Strategy and Tools

Sometimes called Web 2.0 or social media, social networking refers to a group of Web sites that has member-provided content. Nonprofits can create their own profile pages and build their communities of supporters on these social-networking sites.

Social networking can allow a nonprofit organization the ability to communicate and engage new and existing supporters. Before using social media, a nonprofit should decide how it is going to be used. Online tools should be integrated with offline tools. Effective use of social networks will take time and planning.

Chapter 6: Online Fund-Raising

In 2008, the nonprofit sector received 10 percent of its donations online.[23] Experts predict that by 2020, the majority of donations will come from online pathways.[24] This prediction assumes that nonprofits will continue to develop their online fund-raising skills. Online fund-raising is the topic of chapter 6 and introduces the subsequent related chapters.

Chapter 7: Online Volunteer Recruitment

Promoting the nonprofit's volunteer openings online is easy and inexpensive. It allows the nonprofit to reach groups not typically represented in the ranks of current volunteers, increasing the diversity and participation of more groups of people. It also allows the organization to appeal for specific skills sets (e.g., attorneys, accountants, and IT experts).[25]

Online recruitment activities are not meant to replace offline tactics, but to complement them. Like all online marketing tactics, online volunteer recruitment activities must be implemented effectively to produce successful outcomes.

Chapter 8: Online Activism

Online activism refers to the use of online marketing tools to develop grassroots support for an issue in order to change public policy. The online activist must have an excellent Web site. While chapter 8 will deal with this topic in depth, it is important to recognize that activism needs a growing, active grassroots movement. The activist organization should strive to make its Web site the best place for interested individuals to find information on the issue. Comprehensive information that is updated often on a well-designed Web site will help. The Web site should provide materials supporters can use to inform others and provide mechanisms for supporters to communicate with their government officials.

The activist organization should take advantage of available tools for engaging supporters. Social-network sites like Twitter are helpful for sending brief text messages to supporters. Creating a blog on the issue is a good way to allow supporters to provide their comments and to keep them informed. Videos can be uploaded to YouTube and photos to Flickr. Online tools provide a means of disseminating information, drawing attention to an issue, and engaging supporters.

Chapter 9: Online Public Relations

Online public relations should complement offline public relations. Public relations involve influencing public opinion, usually through the news media. Organizations want their issues covered in the media. If news outlets are reporting on an issue, the organization wants to have its position on the issue heard.

Offline public relations activities work toward influencing public opinion through offline media, including print (newspapers and magazines), radio, television (broadcast and cable), conferences, and events. Online media include online versions of traditional offline media. Online media also include blogs, news searches, forums, discussion threads, and social networks.

Effective online public relations require careful planning and effective implementation. Favorable public relations are accomplished through relationship-building. Online tools facilitate communication, which helps establish and develop relationships.

Chapter 10: Research and Measurement

Chapter 10 will focus on online intelligence gathering and evaluation issues. Nonprofit organizations need timely and accurate information to make informed decisions. Nonprofits need to have ways of measuring the effectiveness of their various online marketing activities. Research informs planning. Evaluation allows managers to determine how their activities are performing, to detect problems needing correction, and to find possible solutions to those problem areas.

Summary

The proportion of the population having access to high-speed Internet connections at home, at work, in retail spaces, or in public spaces continues to increase. The Internet is becoming many individuals' first choice for information. While most nonprofit organizations have Web sites, there is a substantial divide between nonprofits that are using online tools in a sophisticated manner and those that are not.

As online applications continue to develop, and as new online applications become available, nonprofit managers will need an array of useful tools at their disposal to further their organizations' causes. Effective managers will continue to learn about new applications, and use them effectively in support of their organizations' mission.

NOTES

1. www.ilovemountains.org
2. Walter Wymer, Patricia Knowles and Roger Gomez, *Nonprofit Marketing: Marketing Management for Charitable and Nongovernmental Organizations* (Thousand Oaks, CA: Sage Publications, 2006).
3. www.fundraising123.org/article/why-do-you-need-be-online
4. www.cdc.gov/nchs/data/nhis/earlyrelease/wireless200812.htm
5. www.blackbaud.com/default.aspx?pgpId=2532&PRID=189
6. www.useit.com/alertbox/nonprofit-donations.html
7. http://hbswk.hbs.edu/archive/4006.html
8. http://nonprofitrisk.org/library/articles/strategy09002003.shtml
9. www.convio.com/convio/news/releases/convio-unveils-nonprofit.html
10. www.reuters.com/article/pressRelease/idUS188348+13-Feb-2008+PRN 20080213
11. www.amazon.com/Financial-Shock-Subprime-Mortgage-Implosion/dp/ 0137142900/ref=pd_sim_b_8
12. www2.guidestar.org/ViewCmsFile.aspx?ContentID=2319
13. www.cnn.com/2009/US/03/26/recession.nonprofits/index.html
14. www.christopherspenn.com/2008/03/02/top-5-non-profit-strategies-for-severe recession/
15. http://features.csmonitor.com/innovation/2008/06/23/donors-warm-up-to-online-giving/
16. www.afpnet.org/ka/ka-3.cfm?folder_id=914&content_item_id=24771
17. www.philanthropy.iupui.edu/News/2009/docs/GivingReaches300billion_ 06102009.pdf
18. http://my.convio.com/?elqPURLPage=104
19. http://features.csmonitor.com/innovation/2008/06/23/donors-warm-up-to-online-giving/
20. http://cnvo-old.pub30.convio.net/resources/newsletter/going-against-the-grain-general.html
21. www.coyotecommunications.com/volunteer/divide.html

22. www.greenpeace.org/international/about
23. www.blackbaud.com/files/resources/downloads/cam/TargetInternetGiving Summary2008.pdf
24. www.useit.com/alertbox/nonprofit-donations.html
25. www.idealist.org/if/idealist/en/FAQ/QuestionViewer/default?section=04&item=19

CHAPTER 2

The Nonprofit Brand in a Digital World

"The digital world has not changed the principles of branding but rather has magnified everything we know to be true about building a great brand. The tenets we've always followed have been made more visible by digital technology. The importance they play in our work has only become more obvious."
—Charlie Wrench, chairman and president of Landor Associates.[1]

CHAPTER OVERVIEW

In this chapter, we discuss the importance of developing a brand identity for nonprofit organizations. Generally, nonprofits are very good at meeting their mission and raising funds and support. But they are less successful at creating a "brand." In fact, for some time, many nonprofits shunned the idea of marketing and branding for nonprofits. However, it is increasingly important to develop a brand identity to break through the clutter. We also introduce the concept of a brand audit, which is part of a strategic planning process but one part that is misunderstood and forgotten. And we will show how activities that are done offline (through traditional means) can be married to online endeavors with great results.

THE AMERICAN HEART ASSOCIATION AND GO RED FOR WOMEN

The American Heart Association (AHA) is known as the expert medical organization regarding heart disease and stroke. The organization funds and conducts medical research, and a majority of its fund-raising goes toward medical research. The AHA has saturated the marketplace with its logo and messages through traditional and nontraditional channels, corporate sponsorships, special events, a food certification program, and licensing agreements. It is considered a premier health organization. Indeed, the AHA was recently ranked twelfth on the Cone Nonprofit Power 100 Report while ranking seventh in brand image and second in personal relevancy.[2] This makes the AHA one of the most valuable nonprofit brands in the U.S. While the organization communicates through various means, it's their Web site that is a key platform for education and communication. The AHA has portals on it's main Web site (www.heart.org) for specific stakeholders—patients, caregivers, healthcare professionals, and researchers and scientists. It Web site acts as an information source for these audiences and provides education about the warning signs of stroke and heart disease.

In addition to medical research, the AHA also works hard to educate various groups about heart disease and related diseases. Heart disease is the number one killer of women and is particularly prevalent in African-American and Hispanic populations. In order to spread this message, the AHA launched the program Go Red for Women to create a fresh, approachable, and innovative cause brand. As a part of this effort, the AHA has partnered with several corporate sponsors, such as Macy's and Merck. The Web site includes several innovative techniques, including celebrity spokespeople, videos, and social-networking platforms. One of the most unique features is an application that allows women to enter information to get a Go Red Heart CheckUp. Here, women enter certain vital statistics into the application and receive relevant information to discuss with their physician about their risks. Recently, the AHA has added the Go Red BetterU program, a 12-week health-and-fitness program and a set of online tools to track progress. To highlight the program and to increase involvement and interactivity, the organization has four women blogging about their experiences. The American Heart Association has done an excellent job connecting with its core target audience for heart disease—women who are at risk for heart disease and heart failure.

Figure 2.1: Go Red for Women

Figure 2.2: Go Red for Women Heart CheckUp

TAKING THE FIRST STEP

While developing a positive and strong brand image is important, there is one step that needs to happen first: determining (and agreeing upon) the mission. It sounds simple. After all, most nonprofits exist to help people in some way. However, it is vital that important stakeholders are in agreement; namely the executive team and the board of directors. Recently, a certain (nameless) nonprofit engaged an outside marketing agency to help with branding. The nonprofit executive team wanted to understand how the organization was perceived relative to other nonprofits that worked in similar areas—in this case, all were aimed at helping kids. Once the research came in, the executives found out two important things: first, not many people who were surveyed even knew about the organization or what they did, despite the fact that the nonprofit had been around for years. Second, of those who did know about the organization, most were unclear about its mission. Its name did not help matters, either—it was too long and gave the impression of being religiously affiliated, even though it was not a faith-based organization. Additionally, its name indicated that it only helped children, but it really helped families—a positioning that would have been unique in the area. However, some members of the board wanted to keep the focus on kids because they felt it was easier to raise money for children than families. Additionally, executive team and board members were too close to the situation; many did not believe the accuracy of the research showing such low awareness levels. After all, they spent their days working for such a worthy organization, helping families and kids get back on the right track. And so it went until the organization decided that before it proceeded further, they needed to do additional internal strategic planning. Eventually, the marketing agency decided to resign the business out of frustration, and the nonprofit remains the same—with an inaccurate name, a "me too" positioning, and a low awareness level.

Sounds like a fluke? Hardly. Many small- and medium-sized nonprofits we have interviewed (along with some large ones, as well) have forgotten or never knew about the importance of maintaining a strong, consistent brand image. And, really, with the daily stress of delivering on a mission and raising money, who can blame them? Even so, nonprofits need to understand that there is plenty of competition—there are 1.5 million other nonprofits[3] in America, and that's not counting churches who don't have to register as 501(c)(3) organizations—and there is only so much attention and money to go around.

So what is the lesson? Take the time to make sure everyone is on the same page about the basics—what you do, who you are, and whether your name conveys your identity. If any of these issues need to be changed, don't take this lightly, and certainly don't embark on a branding campaign before figuring this out. Make sure that the executive team and the board of directors agree on this, as well. Honestly, this is where many battles take place. Disagreement among board members or between executive team members and board members inevitably leads to inconsistent messages, causes fund-raising to suffer, and eventually leads to a failed mission due to a lack of focus and funding.

A strong brand image is the greatest asset that a nonprofit possesses because people tend to automatically anoint nonprofits with positive perceptions. A strong brand image leads to greater awareness and positive perceptions about the mission and ultimately more dollars. Think about it—if a person gets two e-mails soliciting donations, will they donate to the one they know or the one they don't know? It's that easy. So be the one they know.

WHAT IS A BRAND?

A brand has many different related terms and definitions. The American Marketing Association's definition of branding is a "name, term, design, symbol, or any other feature that identifies one seller's good or service as distinct from those of other sellers," as stated on their Web site (www.marketingpower.com). According to Kevin Lane Keller, a leading brand authority, branding reflects a unique social contribution; it comprises a *promise* to target audiences and stakeholders and reflects the mission and values of the organization.[4] Scot Bedbury, author of *A New Brand World* describes a brand as "the sum of the good, the bad, the ugly, and the off-strategy. . . . It is defined by the accomplishments of your best employee—the shining star of the company who can do no wrong—as well as by the mishaps of your worst hire ever."

With almost all of the variations on the definition, some elements are common. Brand identity is the image that the organization creates throughout all of its communications and offerings. A brand image exists in the minds of your stakeholders that is the result of all of the impressions (both good and bad) that exist anywhere. Interestingly, these are often quite different. In other words, what you as a manager think your brand is may be different from what your stakeholders think your brand is. Think about a well-known brand like Nike. Many images come to mind, including sports, soccer, basketball, the swoosh, the "Just Do It" campaign, Michael Jordan, LeBron James, and so forth. All of these are positive. However, the brand image for Nike also includes high prices, child labor issues that arose several years ago, and Michael Vick. These are all impressions of and interactions with the brand, some of which obviously were orchestrated by Nike and others that are perceived by consumers.

Brands are influenced by both rational and irrational perceptions. However, at the end of the day, regular people define the brand—they make it what they believe it to be. It is up to the nonprofit manager to influence these perceptions. Your nonprofit brand lives online whether you put it there or not. So it is best to try to put your best foot forward.

THE IMPORTANCE OF BRANDING FOR NONPROFITS

So why is all of this talk of branding relevant to nonprofits? While many companies know that their brand is one of their biggest assets, to a nonprofit organization, the brand is perhaps its most important. A positive brand is vital for nonprofits since it increases the level of awareness among stakeholders, aids in fund-raising activities, and helps achieve the mission by garnering more volunteer support and media attention. A strong brand creates trust and an emotional attachment. It is the result of a series of good experiences and consistent messages over time. A strong brand builds recognition, which if properly managed, can lead to stronger stakeholder relationships. Phillipa Hankinson, a researcher at University of Surrey Roehampton in the United Kingdom states, "Branded charity organizations are more likely to attract voluntary donations than unbranded charities whose cause and values may be less clearly defined and less well-known. Brands allow donors to identify more closely with what the charity does and the values it represents."[5]

Branding is also monetarily valuable to the organization. The top nonprofit brand, according to the Cone Nonprofit Power Brand 100 Report, is the YMCA of the USA. This organization has a brand value of more than $6 billion, is the top-ranking nonprofit in terms of revenue, and ranks sixth on brand image. The YMCA outpaces the closest competitor by almost $2 billion. The organization started with a social mission and has become one of the largest sports and recreation facilities in 3,000 communities, where it makes most of its revenue from club memberships. YMCA benefits from the awareness of being a ubiquitous "bricks and mortar" presence all over the country and yet still maintains a strong

Table 2.1: The Cone Nonprofit Power Brand 100—Top 10 Nonprofits

Power Brand Rank	Organization	Revenue Rank	Brand Image Rank
1	YMCA of the USA	1	6
2	The Salvation Army	3	2
3	United Way of America	2	3
4	American Red Cross	7	5
5	Goodwill Industries International	6	18
6	Catholic Charities USA	4	53
7	Habitat for Humanity International	9	4
8	American Cancer Society	11	1
9	The Arc of the United States	5	96
10	Boys and Girls Clubs of America	8	21

digital presence.[6] The American Cancer Society was ranked as the nonprofit organization with the best brand image. It stands out as the most personally relevant organization, and it solidified its leadership with stakeholders, including patients, medical communities, the media, and the community.[7]

THE MAKING OF STRONG NONPROFIT BRANDS IN DIGITAL SPACE

Branding an organization online means that more people have an opportunity to experience your organization and engage with your cause. Start at the basics. The brand should be simple, clear, consistent, distinct, inspiring, portable, engaging, and relevant.

The brand idea should be *simple.* A simple idea should be the foundation for the mission and the vision, as well as for the Web site tagline and other ways that the organization communicates with stakeholders. The idea should be the driver for the communication. "The beauty of a simple and memorable brand driver is that it has greater potential to drive inspired branding," said Allen Adamson of Brand Digital. It is not about the media but rather about the idea. If it takes too long to explain, then it is too complicated to convey.

New York City Coalition Against Hunger (www.nyccah.org) has a straightforward mission—to end hunger. It represents 1,200 soup kitchens and pantries in the New York City area. The Web site is dynamic, with a variety of content, such as blogs and research studies, that sets them apart as a thought leader. The organization uses the videos from executives and First Lady Michelle Obama to tell the story of the organization as well as urge people to volunteer under the United We Serve organization banner. The Web site allows for event promotion and provides an interactive map that shows the locations for all its food pantries.

The brand should be conveyed in a *clear, consistent, and distinct* voice. All aspects of communication should have the same voice and come from a distinct personality, for example, one that is conservative, simple, or fun-loving. Consider Greenpeace, which has a liberal, politically active personality compared to other relief organizations. Catholic Charities has a decidedly more conservative image than other organizations serving the poor. This is part of their brand personality. Since there are so many nonprofits out there all disseminating similar messages, having a distinctive brand personality will help differentiate the brand relative to all of the noise.

For example, many cities struggle with the idea of environmentalism. The "green movement" has garnered a lot of attention over the past few years as evidence mounts regarding the impact of greenhouse gases. Additionally, many cities have found themselves with too much concrete and not enough green and open space. But all cities talk about "being green," and pretty soon it all sounds the same. Therefore, it is important to find that distinctive voice. One city, Indianapolis, has found a unique way to communicate this story. Keep Indianapolis Beautiful (KIB), a grassroots organization wanted to create more involvement and ongoing engagement with tree planting in the city and surrounding areas. As a result, the organization and its marketing partner, Mediasauce, created My Tree and Me. This was a small test campaign within the larger national "Neighborwoods" program. The city of Indianapolis has a goal of planting 100,000 established trees over the next few years, and KIB could not do it alone. So the program allowed discounts to homeowners and tree-buyers who registered their new trees. Essentially, KIB and its partners created a microsite that plotted the "new homes" of all trees purchased with coupons from the program. All trees

Figure 2.3: My Tree and Me

Figure 2.4: My Tree and Me

were plotted via Google maps to show prevalence throughout the community, and owners were able to submit names for their trees at the time of purchase as well as giving them "profiles" on the site. The results were 1,750 new trees planted (significant since the starting tree price was $100) and 4,938 unique visitors who averaged almost five minutes on the site. This was significant because, based on planning and budget allocation of some minimal traditional media, the

Figure 2.5: My Tree and Me

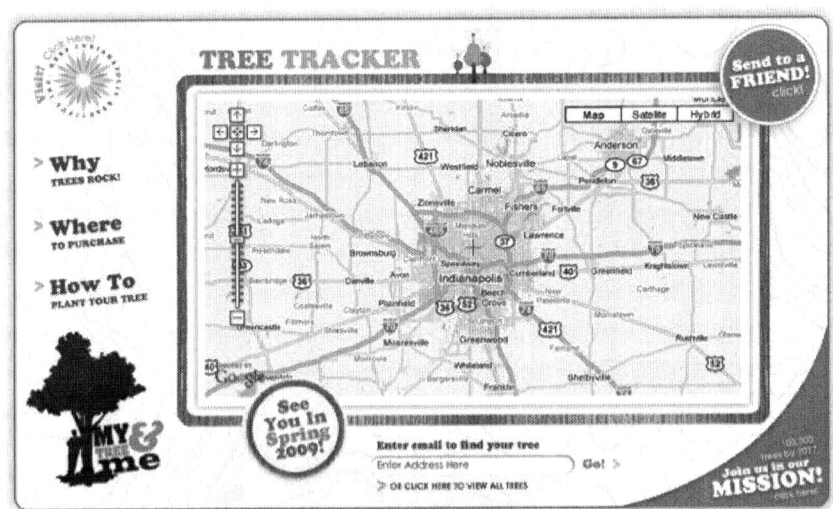

Figure 2.6: My Tree and Me

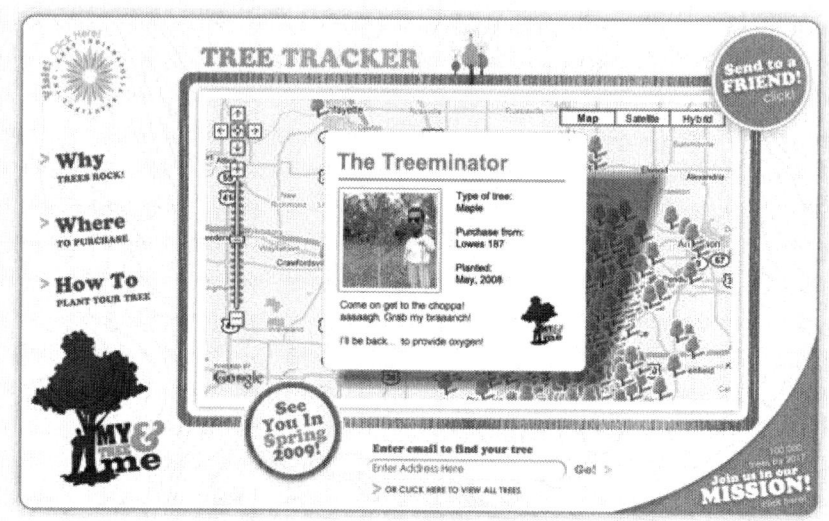

organization felt that having 500 trees would be a huge initial success. In this case, using a branded microsite extended the awareness and the engagement of Keep Indianapolis Beautiful.[8]

A nonprofit brand should be *inspiring* and deliver an *emotional promise*. To a certain extent, nonprofits by their very nature are automatically endowed with a sense of inspiration—the idea of doing something good for others. Many brands start with a functional benefit (e.g., giving food to the poor) but quickly find that they need to move up the branding ladder to provide a more emotional benefit. This emotional connection comes especially easy for nonprofit organizations and is easier to communicate using digital technology. "It is the responsibility of brand managers to tap into some essential human need that a certain group of consumers think about and share. One of the beauties of the digital space in terms of building a brand is that it's interactive. People can engage with other people, and they can engage with the brand," says Donna Hoffman of the Sloan Center for Internet Retailing at the University of California-Riverside.[9]

Having a distinctive image is important, given the competitive landscape within many cause sectors. And having the ability to engage with others is key for nonprofit organizations, given the emotional attachment some donors have with the cause. For example, Modest Needs (www.modestneeds.org) is a program designed to assist families in need. These families can generally pay their bills but have been thrown into financial dire straits (due perhaps to an illness or job loss). Using a microfinance model, donors decide who gets their help, and the organization provides financial assistance. The Web site allows donors to see available projects while these families are able to view the rules and post their testimonials. The idea is simple and emotionally links the donors to the families in need.

Multimedia formats also allow the organization to present its message with impact and meaning. Drew Westen, author of *The Political Brain: The Role of Emotion in Deciding the Fate of the Nation*, relies on research in neuroscience to support his central idea—that people are emotional decision-makers, not rational decision-makers. They make decisions based on how they feel about a specific topic, person, organization, or idea. For a nonprofit organization to make an impact in presenting its case to visitors of its Web site, it must demonstrate the organization's values and principles by showing the difference it makes in people's lives. The nonprofit organization Operation Smile (www.operationsmile.org) does an excellent job on this point. This organization helps fund surgery for children born with facial deformities. The Operation Smile Web site's front page, using images and text, helps the visitor to quickly understand the organization's purpose, who is helped by the organization, and the importance of its mission—in a compelling manner. Mission statements do not motivate individuals to take action. Causes that change lives are what strike responsive chords in people.

Since Internet technologies allow for multimedia formats, video segments containing testimonials and personal stories have the potential of making a substantial emotional impact. Operation Smile presents before and after pictures of children who have had their lives changed by the free surgeries performed on children with facial deformities. Another good example is Democracy Now's Web site (www.democracynow.org), where visitors can download select video clips of compelling news interviews.

The brand should be *portable*. Portability deals with an organization's ability to grow its mission, both through expansion and across communications channels. Brands with very specific names or limited to a specific geographic area are limiting themselves from the start. Even if the scope of the brand is narrow, its name needs to be broad enough to grow as the organization does. As well, effective brands have the ability to be easily communicated on different electronic outlets, including home Web sites, mobile platforms, and social-media sites. Mobile Active (http://mobileactive.org) connects people, organizations, and resources using mobile technology for social change. It recognizes that 4.5 billion mobile phones provide unprecedented opportunities for organizing, communications, and service and information delivery. Therefore, they work together to create the resources for organizations to use mobile phones in their work: locally relevant content and services, support and learning opportunities, and networks that help MobileActives connect to each other. While many organizations can use mobile for communication, there are additional ways to use it for social impact. M4Girls provides educational content to female students in South Africa, resulting in more positive evaluations about mathematics, for example.

The brand should be *engaging*. This means that the ideas are compelling enough to spread organically through both word-of-mouth and digitally. Indeed, donor relationships are partially built on word-of-mouth. We see that for many companies, reputations are made or broken on recommendations. Word-of-mouth information is magnified by digital technology, including posts on social networks, blogs, and video sites. Seth Godin, author of several marketing books and a leading marketing blog (http://sethgodin.typepad.com) says that all organizations should strive to be "remark-able." In other words, nonprofit brands should try to do things to get other people to talk about them and to tell their story. The RED campaign to help end the AIDS suffering in Africa (www.joinred.com) is one example of an organization that is particularly engaging and uses unique ways to build relationships with donors. This site includes links to Twitter and Facebook, as well as including an engaging blog. Room to Read (www.roomtoread.org) was created based on engagement. Founder John Wood saw the need for schools as he trekked through Nepal and decided to create schools in the surrounding areas. The organization focuses on developing literacy and gender equality in education and has worked with foundations and government partnerships to create more than 1,000 schools and more than 9,000 libraries. They have also distributed more than seven million books around the world and have funded thousands of scholarships. The Web site enables the organization to tell its story through social media and by offering both quantitative results and emotional stories to impact donors.

The brand should be *relevant*. What impact does the organization have on the lives of its stakeholders? What would the world be like if the organization no longer existed? It is important to ensure that the organization is fulfilling its mission and providing a positive return on investment to volunteers and donors. This information needs to be communicated effectively, and the Web site can be a wonderful tool to accomplish that goal. Some stakeholders are looking for stories and some are looking for numbers. In order to be relevant for both groups, have many types of information available on the Web site.

Communities in Schools (CIS) started thirty years ago in New York City to help kids who were high school dropouts or in danger of dropping out. CIS Dallas has been especially successful at placing professionals in the schools to provide much-needed services. While CIS Dallas gets most of its financial support from corporations, the Web site (www.cisdallas.org/) allows for engagement with various stakeholders. CIS Dallas shows that donations to the organization have a very positive return on investment.[10] Most importantly, this organization deals with results and clearly posts it on the Web site.

COMMUNICATING YOUR BRAND

Digital Storytelling and Nonprofit Organizations

Consider that your nonprofit organization's brand is really a collection of stories and pictures. The brand is the total experience that a person has with your organization, and compelling stories help the brand enhance its uniqueness and reputation. People don't necessarily remember facts, but they will remember stories. Luckily, social media allows nonprofits a much easier way to create and tell stories and then share them with the world.

So how should your organization tell stories? In their book *Made to Stick*, Chip and Dan Heath provide some great tips on storytelling. They argue that stories should be simple, unexpected, concrete, credible, and emotional, just like the brands they are communicating. Stories can be told in several contexts: PowerPoint presentations, blogs, podcasts, photo sharing, video sharing, and through user-generated content. While some of these do take some investment in terms of time and money, having stories is incredibly effective for nonprofits. Table 2.2 outlines some tips for effective storytelling on blogs, podcasts, and photo and video sharing sites.[11]

Epic Change is a nonprofit that is all about stories. According to its Web site, "Epic Change believes that people's stories are assets that can be used as resources to improve their lives. They help people in need share their 'epic' true stories in innovative, creative, and profitable ways to help them acquire the

Table 2.2: Tips for Social Media Storytelling

Blogs	Podcasts	Photo Sharing	Video Sharing
Choose a topic and be passionate about it	Determine who your audience is and what they want to hear	Find a good staff photographer to be the official documentarian	Buy a good video camera (again, they are inexpensive)
Create resources to post and have a strategy for regular posting	Find a niche and offer valuable and unique content	Buy a good digital camera (they are inexpensive now)	Set up a nonprofit channel on YouTube
Have staff buy in and use guidelines for blog authors	Plan your content and production schedule	Learn basic photo composition rules (a good photography or design book will suffice)	Select content with the most impact: that engages audiences and offers them ways to support the organization without high barriers to entry
Set goals for the blog (visitors, links, subscribers, etc.)	Get the equipment		
	Promote through RSS feeds and iTunes as well as other podcast directories	Take a lot of pictures	
Respect fair use and copyright (see Creative Commons attributions)		Upload all good photos into a public directory or other outlet (like Flickr)	Decide what product quality is appropriate
Do you homework on who else is blogging	Examples: Idealist.org, The Nature Conservancy: Nature Stories"	Solicit participation with supporters through sharing photos and comments	Learn some video editing (Mac computers come loaded with video-editing software that is quite good)
Don't over edit—it does not have to be perfect			
Promote blogs through ping backs and RSS feeds		Examples: The Learning Community, Homeless Prenatal Program	Recycle and edit existing content for additional impact
Examples: Idealist in NYC, Urban Sprouts School Gardens blog			Examples: United Cerebral Palsy, Kiva

From Tactical Track Module 3: Sharing your Story Social Media Style, www.wearemedia.org.

Figure 2.7: Epic Change

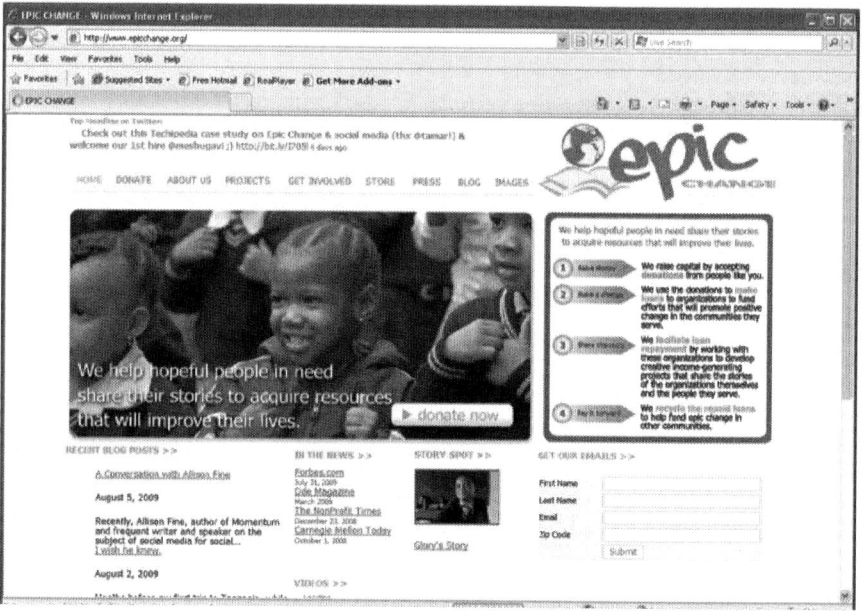

financial resources they need to create positive change in their communities." Epic Change (www.epicchange.org) includes a blog that is a diary of an experiment in social entrepreneurship that has catalogued the organization's activities. They include a story spot that highlights different projects using video and photos. Epic Change believes that using these social-media tactics to tell the stories of people who are trying to change their lives is effective for gaining support and resources for the organization.

Digital Engagement and Brand Touchpoints

One of the most difficult things for nonprofit organizations to do is to translate traditional media tactics—such as television, print, and outdoor ads—into digital touchpoints. Touchpoints are all of the ways that stakeholders can experience your brand—everything from meeting a board member to visiting a Web site to receiving a gala invitation to reading an article in a local newspaper. Digital touchpoints simply limit those experiences to those online. While this may sound small, think about all of the places that someone can interact with your brand—through a search engine, a Web site, Facebook, Twitter, LinkedIn, and review sites, just to name a few. Figure 2.8 illustrates the many ways to engage visitors using digital brand touchpoints.

In marketing, the concepts of strategy and tactics are different. Strategy is tied to objectives (where you want to go), and tactics are how to get there.

Figure 2.8: Digital Engagement and Brand Touchpoints

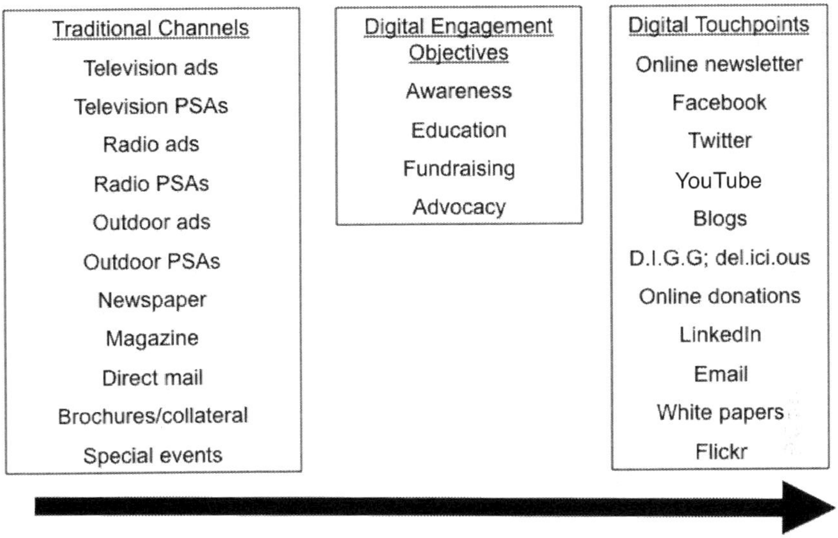

Traditional Channels	Digital Engagement Objectives	Digital Touchpoints
Television ads	Awareness	Online newsletter
Television PSAs	Education	Facebook
Radio ads	Fundraising	Twitter
Radio PSAs	Advocacy	YouTube
Outdoor ads		Blogs
Outdoor PSAs		D.I.G.G; del.ici.ous
Newspaper		Online donations
Magazine		LinkedIn
Direct mail		Email
Brochures/collateral		White papers
Special events		Flickr

Nonprofits are quite used to using traditional tactics—like postcards, ads, or public service announcements—with a concrete strategy behind them. The digital environment should be treated the same way, but because social media is easy-to-use and inexpensive, there are times when digital touchpoints are quickly implemented without any real known goals or strategies. Determine the objective of each digital touchpoint in order to use them most effectively. There are several touchpoints that are useful for educating the visitor; for example, developing a quality online newsletter, an engaging blog, or a set of white papers to highlight the organization's level of expertise works well. If the objective is to create a forum for updates, a good mobile technology program would be effective. If the objective is to raise funds, make sure there is a dynamic and useful online donation system. Sort these out, because while social media is less expensive than traditional media, it is still a crowded space (and getting more so each day). Understanding what each touchpoint should ultimately do will lead to an idea of how your organization will measure success.

STARTING FROM SCRATCH: THE BRAND AUDIT

Throughout this book, we will present nonprofit managers with tools to assess various aspects of communication elements—the Web site, fund-raising systems, public relations. For example, the Web site (the core of the digital strategy) is examined in great detail, and we have developed a Web Site Assessment Tool that allows managers to methodically examine how well the Web site is communicating to various stakeholder audiences. But it all starts with the brand.

The brand audit is a tool that allows an organization to assess its communication effectiveness. There are various audits available—a simple Google search will find many such tools, some based in academic research (work by Kevin Lane Keller and David Aaker) or years of testing on major brands (e.g., Y&R BrandAsset Valuator) and some based on little more than fluff.[12] Generally, a brand audit can be divided into three areas: an internal brand audit, a communications audit, and an external brand audit.[13] Some of the methodologies are qualitative, consisting of interviews and projective techniques (e.g., association techniques, construction techniques, and laddering methodologies), while some are more quantitative, encompassing statistical analysis of survey data, conjoint analysis, and financial analyses.[14] Obviously, some of these take significant technical expertise, and if a nonprofit can afford a good consultant, we do encourage that. But for most nonprofits, this would be a luxury, so we have developed a few key ideas that can be used for brand audits. Consider conducting a good brand audit every three years and have a checkup each year, especially if there is substantial growth in the organization. As more staff members are hired, it is likely that some of the brand vision can get lost in the day-to-day work of achieving the mission.

Internal Brand Audits

The internal brand audit consists of the perspectives of internal stakeholders (we talk about them again in chapter 9 regarding public relations). Generally, the internal stakeholders include the executive team and other employees, volunteers, and board of directors. Interviews are used to determine each stakeholder's perspective on a few issues, such as:

- What is the mission of the organization? Is it meeting that mission? How effectively? What can be done more effectively?
- What is the most pressing need for the organization? What is being done to meet that need?
- How does everyone work together? What is the relationship between the executive staff and volunteers? Between executive staff and the board of directors? What is working and what is not working?
- How does each stakeholder believe the organization is seen by the community? By donors? By volunteers?
- Who is the competition? How is the competition defined (e.g., by cause, geographical boundaries, constituency)? How does the organization "fit" within the larger set of competition?

Of course, there are questions that are unique to each cause and, indeed, each organization that can be added. For the most part, the internal brand audit is qualitative and consists of one-on-one interviews or small focus groups. One thing that should be noted: these interviews should be done by a neutral party.

This can be a nonprofit consultant, a marketing consultant, or some other neutral party. If that is impossible, be aware of any assumptions or biases that can be brought in by the interviewer. For example, if the development director does the interviews due to her marketing background, understand that she will be wary of criticizing the executive director. Note that this is an issue for all parties—a consultant may also be wary of criticizing the director who hired her. While questions can be set upfront, ensure enough time for free discussion to take place, as these typically yield valuable insight.

One of the authors worked in conjunction with an advertising agency for the Campfire USA First Texas Council last year to develop a strategic plan to prepare the organization to launch a $10 million capital campaign. While the researchers were interviewing executive team members, some interesting insights were uncovered. For example, executive team members believed that some of the more wealthy campers were attending other camps in the area that had more amenities. Executives felt that this was giving their camp a negative comparison with other area camps. However, when an analysis of the database of past campers was revealed, it showed that the actual campers had a higher household income than expected, which had major implications for pricing. Indeed, many executives were surprised to find out the profile of many of their campers. Internal audits can reveal insights vital to building a good brand foundation.

Communications Audits

Communications audits are good for medium-sized nonprofits or nonprofits with multiple constituencies or programs. A communications audit examines all of the materials that are produced by the organization, including newsletters, press releases, letters to editors, interviews, brochures, Web sites, social media, blogs, tweets, and logos. Analysis determines the consistency and cohesiveness of the elements in terms of design and appearance, message tone and content, and general adherence to brand standards. This is relatively easy to do and can be accomplished in-house. Some issues to consider are:

- What are the key messages? How is the organization communicating the key messages?
- Are there any confusing messages? Are there elements that are not consistent?
- What is missing? Are there ways to communicate with stakeholders who are missing or wrong? Be sure that any additional platforms (namely social media) have a purpose and are measured for effectiveness.

Again, there are several elements that need to be considered. For example, if the nonprofit is a medical charity, is there sufficient medical information on the Web site? Is it written in a way that stakeholders can understand it? The American Heart Association, one of the largest nonprofits in the world, is an

Table 2.3: Communication Audit Elements

Advertising (events, programs, services, etc.)—any paid advertising in print, outdoor space, radio, television, online

Other brand marketing elements, such as signage, packaging, distribution, direct marketing, sponsorship, retail

Press kits

Press releases

Brochures

Web sites

Social-media sites (Facebook, Twitter, YouTube, blogs, etc.)

Internal communication systems

Business cards, letterhead, and other collateral

Event material (planning, collateral, etc.)

Research (primary and secondary) relating to communication

Staff training

Volunteer training

Board training

Manager training

Program training

Competitive information (advertising, promotion, etc.)

Based in part on "Anatomy of a Brand Audit" *Branding Strategy Insider* (November 27, 2007), www.brandstrategyinsider.com.

organization based on medical research. However, the information on their Web site is clear and not written with excessive jargon. Ideally, the communications audit should be able to examine a 360-degree review of all of the touchpoints (digital and otherwise) for the ways that stakeholders experience the organization. How is the nonprofit advertised? What are the messages for the donors? Are emotional or rational appeals being used? What is the experience like for those who use it? How are they treated?

External Brand Audits

The external brand audit examines how external stakeholders view the organization. This is typically where more sophisticated analysis comes in, such as statistical survey analysis to understand the community's perceptions of the organization. It is important to identify who is important—is it local governmental officials, community members, media, influential bloggers, donors? Once this is determined, then a strategy can be developed. For example, if the media and local government are the two most important stakeholders, interviews will suffice, using much of the same ground rules as the internal brand audit interviews. However, if it is important to understand the perception of a large number of donors or community members, then a survey may be warranted. We will talk in more detail about ways to use the Internet to gather information in chapter 10, but some issues to consider in the external brand audit include:

- What does the organization mean to you (the stakeholder)?
- Do you contribute money? Why? Do you volunteer time? Why?
- How do you get information about the organization? What is most useful for you?
- What types of information do you want to see? How do you want to see it?
- Who else do you see providing the same services as organization X? Do you also contribute money and/or time to them?
- Which causes are most important to you? Why?

Again, there will be some tailoring that is required based on the type and size of the organization. If the organization has recently lost donors or other types of support, using some of these questions to find out why people have defected can be quite insightful (if not brutally honest). Sometimes finding out why something is not working is more important than finding out why something does work.

If time is of the essence or resources are at a minimum, interviewers can ask a group of internal and external stakeholders two questions: first, in three words or less, what does the organization stand for?; and second, what does the organization offer and do they consistently back up that promise? This can yield some quick information of how well the organization's brand is performing in the areas of brand awareness.

What Are You Looking For?

Throughout all three sections of the brand audit, the organization should be looking for consistency. Ideally, each stakeholder should hold similar perceptions about the organization and its mission. Remember, perception is reality. So if there are breakdowns in perceptions among the stakeholders, this will lead to a diminished brand image. The communication coming from the organization should reinforce a cohesive image. If there are breakdowns or if there is low awareness or faulty knowledge, this needs to be corrected. Oftentimes, executive team members are so close to the organization and its brand that they have no clue what people are really thinking.

Brand audits are tools that can aid organizations to develop a memorable, simple, and differentiated brand image. These tools take the perspectives of all stakeholders and, by gathering insights from all parties, will ensure that the brand is meeting objectives set by the leadership of the organization. Conducting these audits periodically will help your organization stay true and consistent.

THE ULTIMATE DIGITAL BRANDING EFFORT: THE OBAMA CAMPAIGN

Regardless of your political beliefs, it is hard to deny that the 2008 presidential campaign was anything but historic. For the first time in many years, there was no vice presidential "incumbent." Second, in the Democratic primary there was the first female candidate and the first African-American candidate with widespread support. Third, the Republican candidates were few; indeed, John McCain was known more for his independent spirit than this conservative appeal and was never a favorite with the base. So think about this campaign from purely a branding and digital engagement perspective, and it serves as an effective guide.

Think of the Obama brand. Not exactly well-known in 2004 when he gave his now-famous speech at the Democratic National Convention that introduced him to America, Barack Obama was a freshman senator from Illinois with little political experience but a strong educational background. And he had a great story. He was a young, unknown black man with an African father, a white mother, and a Muslim-sounding name. And he had, for a time, lived in Indonesia. No one really knew what he was about, and his family background was hardly typical of presidential candidates.

Obama's first opponent, Hillary Clinton, was the best-known woman in America, a former first lady and senator from New York who had worked hard to create bipartisanship on several issues. She was highly educated and considered the most formidable force in the Democratic Party. His second competitor, McCain, was a popular and respected war hero (indeed, a POW who survived more than five years in enemy custody) with forty years of senatorial experience and with a record of extending hands across party lines. But Barack Obama had a better marketing strategy than either one of them: change.

Obama's presidential campaign launched in February 2007, started with the message of change, and did not deviate from it. Ever. The message resonated with American voters. He kept the message simple and consistent through endless repetition. Voters identified with the message of change, and Obama effectively defined that message so that all the other candidates were also forced to address it. Clinton started her campaign with the "experience" message. When she saw that Obama was making progress with his "change" message, she developed "countdown to change" until critics complained of her lack of a unique positioning. She then shifted to "Solutions for America." Too many messages in a short amount of time. John McCain should have learned some lessons from Clinton but didn't. While Obama kept with the "change" message, McCain used several messages: conservative, maverick, hero, straight-talker, commander, bipartisan, experienced, patriot. Too many messages in a short amount of time. He settled on "country first," but it was late in the game and held little relevance with voters.

Obama stuck with one simple message—change—and did not deviate from it, regardless of what the competition said about him. This is a classic positioning principle. The lesson is that the best message is simple, consistent, and relevant.[15]

Use of Effective Design and Functionality

Before anything could happen, the campaign needed a look. A logo. While most companies spend several months and hundreds of thousands of dollars or more developing a brand and logo, the Obama campaign did not have that time. According to Scott Thomas, the campaign's design director, they were designing on the fly.[16] Eventually, the hardest issue would be getting everything consistent—from the use of the logo, to the colors, to the fonts, to the various Web sites and social-media sites that would be so crucial to the campaign's success. Each time a voter engaged with the Obama brand (via a button, Web site, profile, or poster) they were greeted with the same blue, gray, and red colors and familiar "O" logo. The cornerstone of the presidential campaign in terms of communication was the campaign Web site (barackobama.com). It was kept simple, and the site was optimized for the two major types of search: organic, where keywords are optimized for searching, and paid, where key words are purchased. The campaign Web site also had related sites for each state (e.g., ny.barackobama.com in New York) and for specific audiences. For example, there was a Spanish site that emphasized Hispanic campaign elements such as miGente.com and a Latinos for Obama microsite. The site allowed for content from Barack Obama, Michelle Obama, and the Bidens to connect with viewers, and the team kept the content relevant and timely. Users could access videos of speeches and transcripts, press releases, and facts. The site featured information on special issues and groups (e.g., women, seniors, Americans with disabilities, veterans, and environmentalists). The site was designed as a comprehensive resource for helping users to become active campaigners.[17] Ideally, visitors to the site were encouraged to join the social-networking site mybarackobama.com in order to further engage with the campaign. Key lessons include:

- Keep visual representations of the brand consistent across platforms.
- Consider tailoring messages to various constituents within the Web site.

Use of Social Media

Many people think that Barack Obama won the election with the Web, particularly with social-networking technology. Indeed, this was a campaign with a chief technology officer, a core staff of eleven people (including one of the founders of Facebook), a total staff of thirty that grew with the campaign, and a $2 million infrastructure. The team proved to be tech-savvy from the start. "They leapfrogged the mainstream media by producing content that they knew would get distributed for them once it was uploaded," said TechPresident.com founder Andrew Rasiej.

Probably the biggest initiative, mybarackobama.com was a proprietary social-networking site. Two million people developed a profile and then many volunteered information to the campaign, joined the network to find local events, volunteered, and coordinated other grassroots efforts. Supporters could create their own Web sites, establish their own communities, upload photos, and keep personal blogs—all tools that fostered greater engagement. The campaign team provided all of the tools (within the "action" center) for supporters to develop their own active campaigns. They encouraged slicing and dicing content. They provided guidelines for planning a voter-registration drive, developing a neighborhood-visit campaign, hosting a debate party, making phone calls, knocking on doors, and more. Additionally, users were able to form groups (e.g., Students for Barack Obama, Macs for Barack), and these were given a homepage, directory, blog platform, e-mail list, group fund-raising page, and other tools. Access was granted to databases of information for supporters to utilize. This eventually led many supporters to engage in grassroots campaigning late into the election cycle, especially in battleground states. Overall, there were 35,000 groups created by volunteers. The entire goal of the social-networking site was to drive offline behavior, such as organizing, calling, voting, and attending events. Indeed, more than 200,000 offline events were organized through the social-networking site, including everything from dinner parties to fun runs.[18]

In addition to a proprietary social network, the team utilized existing social networks very effectively. Team Obama used streaming video throughout the campaign and posted all content on the Web site. They edited it and uploaded it onto iTunes and YouTube. They used sites like Flickr and Scribd to get additional exposure. Team Obama used Twitter, LinkedIn, MySpace, Facebook, and specialty social-network sites aimed at specific groups (e.g., eons for baby boomers; BlackPlanet for African-Americans). Overall, the team maintained more than fifteen carefully selected online communities and had more than five million supporters. Importantly, the team spent some time getting to know each site as opposed to jumping right in. That way the content was catered to the audience and the purpose of the site—not a one-size-fits-all solution. They provided each audience with the right experience, making sure all information was up to date and accurate. Everything worked together. According to David Carr writing in the *New York Times*, "Like a lot of Web innovators, the Obama campaign did not invent anything completely new. Instead, by bolting together social networking applications under the banner of a movement, they created an unforeseen force to raise money, organize locally, fight smear campaigns, and get out the vote that helped them topple the Clinton machine and then John McCain and the Republicans."[19] Key lessons include:

- Use social networking to allow people to connect with others who share similar interests.
- Make sure that social networking is used to drive offline behavior (e.g., volunteering, event attendance).
- Allow users the freedom to create a unique presence.
- Research before reaching out to existing social-networking sites (e.g., Facebook).

Creation of Advocacy

"The campaign was not successful simply because it got a lot of people out to vote. It was successful because it got a lot of people out getting others to vote," wrote Jalali Hartman, CEO of Yovia.com. By using mobile technology and iPhone apps, as well as online tools and social networking, the Obama campaign was able to engage thousands of supporters who had never campaigned before. The database of thirteen million e-mail addresses was used to develop grassroots support for not only the campaign but also the ideas that the campaign embodied. Three million people signed up to receive text messages from the campaign. Supporters traveled to battlegrounds states, they made calls, they held parties, and they voted. And they got their friends to vote and their friends' friends to vote. Indeed, the day after the election, Obama sent an e-mail to supporters indicating that the real work had yet to begin. This set up the mindset for continued advocacy after the campaign was closed. Key lessons include:

- Know your audience; know what tools will allow them to act.
- Be creative and take some risks with technology.

Groundbreaking Fund-raising

In September 2008, Obama amassed more than 65 percent of his record-shattering fund-raising haul—$100 million of the $150 million that was raised online. Indeed, the campaign raised $10 million in the twenty-four hours after the selection of Sarah Palin as the Republican vice-presidential candidate. Overall, more than three million donors made a total of 6.5 million donations, adding up to more than $500 million in campaign contributions. Most of these were online. Of those, six million of the donations were less than $100, with the average donation being $80 and the average donor giving more than once. Compare that to the $75 million that McCain raised online out of a total $360 million.[20] Key lessons include:

- Don't underestimate the power of everyday people to give; small amounts add up.

- Provide multiple ways to give—personal pages, Web site, social-networking sites.
- Know that people will give to a compelling movement.

Use of Research

The Obama team was smart about segmenting messages to different audiences. They used behavioral targeting to segment their voter audience so that each message was tailored specifically to the individual voter. When a prospective voter visited the candidate's site, an Internet tag was placed on the user's browser that could identify what types of sites the user visited afterward, thereby making the political ads served up more effective.[21] The team used various media types depending on the audience (e.g., text for college students, traditional television for older voters). The campaign used traditional media in untraditional ways, specifically by purchasing time on big events, such as the summer Olympics and a thirty-minute infomercial on seven networks just days before the election. They used search-engine optimization to dispel negative information and Internet rumors. An analytics team measured everything that went in and out of the Web site and tracked which ad drew the most traffic and what kinds of e-mails from the campaign got opened and read.

Chris Hughes, one of the youngest members of the Obama team, told the *Washington Post*, "Whatever we've learned from this campaign is that there's huge potential for people that haven't been involved in politics to discover that,

Table 2.4: Obama by the Numbers

E-mail	13 million on e-mail list; 7,000 e-mail variations and more than 1 billion emails sent
Donors	3 million online donors who contributed 6.5 million times
Social Networks	5 million "friends" on more than 15 social networking sites and more than 3 million friends on Facebook
Web Site	8.5 million monthly visitors to MyBarackObama.com (at the peak); 2 million profiles with 400,000 blog posts; 35,000 volunteer groups that held 200,000 offline events; 70,000 fundraising hubs that raised $30 million
Video	Almost 2,000 official YouTube videos watched more than 80 million times with 135,000 subscribers; 442,000 user-generated videos on YouTube (including many that went viral)
Mobile	3 million people signed up for the text-messaging program; each received 5 to 20 messages per month
Phone Calls	3 million personal phone calls placed in the final four days of the campaign
Votes	365 electoral votes; 66.8 million more popular votes

Digital Public Affairs, *The Social Pulpit: Barack Obama's Social Media Toolkit* (Edelman, 2009).

Conversation with the Pros:
Scott Henderson, Managing Director, Cause Shift

Scott Henderson is the former director of cause marketing for MediaSauce in Indianapolis, a marketing agency focusing primarily on the digital environment (www.mediasauce.com). He blogs at Rally the Cause (www.rallythecause.com) and Cause Shift (http://causeshift.com), where he is now managing director. Scott thinks that developing a strong brand is important for nonprofit organizations for one simple reason: relevance. Every organization is fighting for the attention of people surrounded and bombarded by media everywhere they go. If people can't understand quickly what an organization does and why it matters to them, they will move on to other things. To have a strong brand, nonprofits need first to understand what they stand for and what unique value they bring to the greater community. Then they need to communicate through every touchpoint they have with their stakeholders. Henderson thinks every organization benefits when more people (internally and externally) understand these two things.

The biggest mistake that nonprofits make is not understanding the concept of branding. "Strong branding is not just a logo," Henderson says. "It is a mosaic of interactions—for example, print, radio, personal, direct mail, events, and so on—that clearly and consistently states what a nonprofit stands for and the unique value they bring to the community. You can't change your brand by adjusting a logo. It requires many different little things to be aligned with each other. That takes vigilance and constant attention at all levels of the organization."

Henderson feels that nonprofits can use social media very effectively. He sees several trends regarding the use of technology. First, he states that most nonprofits realize that they can no longer have a Web site that mimics a brochure and are seeing the benefits of bringing their cause alive using social media and more robust Web sites. Henderson expects to see pioneering nonprofits to integrate online giving in a more effective way because right now most online fund-raising still approximates direct-mail solicitations. Second, there is a call for better measurement of success. Despite their low costs, social-media efforts do take time, and nonprofit boards and executive directors want to understand the return on that investment of time. This continues to be a struggle for many organizations (not just nonprofits), but it is easier to measure online media usage than traditional media usage.

Henderson advises nonprofits to create a strategy and build a game plan that brings that strategy to life. The number one responsibility is to tie the branding efforts to specific organizational objectives. "If you can't point to how it is going to help create more resources for your organization, save yourself the frustration," he says.

yes, this is something that impacts me. Even before I joined the campaign, the fundamental premise was to help put the political process into people's own hands. That was the value from the start of the campaign, that was the value at the end of the campaign, and it's not going away."[22] Indeed, this awakening can be harnessed by many nonprofits to engage them in participation, advocacy, and fund-raising.

Developing a strong brand image is the key to all other aspects of communicating about the mission of the nonprofit organization. The rest of this book deals with several issues that are aided by having a strong brand. The Web site is the hub for digital branding. In the following chapters, we discuss the importance of both Web site functionality and effective Web site design. We discuss how fund-raising, volunteer recruitment, and advocacy is facilitated by online engagement with key stakeholders. Public relations, especially media relations, is aided by the Internet by making it easier to communicate key messages.

LESSONS LEARNED

- Understand that before anything, agree on the mission and purpose of the organization. Have everyone on board with this position.
- Nonprofits often forget about the importance of brand image. Typically, they are spending their time meeting their mission and raising money. But having a strong brand image makes both of those tasks easier.
- Brands should be simple, clear, consistent, distinct, inspirational, portable, engaging, and relevant.
- Stories are the key for nonprofit brand images. Digital technology makes this much easier and effective.
- Tie all digital brand touchpoints to objectives and metrics.
- Consider conducting a brand audit in order to better understand the positioning of your brand.

FURTHER READING

Brand Digital: Simple Ways Top Brands Succeed in the Digital World by Allen P. Adamson
Cause Wired by Tom Watson
The Art of Digital Branding by Ian Cocoran
Marketing to the Social Web by Larry Weber
Nonprofit Internet Strategies by Ted Hart, James Greenfield, and Michael Johnston
Branding for Nonprofits by D.K. Holland

NOTES

1. Allen P. Adamson, Allen P., *Brand Digital: Simple Ways Top Brands Succeed in the Digital World* (New York: Palgrave Macmillian, 2008).
2. The Cone Nonprofit Power Brand 100: In collaboration with Intangible Business (Cone Communications, June 2009), www.coneinc.com.
3. National Center for Charitable Statistics, http://nccs.urban.org/statistics/quickfacts.cfm.
4. Kevin Lane Keller, *Building, Measuring, and Managing Brand Equity, 3rd Ed.* (Upper Saddle River, NJ: Pearson Prentice Hall, 2008).
5. Kristine Kirby Webster, "Branding the Non-Profit" (Marketing Profs, April 30, 2002), www.marketingprofs.com.
6. Cone Nonprofit Power Brand 100.
7. Ibid.
8. Personal correspondence, Mitch Maxson and Scott Henderson, August 14, 2009.
9. Adamson, *Brand Digital*.
10. Communities in Schools Dallas 2007–2008 Annual Report, www.cisdallas.org.
11. Tactical Module 3: Sharing Your Story Social Media Style, www.wearemedia.org
12. Pierre Chandon, *Note on Brand Audit: How to Measure Brand Awareness, Brand Image, Brand Equity and Brand Value* (Fontainbleau, France: INSEAD, February 2004), 5191.
13. Mark Shipley, "Brand Audits," Fusion Brand, www.fusionbrand.com; "Keeping the Brand Healthy: The Annual Brand Checkup" (March 13, 2007), www.marketingprofs.com.
14. Chandon, *Note on Brand Audit*.
15. Al Ries, "What Marketers Can Learn From Obama's Campaign," *Advertising Age* (November 5, 2008), www.adage.com.
16. Rahaf Harfoush, *Yes We Did: An Inside Look At How Social Media Build the Obama Brand* (Berkeley, CA: New Riders, 2009).
17. Kimberly Smith, "Special Report: How the 'Obama for America' Campaign Used Digital Media to Turn Ordinary Citizens into Campaign Evangelists and Win the Election," www.marketingprofs.com (January 20, 2009).
18. Harfoush, *Yes We Did*.
19. Ibid.
20. Jose Antonio Vargas, "Obama Raised Half a Billion Online" (November 20, 2008) www.washingtonpost.com.
21. Chris Dannen, "How Obama Won It on the Web" (November 5, 2008), www.Fastcompany.com.
22. Vargas, "Obama Raised Half a Billion Online."

CHAPTER 3

Web Site Design and Functionality for Effective Communication

"Usability is much more about human nature than technology. Technology changes quickly; human nature very slowly."
—Jakob Nielsen Ph.D, Founder of Nielsen Norman Group, called the "guru of Web page usability" by the *New York Times*[1]

CHAPTER OVERVIEW

The Web site is the communication cornerstone for many organizations. The purpose of this chapter is to help managers understand why design is important for effective communication with all stakeholders. This chapter will also help managers understand the priorities of the various Web site user types since all visitors are not created equally and should not garner the same resource attention. We will also provide managers with a roadmap regarding various types of interaction with the Web site and finally introduce managers to the Web Site Assessment Tool that will help them assess their nonprofit Web site.

DO SOMETHING AIMS TO ENGAGE TEENS AND TWEENS

Research on Millennials (those eighty million people born between 1980 and 2000) states that they are, as a group, a very cause-oriented bunch. Nonprofits have, to varying degrees of success, tried to capitalize on that. However, Do Something is one of the biggest success stories. Do Something (www.dosomething.org/about) is the largest organization focusing on engaging young people, those twenty-five and under, with causes and volunteerism. Their aim is to "inspire, support, and celebrate a generation of doers: people who see the need to do something, believe in their ability to get it done, and then take action." The purpose is to facilitate volunteering for teens, to provide action guides for important causes, and to choose a cause and run a monthly campaign. Do Something is supported primarily through corporate partnerships and has seen miraculous growth over its sixteen-year history. It was founded by *Melrose Place* star Andrew

Shue and his childhood friend, Mike Sanchez, in 1993. Over the past year, Do Something has undertaken a massive redesign of its Web site to accommodate the organization's growth. Two years ago, it supported fifteen causes; today it supports eighty-five. Some of the tools that were important to its target audience of teens and tweens include social-media access (such as Twitter and Facebook); the Act Now Matrix, which is a database that allows teens to select their cause, who they are working with, place of volunteering, and length of time; and the Volunteer Database, a volunteer opportunity aggregator that allows teens to type in their zip code to find local volunteer opportunities. Volunteers even get updates on their cell phones. In 2009, Do Something won a Webby Award in the Youth Category, beating out several well-known youth brands. Do Something is a good example of an organization who clearly understands its target audience and has designed an effective Web site that engages its audience to act.[2]

MORE THAN A PRETTY FACE: THE IMPORTANCE OF DESIGN

Designing a Web site has become easier in the past few years. Just about anyone can do it. Managers can use software like Dreamweaver and Flash or iWeb to develop their Web sites. There are also Web sites (e.g., Boxed Art, Dream Templates, Template Monster) that allow users to download designer templates to get started to edit in one of these software packages. If you want to use a dynamic Web site (such as a blog format), getting started is even easier. In just a few short clicks, you can be blogging on Blogger (www.blogger.com) or WordPress (www.wordpress.com and www.wordpress.org) using preexisting templates or one you design on your own. Indexhibit (http://indexhibit.org) is a plain source package that allows users to set up a portfolio or gallery. Or you can use a content management system like Joomla or WordPress to develop an interactive site.

Regardless of what tools you use, one thing remains vital: the importance of effective design. By "effective," we don't just mean "pretty." Indeed, the visual design is only a part of the plan, albeit an important part. Visual design is what makes a positive first impression. If your organization can afford it, the best option is to get a good graphic designer. Using a designer allows the organization to have a customizable Web site tailored to the needs of the brand. However, if you cannot afford a good designer, using templates can help anyone make a visually pleasing Web site. While there are tools that make developing Web sites quite easy (much easier, at least, than writing HTML code from scratch), it also means that there are thousands of Web sites out there that are, well, just bad. They are hard to read. They are hard to navigate. Some Web sites are not updated regularly. Some use fonts and colors that are hard to read on a monitor. Some sites use tools that are not effective for their site or not meaningful for their audience.

A usability review or usability test assesses how well a visitor can get through a Web site. It includes issues such as interaction design (what happens after this click and that click) and information architecture (how everything is organized).³ Some of the areas included in usability are the effectiveness of the navigation, browser compatibility, how the pages are linked, the ability to search within the site, and so on. Other areas important for Web site design include the visual design, the value of the content, and the interactivity. Most of these principles are valid even as technology changes rapidly. But the idea is: when a visitor finds your homepage, is it clear what they can do next?

Steve Krug, author of *Don't Make Me Think: A Common Sense Approach to Web Usability*, starts with one primary "law" of usability that is applicable to all Web sites. This law is: "Don't make me think." Sounds simple—and it is. Essentially, the Web site should make intuitive sense. It should be obvious and self-explanatory. No directions required. It should be easy to find things like the mission, additional information, and how to contact the organization. Visitors to your Web site don't want to have to think too much. They typically don't read pages, they scan them, so make sure that pages are easily interpretable. This goes for design elements, as well, since visual design is typically what catches visitors' attention. Also, visitors aren't necessarily looking for the best option for finding things, but rather the first reasonable option that they find. So you need to make sure it is clear where visitors should go next.

With the maturation of Web 2.0 (which essentially means that instead of a visitor communicating only with the Web site, now they can communicate with each other, as well) there is a concept called the social web. As defined by Joshua Porter in his book *Designing for the Social Web*, social web design is the "conception, planning, and production of Web sites and applications that support social interaction."[4] This concept incorporates social behavior—that need for people to share, to talk, to care, to advocate, and so on. This group interaction is what separates social Web sites from traditional Web sites. Some mainstream examples of the social web include eBay, Amazon, Wikipedia, and Facebook. However, recently there have been several nonprofits that have organized almost exclusively using the social web. One such example is Kiva, a microfinance site.

Kiva (www.kiva.org) is a social-network site that allows people to lend money to entrepreneurs all over the world. Started in 2003 by Jessica and Matt Flannery and Premal Shah, the site includes profiles of the entrepreneurs with a request for a specific amount of money and an explanation of how they plan to use it. A bar chart describes how much has been raised, so that it is easy to see how a donor can complete a working project. The site also includes updates from the entrepreneurs about what progress they have made with the loan. The money is paid back, and donors typically then lend to another entrepreneur. There is a place on the Web site for donor profiles and ways for donors to get more involved by sending information to their friends and colleagues via e-mail. To date, Kiva has helped hundreds of thousands of lenders raise millions of dollars to help entrepreneurs in more than forty countries. It has enjoyed exposure on *The Oprah Winfrey Show, The Today Show*, and in Bill Clinton's book *Giving*. It has become the world's best-known online micro-lending service.[5]

Porter argues that it is important to consider flexibility when designing these social interfaces. If it is too confining, people won't use it, and if it is too flexible, people won't know how to use it. So the challenge is to "design interfaces that support the current and desired behavior of the people who use them."[6] In the case of Kiva, the interface is simple to use and allows for easy engagement between the donor and loan recipient.

ALL VISITORS ARE NOT CREATED EQUAL: THE VISITOR ENGAGEMENT CYCLE

When considering Web site design and development, managers often fall into the trap of thinking that everyone coming to the Web site is the same. There are obvious differences: some are looking for information on the cause, some are looking for volunteering information, some may be with the media looking for contact information, and some may be looking for financial information. Typically, these concepts fall into the realm of user experience, and all Web site managers should understand how visitors interact with the site. All of these highlight different visitor motivations. However, it is also important to consider their broader relationship with your organization. As such, we have adapted the visitor engagement cycle to describe how visitors to the Web site differ in their motives and needs. The visitor engagement cycle includes four distinct visitors.[7]

The first visitor is not really a visitor at all. These are the millions of people who are completely unaware of your organization. They are called the *unaware public*. While every once in a while someone may serendipitously stumble upon your organization through a search engine, word-of-mouth, or a news article, most of your energy will not be spent with the unaware public.

The second visitor is the *first-time visitor*. These are people who are at least somewhat aware of your organization. This awareness can be the result of a traditional awareness campaigns, a story in the media, an interest in your overall cause, a link, or a mention from a friend. There is really a host of ways that a first-time visitor initially becomes aware of your organization and then takes the time to visit your Web site. The key here is the visitor takes the initiative to visit. This early engagement is important because the visitor is at least curious if not already interested. Your primary goal for the first-time visitor is to give them enough content and information to keep them there and keep them coming back. Move them to the next phase of the visitor engagement cycle. This is no small task.

Regular visitors have been to your site before (probably for one of the reasons listed earlier). They come back to your site for some reason—and you need to find out why. You may be able to group these regular visitors according to motivation—are they volunteers? Are they donors? How do we define "regular"? We are actually leaving that open—for some organizations, regular may be every day, and for some it could be every few months. Your primary goal for regular visitors is to find out as much as you can about them and ensure that you are providing new and engaging content to keep them returning. Ideally, you want to get them engaged by asking them to sign up for a newsletter or blog or to make a small donation to a program or cause. Invite them to an event. Get them involved. Ben Rattray, founder of Change.org, stated in Tom Watson's book *CauseWired* that online activity (particularly fund-raising) includes awareness, engagement, activism, and recurrence, and the hardest thing to do is to get people into the activism and recurrence phases.[8] It is imperative to give visitors enough information to keep them interested.

The last visitor is called the *advocate visitor*. This person has a strong relationship with your organization. These can include major donors, regular donors, ongoing volunteers, staff, constituents, board members—really anyone who has a passion for your cause and your organization. Ideally, you want to turn as many of your visitors into advocates, since you will likely be able to count on them for time and monetary donations.

You cannot possibly pay attention to all of your visitors. And indeed, some deserve more attention than others. Think of this as an inverted pyramid (see figure 3.1). At the very top is the unaware public. They make up millions. You don't have the resources to really worry about them. We will discuss some ways

Figure 3.1: Visitor Engagement Cycle

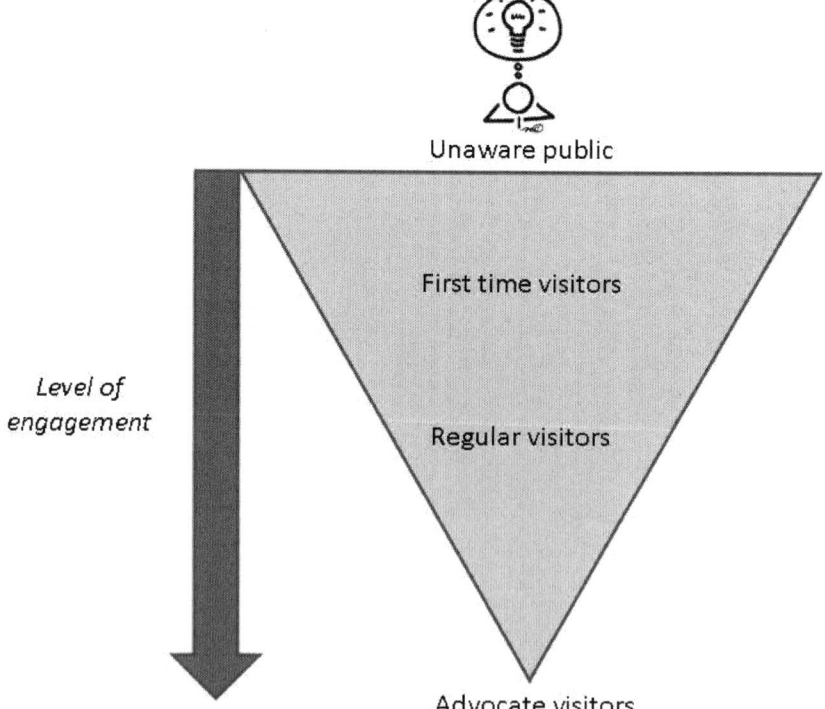

that you may be able to get at least some of them to first-time-visitor status through search-engine optimization, but essentially you will spend the least amount of effort on this group. Next in the pyramid is the first-time visitor. These are important because, again, you want to provide them with the content they are looking for and also pique their interest enough to return on a regular basis. You will spend a fair amount or time and energy on them, but know that they won't all become regular visitors. Next you have the regular visitors. Your goal is to engage them consistently and find out as much as you can about them. Later in the book we will talk about some research tools available to help you find out as much information as possible about this group. Last, the advocate visitors will make up a small number of your visitors, but they are the most engaged. You don't want to lose them. It is easy to take them for granted, but it is important that you don't make this mistake. Think about the 80/20 rule. This rule says that 80 percent of your donations, volunteer hours, and revenue comes from about 20 percent of your constituents. This generally holds true with some variation on either side.

What does that mean to your nonprofit? Many nonprofit organizations spend their time and limited resources trying to go for the masses—the unaware public or those first-time visitors. While it is important to always keep a new stream of potential donors, it is typically more useful to keep the regular and advocate visitors happy so that they are not tempted to go elsewhere.

In order to get more information on the visitor engagement cycle, managers can use several tools to see how many people fall into these categories (this will be discussed later in the book). For example, you can find out exactly how many people fall into the regular-visitors category, and managers can further find out how long they stay on each page and what they do on the Web site (e.g., donate, sign up for newsletter, bookmark the site, get more information on an event) using Web analytics. In addition, using this information, managers can also find out what is not working with the site. For example, if a regular visitor is reviewing the information on newsletter sign-up and does not follow through, what is the reason? Perhaps the sign-up form is too long and needs to be shortened. Or perhaps the navigation needs to be tweaked because visitors are using the search box for simple terms. Therefore, this visitor engagement cycle inverted pyramid function is an effective tool to identify areas that require improvement.

THE BIG PICTURE: FUNDAMENTAL QUESTIONS ABOUT YOUR WEB SITE

In order to design more effectively (and tweak existing sites in the right way), it is important to consider each of the following questions. The answers will give you insight so that when you are ready to conduct the assessment discussed later in this chapter, you have a good perspective.

Who Is Your Web Site Designed For?

Obviously one answer is donors and potential donors. But you also need to consider the other stakeholders—and primarily your constituents. Constituents are those people who actually use your services. For example, they include the cancer patients seeking information or the low-income parents seeking rent or mortgage assistance. It is important to consider who your most important stakeholders are and how you plan to communicate with them.

What Type of Web Site Do You Have? What Are Its Capabilities and What Would You Like Its Capabilities to Be?

Here you will have slightly different goals, depending on whether you have a microsite (e.g., promotion of a 5K run), a social Web site (e.g., allowing interested parties to communicate via an online community), or a large Web site serving multiple stakeholders. Depending on where your organization is right now, you may also want to consider what capabilities you wish your site to have in the future. For example, does your organization want to create an application that allows interested parties to share information on their Facebook or LinkedIn pages? Does your organization want to eventually capture additional information such as cell phone numbers? Will you want an iPhone app? These future needs should also be considered.

Where Can Visitors Use Your Web Site? Does It Have a Mobile Version?

Is it important for your Web site to be mobile? If so, what do you want visitors to do with your site on their phones? This is above and beyond the need to have your Web site applicable for various browsers. Browser technology differs in that Web sites can be displayed differently on various browsers.

Why Do Visitors Come to Your Web Site?

Understand the mission of your Web site. Again, is it geared toward donors, volunteers, or constituents? Here are some reasons for visiting nonprofit organization sites: to donate, to learn about the cause, to sign up for volunteer opportunities, to hear stories about the mission, to learn about programs and services for constituents, to learn about special events, and so on. It is important to figure out which one or ones are the most important for your organization.

GETTING STARTED: PLANNING YOUR WEB SITE

Before you get started, especially if you are starting from scratch, it is important to plan ahead. You can do this with your existing site, as well, to ensure that everything is organized.

What Is the Purpose of the Site?

Given you have identified the answers to the above questions, generate some objectives. Is it to increase awareness of the cause? Is it to position your organization as an expert in the area? Is it to generate connections with new donors? Is it to generate additional funds? There are a host of objectives that can be considered; try to determine which ones work for your organization.

How Is Your Site Going to Be Organized?

It is tempting to just start creating, but the best use of your time and energy is to outline how you think the site should be organized, including what information should go where. Ideally, this can also be done using index cards and a bulletin board, which allow you to move things around easily. Seeing the site visually often helps view the bigger picture and identify areas of opportunity or weakness early on. This is also important because how a user actually navigates your site may be very different than what you intended. This will become apparent during the usability tests.

What Information Do You Need?

Make a list of the information you need, including logos, photos, illustrations, and stories. Secure any permissions necessary for the content. Make sure your domain name is registered and up to date. Collect any required disclaimer information, trademarks, or copyright information. Gather any audio elements you may need.

What Are Your Preferences?

Make a list of any preferences and requirements you may have for communication purposes. For example, if your logo uses a certain color, identify it for the site. State any preferences for typeface or color schemes.

What Are Your Basic Page Elements?

Make a list of what you are going to name your pages and what elements you want on your site (such as video or blog capabilities). Include the number and type of forms you want and the purpose of each one. Include all contact information. Include the navigation system you want to use and how it should be labeled.

What Is Your Plan?

Consider how to promote your site. Definitely include your domain name on all other printed material. Secure your hosting service contract and define your key words (the words you want to be used in search engines). Key words can include a wide range of words and phrases, including your nonprofit name, the cause, and your competitors and partners. These will be used for search-engine optimization and for social-media monitoring.

Who Needs to Approve It?

The last issue is to determine who has approval. Some nonprofit leaders like to get as many opinions on the Web site as possible. While that is fine for input, ultimately only a few people should have decision-making power. Make this line of approval clear or you will forever be changing things because Betty the volunteer likes blue better than red.

THE WEB SITE ASSESSMENT TOOL

In order to explore the opportunities and weaknesses that your site may have, especially relative to your competition, we have developed a tool called the Web Site Assessment Tool. The purpose of this tool is to allow nonprofit managers a way to assess current Web sites. Additionally, organizations can conduct analyses on competitor sites to see what they are doing well (and not so well). This tool includes information about usability, visual design, content, and interactivity. Managers review their site and evaluate their site according to the criteria using a scale of 1 to 5. The lower the number, the lower the score. We have also allowed space for comments. For example, if your site does not have blogging capability, then this area is not applicable to you, but you may want to note that this is an area where you want to develop a capability.

After reviewing the information in figure 3.2, have several other people within your organization complete the questionnaire. In addition, you may also use this questionnaire with users to conduct your own usability test.

Figure 3.2:   Web Site Assessment Tool

Organization: _____
Target Audience(s): _____

Criteria	Evaluation	Comments
		Include any relevant comments
Usability Home Page *Does the homepage introduce the organization's brand well?*	1 2 3 4 5	
Browser Capability *Is the site applicable for Internet Explorer, Safari, and Firefox?*	1 2 3 4 5	
Links *Are the links good signals that are consistent and clear?*	1 2 3 4 5	
Navigation *Does the navigation make sense? It is consistent?* *Is it in a standard place?*	1 2 3 4 5	

Loading Time Does the site load quickly? Does it allow the user to skip an interactive introduction if you have one?	1 2 3 4 5	
Search Capability Is the search box intuitive, clear, and functional?	1 2 3 4 5	
Design of Forms Are the forms short? Are they functional? Do they only include the vital information?	1 2 3 4 5	
Usability of Donation Button Is the donation page branded by a third party? Does the process have too many clicks? Do the donors feel that they have left the site?	1 2 3 4 5	
Contact Information Is the contact information clear? Have you provided multiple ways for users to reach your organization?	1 2 3 4 5	
Call to Action Does the site have a call to action such as donate, volunteer, or find out more?	1 2 3 4 5	
Visual Design		
Alignment Are all items aligned properly within the frames?	1 2 3 4 5	
Proximity Are related items close together?	1 2 3 4 5	
Repetition Are elements repeated throughout the site? Are they consistent?	1 2 3 4 5	
Contrast Do elements draw attention and maintain the audience's focus?	1 2 3 4 5	
Use of Photos and Illustrations Are the photos and illustrations appropriate for the Web? Is the quality high?	1 2 3 4 5	
Use of Color Does the site use proper Internet-safe colors? Are the colors consistent across the site? Is it visually appealing?	1 2 3 4 5	
Consistent Focal Points Is there one main issue on each page—one dominating force?	1 2 3 4 5	
Typography Does the typography read well on the Web? Is the type size appropriate?	1 2 3 4 5	
Scanability Is the information easy to read quickly?	1 2 3 4 5	
Clutter Is there too much clutter?	1 2 3 4 5	
Use of Instructions Are instructions clear, consistent, and relevant?	1 2 3 4 5	
Content		
Audience/Stakeholder Consideration Does the site match with the intended audience(s)?	1 2 3 4 5	
Informative Content Is the site informative? Is this information of high quality?	1 2 3 4 5	

Entertaining Content *Does the site have elements that are entertaining?*	1 2 3 4 5	
Variety of Content *Is there a variety of content on the site? Does the site change content regularly?*	1 2 3 4 5	
Third-Party Endorsement *Does the organization have a rating from a third-party organization such as Charity Navigator? Is this displayed?*	1 2 3 4 5	
Interactivity		
Degree of Interactivity *Is the site considered more interactive than static?*	1 2 3 4 5	
Inclusion of User-Generated Materials *Does the site allow users to upload their own content, including blogs?*	1 2 3 4 5	
Multi-Media Elements *Does the site contain multi-media elements, such as video, audio, discussion boards?*	1 2 3 4 5	
Social-Networking Capability *Does the site allow for social-networking capability with tagging (e.g., Delicious), social-networking (e.g., Facebook)?*	1 2 3 4 5	
Ability to Share Information *Is there a RSS feed?*	1 2 3 4 5	
Total Score		

Usability

This first section deals with basic usability issues. Remember, usability deals with how well users are able to go through your Web site. These are areas that all Web sites need to have working well. Below we discuss a few additional details regarding each subsection.

Home page. The home page is the first thing that your users will see. Is it interesting? Does it address what you do? Remember that the home page needs to introduce your organization's brand image to users, including the identity and mission of the organization, the site hierarchy, and a place for site search. It also needs to include relevant content, stories, and any registration or signup that you want users to do (see table 3.1). Make sure that it is not cluttered, as this would leave a bad impression. Make sure that you include logos and graphics. Remember not to overlook the obvious.

Browser capability. Everyone uses a different browser, especially depending on whether your user is using a Mac or a PC. Be sure to test your site on all browsers, including Explorer, Firefox, and Safari. Remember that every-

Table 3.1: Home Page Must-Haves

Be sure to include something that tugs at the heartstrings and try to make it visual through video or photos

Have a two-second statement that is *not* your mission statement

Include a case (or link to one) for your nonprofit that identifies what you are doing differently

Include a way to capture interest (such as a form to sign up for a newsletter)

Provide ways to donate that include online donations, an address for snail mail, and a phone number

Include something portable so that people who use social-networking tools can share (through Twitter, blogs, vlogs, Facebook, etc.)

Have clear navigation

Show where the money goes since people are more likely to donate if they know exactly where their money is helping

Provide links and information to events and other opportunities for engagement

Make sure your logo is on all pages; but that your mission statement is not. Include the full mission statement on the "about us" page

---

Adapted from Kayta Andreasen, *Ten Things Your Home Page Must Have*, retrieved May 29, 2009, and Gayle Thorsen, *Nonprofit Homepage Tips*, retrieved March 9, 2009, from Network for Good, www.fundraising123.org.

one might not have the plug-ins you require, such as Flash, so give them an option to skip over any content that would require special plug-ins. Also, be aware of new browsers; cell phones work on different platforms than computers.

Links. Are the links obvious? Are they in another color? Do they all work? Make sure you test them regularly, as content does come down from other sites you may be linking to. Make sure the links make sense and that they provide good signals for users.

Navigation. Navigation is the organization layout for your site. You will want to make sure your navigation is well-organized, is in a standard place on the Web site, and is consistent from page to page. While your home-page navigation can be different from the rest of the site (it can be bigger or with different section descriptions or have a different orientation), you do want to ensure consistency across the other pages. Some of your users will want to browse, so make that intuitive; some users will want to use your search functions, so make sure that it is labeled well.

Loading time. For the most part, the days of dial-up are gone. That said, modem speeds do vary, so you want to make sure that your site is not taking too long to load. It shouldn't take more than a few seconds for a page to load; if users have to wait, they leave. So if you have many visuals or video effects on your site, this will require more loading time. Be careful to strike a good balance.

Search capability. While some people browse sites, others go straight to the search box. You want to ensure it is labeled well; don't use words that are creative. You can always have a basic search function and then more advanced search options, depending on what you think people are looking for. This is an area that should be researched during the usability testing.

Forms. You will probably have at least one form on your Web site, and you'll have more if you want to receive donations online or permit sharing of information through e-mail or RSS feeds. Make your forms simple. Don't ask for more information than you need—people don't like to give too much personal information. This is especially important for first-time users, since they have not established trust with your organization yet.

Usability of donation button. If you are collecting donations to your organization through the Web, you probably have a third-party processor. Make sure it is easy for users to donate to your organization by ensuring that the processor is trustworthy, that the process is short and simple, that there are not too many steps that require separate clicks, and that the users do not feel that they have left the Web site. Network for Good has conducted some research that shows that branded donation pages like Custom DonateNow brings in more money and improves the donor's experience. This allows for the donate button to match the site and provides easier administration and banking.

Contact information. Some Web sites will only allow contact electronically. However, most of those are e-commerce sites. It is important to give users a way to contact you. After all, you are building relationships; make sure it is clear where people can contact you for additional information. Some professionals advocate having a contact link on each page.

Call to action. Does your site ask the visitor to do something? While most sites do provide good information, it is a wasted opportunity if visitors are not able to act. Be sure to include calls to action to make it easy to volunteer, donate, or learn more about the cause. Add ways that allow people to share the information such as RSS feeds and links to social-networking sites. RSS stands for Really Simple Syndication. Visitors with RSS readers, a software add-on for an Internet browser or a feature of some e-mail applications, will poll Web sites with which an individual has subscribed, posting the most recent stories available from each Web site. Many people prefer RSS readers because they can get the latest news from a variety of online sources.

Chapter Insight: What is RSS (Really Simple Syndication)?

RSS is a family of Web feed formats used to publish frequently updated works, such as blog entries, news headlines, audio, and video—in a standardized format. A RSS document (which is called a "feed," "Web feed," or "channel") includes full or summarized text, plus metadata such as publishing dates and authorship. Web feeds benefit publishers by letting them syndicate content automatically. They benefit readers who want to subscribe to timely updates from favored Web sites or to aggregate feeds from many sites into one place. RSS feeds can be read using software called an "RSS reader," "feed reader," or "aggregator," which can be Web-based, desktop-based, or mobile-device-based. The user subscribes to a feed by clicking an RSS icon in a browser that initiates the subscription process. The RSS reader checks the user's subscribed feeds regularly for new work, downloads any updates that it finds, and provides a user interface to monitor and read the feeds.[9]

RSS allows for dissemination, aggregation, and research. When releasing news, simply incorporate tags to be readable in RSS readers. You can use RSS for audio and video, as well. RSS allows for content to be aggregated. This allows for your organization to pull together news and other types of information about the cause and drive traffic to your Web site. RSS can be used for insight-mining and market research, as well. Organizations can monitor RSS feeds to find out valuable information about the cause in general and other organizations serving the same constituents. Most of this monitoring is free, but there are also some companies who offer more in-depth research services.

Visual Design

The next section deals with "making it pretty." Below we discuss some basic design principles that, while simple, are crucial to maintaining a visually appealing site. It is here where many people tend to get creative and as such break some of these rules. Don't do it. Robin Williams and John Tollett offer some great tips for designing in their book *The Non-Designer's Web Book*.[10]

Alignment. Alignment means whether the items on the Web page are lined up with each other. Alignment does not mean that everything is aligned along the same edge but that everything has the same alignment. This seems simple but it usually the most prevalent problem.

Proximity. Proximity refers to the relationship among items when they are close together on your Web site. Put things that belong together close together. This includes photos, illustrations, copy, and headings.

Repetition. Repetition here refers to the fact that you want to repeat certain items throughout your site to maintain consistency. This can include navigation, colors, logos, typography, and taglines—something that you want on each page.

Contrast. Contrasts are elements that are different that draw your attention and guide your eyes around the Web site. Contrast can occur through color or typography (e.g., making a headline bigger or bolder).

Use of photos and illustrations. The most important issue to remember here is the file format. Graphic formats for the Web are usually GIF or JPEG. You can create original art using vectors, which smooth out the edges of the image. GIFs are best for images that are flat with a large area of color, simple illustrations, logos, and cartoons. Use JPEGs for photos and images with subtle color changes or graduations.

Use of color. Remember that color on the Web is a little different than anywhere else. Make sure you are using Web-safe colors (RGB values), and make sure you pick a color theme for the Web site and stay consistent. Remember to consider issues like monitor resolution when conducting any Web site tests.

Consistent focal points. There should be one dominating force on the page, whether a photo or video or story. You need to give something priority. This will help with the contrast effect.

Typography. This is another area where the typeface on the Web can be different than other places. The key is legibility and readability. Large blocks of text should adhere to the readability standards; that the font is between eight and eighteen point size for body copy and that it is generally a simple, sans serif font. Make sure headlines are legible and are typically sans serif, not in all caps, and large enough to read. Don't mix multiple typefaces—generally one serif font and one sans serif font will suffice. Also remember that exotic fonts often don't translate well to the Web.

Scanability. As stated earlier, people tend to scan sites instead of read them, so organize information in a way that allows users to quickly scan the page to find what they are looking for. Make sure key words or phrases are prominent displayed.

Clutter. It is tempting to put everything on your Web site. Resist that temptation, especially for the home page. Keep it clean and simple. You can have additional pages, but if you decide to do this, keep information organized around themes (stories, programs, volunteers).

Use of instructions. People tend not to read instructions. So if you must have instructions, make them simple and to the point.

Content

This section deals with the actual information that you have decided to put on the Web site. This content (the type and amount) will vary somewhat depending on your mission. For example, an organization like the American Heart Association is a research-based nonprofit to research heart disease and stroke. Because of that mission, there will be quite a lot of content on the Web site, some of which will be medically technical. However, if your site is a simple "flash cause" site, where you are developing a site to help a local family whose house burned down, your content will be minimal. Keep this in mind as you develop specific content types.

Audience/stakeholder consideration. In some cases, your site will be speaking to multiple audiences. For example, a local food pantry may be speaking to (1) donors of food and money, (2) people who need food, (3) the community at large to raise awareness for hunger, (4) corporations wishing to donate large amounts of food or money, and (5) the media. Make a conscious effort to determine your core stakeholders and then determine how and what you will communicate to them.

Informative content. Ideally, you want to have content that provides value to the user. There are a number of ways you can do this. You can tell stories of the people your organization helps, you can provide information on how many people your organization helps, you can provide research, and so on. Make sure that the content evolves so that visitors will know they are learning something new each time they visit. This is the "hook" to keep them coming back.

Entertaining content. The most valuable entertainment that nonprofits have is in the stories. Does your site have compelling stories or videos? Consider adding these as many people tend to get involved when they feel that they have a connection with the cause or someone it helps.

Variety of content. While it is tempting to sit back once the site is completed, you need to remember to update the site with new information regularly. You have to give people a reason to come back. There is no magic rule as to how often to change content; however, you need to do it relatively often, especially to remove out-of-date information.

Third party endorsement. If your organization is positively rated on one of the many third-party organizations such as GuideStar or Charity Navigator, be sure to have a link to that on your site. Some people do additional research on

Table 3.2: Content to Aid Credibility

White Papers: Short papers that typically argue an issue and solution and are not necessarily a sales tool but offer some unique intellectual capital. A white paper sometimes requires a fee or registration.

E-books: Shorter and more visual than white papers, these e-books are typically a PDF that can be downloaded from a Web site for free.

E-mail Newsletters: Information sent out to a list of stakeholders highlighting the news from the organization. These typically are produced on a schedule (e.g., monthly or quarterly).

Research and Survey Reports: Reports from proprietary research conducted by the organization; if the research is conducted well, this adds immediate credibility as a research oriented organization.

Wikis and Blogs: Wikis are editable sites for storing information; blogs are sites that are dynamic and allow for rapid updating; both of these (if done well) can position the nonprofit as an expert in the field.

Webinars: These are multimedia presentations about a specific topic or problem which sometimes feature guests from other areas or causes; sometimes stored on a slideshare site for additional dissemination.

David Meerman Scott, *The New Rules of Marketing and PR: How to Use News Releases, Blogs, Podcasting, Viral Marketing and Online Media to Reach Buyers Directly* (Hoboken, NJ: John Wiley & Sons, 2007).

nonprofit organizations before getting involved. Alternatively, you can include testimonials from volunteers and constituents, which heightens the validity of your message.

Interactivity

Degree of interactivity. Interactive sites offer the opportunity to engage visitors using two-way communications. Interactivity leads to a more personalized relationship with visitors because they are able to respond to content and have a voice. Visitors today expect more interactivity on Web sites, so it is important to have elements on the site that lead to engagement.

Inclusion of consumer-generated content. Consumer-generated content (CGC) allows the visitor to develop content. There are several ways to do this through blogs, vlogs (a video blog), mashups (where people take content from various places and edit it together to create something new), discussion boards, and sharing on social networks. Make sure that if your site contains blogs that the comment feature is enabled, allowing people to respond.

Multimedia elements. Multimedia elements include photos, audio, and video. Videos can be posted on the site or shared through YouTube. Audio can be transmitted via podcasts. The idea is that the site contains more than text and simple photos.

Ability to share information. With Web 2.0, the ability to share information is vital. There are tools, including RSS, that allow for information to be shared. These include Digg, Delicious, Mixx, Furl, and so on.

THE FUNCTIONALITY OF NONPROFIT ORGANIZATION WEB SITES

A study was conducted by one of the authors which examined how nonprofit organizations were using their Web sites and how well they were taking advantage of available Internet applications. The study included observations of the Web sites of 564 nonprofit organizations in the United States. The organizations were located in thirty-nine states and the District of Columbia. A number of different types of nonprofit organizations were represented in the study.

Nonprofit Organization's Mission and Programs

In the study of nonprofit Web sites, 60 percent of organizations did an excellent job of providing information about their missions and their programs. An additional 26 percent of organizations did a good job, while the remaining organizations were rated as being fair or poor in providing this information to visitors. Therefore, approximately 85 percent of Web sites did a good job making it easy for visitors to remember the organizations' programs.

A nonprofit organization would naturally want to use its Web site to communicate its purpose and programs to its various audiences. Any organization must assess how well it is communicating this information. The Web site provides an opportunity to present the organization's story to the world. Better Web sites anticipate the information visitors want most and present this information first, making more in-depth information easy to access through appropriate navigation links, but not necessarily on the Web site's front page.

Gathering E-mail Addresses

Among the Web sites in the study, about 63 percent of nonprofit organizations' Web sites had a mechanism for collecting e-mail addresses of visitors. This is not surprising given the ease of putting this capability on a Web site. However, it is surprising that 36 percent of Web sites did not allow visitors to provide the organization with their e-mail addresses.

There are several advantages of collecting e-mail addresses from visitors. Individuals who visit an organization's Web page do so voluntarily. Many have sought out the organization's Web site intentionally by entering the organization's name in their Web browser's address box, or they have found the Web site of interest through a search engine like Google. In this case, the visitor to the Web site has an interest in the organization. Why not allow visitors to an organization's Web site the option to add their names to its e-mail list? This could be the first step to develop a relationship with someone who has shown an interest in the nonprofit organization.

Collecting e-mail addresses of visitors is typically accomplished by allowing visitors to sign up for the organization's e-newsletter. Our study found that 50 percent of the Web sites allowed visitors to sign up for an e-newsletter and about 55 percent of the Web sites allowed visitors to add themselves to an e-mail list. The Union of Concerned Scientists' Web site (www.ucsusa.org) is an example of a Web site that allows visitors to subscribe free of charge to a variety of e-mail lists, depending on their interests. By signing up for the organization's e-newsletter, an individual is letting the organization know that she desires to be kept informed of the organization's activities.

In addition to e-newsletter enrollments, some organizations allow visitors to provide their e-mail addresses in order to be notified of important events. Examples of events may be scheduled showings for an art gallery or performances for a theatre company or they may be action alerts from activist organizations. In any case, the organization is allowing individuals to select a specific type of event or a specific topic of interest. This function allows the nonprofit organization to distinguish sub-groups of Web site visitors based on their interests. Organizations can direct future communications to these individuals that are more likely to be valued by them.

"Visitors to nonprofit Web sites are more likely to donate money, volunteer time, and recommend the nonprofit to others if they are satisfied with their online experience,"[11] says Sarah Allen-Short, director of media inquiries and analyst relations at ForeSee Results. Through thoughtful, targeted communications with individuals expressing interest in the organization, over time those individuals get to know the organization better, have more positive feelings toward the organization, begin to care more about the organization's purpose, and eventually support the organization through their behaviors, such as financial contributions and volunteering.

Therefore, care must be taken to protect personal information of those supporters. When collecting information online, be sure to explain the purpose of collecting that information. Everything should be permission-based; from e-mail campaigns (e.g., allow them to opt in) to online donations. A good example of a code of ethics can be found at www.fundraising123.org. Take a look at their ePhilanthropy Code of Ethical Online Philanthropic Practices. It includes information on philanthropic experience, privacy and security, disclosures, complaints, and transactions.[12]

Online Donations

In the study of Web sites of U.S. nonprofit organizations, the ability and convenience of making online donations was examined. The investigation found that 68 percent of the Web sites allowed supporters to make online donations. Unfortunately, this means that 32 percent of Web sites *did not* allow interested persons to make an online donation to the organization.

> **Chapter Insight: Double Opt-In**
>
> Nonprofit organizations are vigilant about fostering supporter relationships and about maintaining the nonprofit's good reputation. Sending information to interested groups through e-mail distribution lists is an important tool for accomplishing both objectives.
>
> It is important to use this tool effectively. Effective use begins with authenticating the enrollment of individuals when they have subscribed to a newsletter or e-mail list. A double opt-in procedure is typically used. A double opt-in procedure requires visitors to indicate two separate times that they want to subscribe to a newsletter or distribution list. First, for example, a visitor provides his or her e-mail address in a subscription box on the Web site. Next, the organization's software automatically delivers a message to that e-mail address, thanking the visitor for subscribing and asking the visitor to verify her or his desire to subscribe by replying to the e-mail message.
>
> The purpose of the double opt-in process is to prevent an individual from being added to an e-mail list by someone else against the individual's wishes. This process demonstrates respect for an individual's privacy and also prevents the organization from being used to annoy unsuspecting persons with unwanted e-mail.
>
> Once subscribed, the organization should continue to demonstrate its respect for members of its lists by making it easy to unsubscribe. This is typically done by including a simple notice at the bottom of e-mail messages that allow the e-mail subscriber to opt out by clicking on an "unsubscribe" link.

Forty-seven percent of Web sites were considered excellent; 24 percent were rated "good" in making it easy for visitors to donate online on the organization's Web site. The remaining Web sites were rated fair or poor.

Only a small proportion of visitors to an organization's Web site will be sufficiently motivated to make an online donation. If it is inconvenient to do so, only a group of the most highly motivated supporters will bother to donate. Furthermore, poorly constructed Web sites communicate a message to visitors that the nonprofit organization is careless or unprofessional—not exactly the signals most nonprofit managers want to send to potential supporters.

In order to enhance the convenience of online giving, the tools used on the Web site for online donations must be easy for visitors to find and the software must work properly. Many organizations find that placing online giving prompts on the first page of the Web site to be effective. Some organizations emphasize online giving by using large symbols and bold, colorful text featured prominently on the first page.

Smaller organizations that lack the resources to offer supporters this function can outsource this capability to vendors. For example, Click and Pledge is an organization that provides this service for nonprofit organizations, charging a onetime $25 application fee and a 4.75 percent processing fee for most credit card donations. Click and Pledge claims to be able to add this function to a nonprofit organization's Web site in five minutes. PayPal also offers nonprofit organizations the ability to accept online donations. PayPal handles the donation transaction so the nonprofit never has donor credit card information (no security concerns for nonprofit). PayPal charges about 30¢ plus 2 percent of the donation.[13]

When the organization accepts donations through its own application, it must make sure it is using up-to-date security. In a recent study of Australian nonprofit organization Web sites,[14] only 22 percent of Web sites offered donors secure (encrypted) transactions. Some donors may assume their credit card information is being protected and may be put at risk by an organization's unsecured Web site. Nonprofit organizations can subscribe to a security certifier like VeriSign (www.verisign.com/ssl/) or GeoTrust (www.geotrust.com/). These vendors can assist the organization with the technology as well as to provide their logos for display, which let visitors know their donations are secure.

Internet browsers are beginning to offer an add-on that rates a given Web site's security and trustworthiness. For example, Firefox offers the add-on WOT (Web of Trust). The WOT (see www.mywot.com) add-on rates each Web site the visitor views in terms of its trustworthiness, vendor reliability, privacy, and child safety. When going to a Web site that is problematic, WOT will issue a bold warning message. These features are expected to become standard. Nonprofit organizations will need to make sure their Web sites are rated favorably.

Planned Giving

Planned giving represents a variety of ways in which donors can give money or other assets to a favorite nonprofit organization now, in the future, or after they die. Professional help in legal matters is usually needed at some time in the planned giving process. These professionals may be accountants, lawyers, bankers, or financial advisors. Most nonprofit organizations view planned giving as a type of major donation from wealthy individuals. Major donors are usually dealt with in a more personal manner than the much larger number of donors contributing more modest sums.

It is customary to view only affluent individuals as potential planned givers. Since wealthy individuals often attract personal visits from key staff members, organizations tend to overlook relevant planned giving content on their Web sites. Web sites are often seen as a means of communicating with large numbers of individuals, but not major donors. The study found that only 26 percent of Web sites provided information to viewers on planned giving. The remaining 74 percent of Web sites did not provide this content.

Nonprofit organizations would be wise to provide information on planned giving on their Web sites. Research shows that many people would consider making a bequest in their wills if they were asked to do so or were provided with appropriate information. However, most people who are not wealthy are never asked to consider such an option.[15] Progressive nonprofit organizations put information and notices regarding planned giving in their communications to supporters, not just leaving this to staff members who develop relationships with affluent individuals.

Many people who consider making bequests in their estate plans research nonprofit organizations of interest by visiting their Web sites. Therefore, it is important for nonprofit organizations to have relevant information available online. This obviously includes information about the organization, its history, purpose, good works, and good stewardship of resources. However, nonprofit Web sites should also contain pertinent legal and financial information. Legal information needed, containing the proper wording to be included in wills, should be available on the nonprofit Web site's planned giving section. Also, financial planning calculators that assist individuals in determining the financial and tax implications of alternative approaches to planned giving need to be available. Habitat for Humanity's Web site (www.habitat.org) does a good job with respect to planned giving information, and readers may want to visit its Web site for some insights.

Send to a Friend

Effective Web sites make it effortless for visitors to e-mail something interesting they find on an organization's Web site to a friend or associate. An example of this could be an interesting article, an evocative testimonial, a press release, or video. Organizations typically provide this capability by including an "e-mail this article," "send to a friend," or similarly worded link at the top and bottom of the content item. This is a great way for visitors to help the organization gets its message out. Marketers understand that people are much more likely to open and read e-mail messages from people they know than from people they do not know or from organizations with which they do not have a relationship. Also, e-mail junk mail filters are unlikely to filter a message from an address in the recipient's e-mail address book.

The study of nonprofit Web sites found that only 21 percent of Web sites provided a "send to a friend" option. This capability is easily added, making it surprising that 79 percent of Web sites did not provide this simple but useful option.

Accountability and Stewardship

Most nonprofit organizations rely upon the support of others in order to further their missions. Perhaps one of the most important assets of nonprofits is their reputations. Supporters expect nonprofit organizations to be good stewards of their resources. People would naturally want to avoid contributing to an organization that squanders its resources.

Nonprofit organizations should provide stewardship information, demonstrating their efficient and accountable use of resources, on their Web sites. This type of information should be conveniently found by a link to accountability information on the front page. Energy Outreach Colorado (EOC)[16] (www.energyoutreach.org) does an excellent job on its Web site with respect to accountability information. EOC prominently features a graphic near the top of its front page stating that it leads a national charity ranking list. The charity rating site is linked, and the visitor can click on the link and read a charity rating organization's praise of EOC's stewardship practices. EOC is successful in using its accountability practices to differentiate it from other nonprofit organizations.

In the study of U.S. nonprofit organization Web sites, the study examined how well organizations' presented online stewardship and accountability information. The study rated 21 percent of the Web sites as excellent on this feature; 34 percent were rated as good. The remaining 45 percent were rated fair or poor, indicating that many organizations could do more to provide this information to Web site visitors.

We recognize that there is some controversy among nonprofit managers about the work of charitable rating sites. To Web site visitors, however, this does not matter. Nonprofit managers cannot ignore their ratings by these sites even if they disagree with the fairness of the methodology used by the rating organization. Managers are advised to try to obtain the best rating on these sites that they can.

It is important to communicate to visitors the tax-exempt status of your nonprofit organization. Tell visitors what type of tax deduction they can expect,

---

Chapter Insight: The Smile Train

The Smile Train (www.smiletrain.org) is a nonprofit organization which provides free corrective surgery to children who have cleft palate deformities. There is another nonprofit with the same mission called Operation Smile (www.operationsmile.org).

The Smile Train's marketing strategy to attract support and to differentiate itself from Operation Smile relies on promoting its good stewardship of contributions. Both organizations do a good job of featuring visually compelling before-and-after pictures of children who have been helped. However, the Smile Train features stewardship information prominently on its Web site's front page. On the front page, an emotionally provocative picture of a child with a deformed cleft is the first content item noticed by a visitor. The text on the front page tells the visitor that the child can be helped with a surgery costing only $250 and that 100 percent of donations go to programs. In other words, every penny given will go into helping an individual child—a compelling message.

if any, and provide an electronic receipt for their donation. Some organizations do not have tax-exempt status. These organizations should make clear that donations to them are not tax-exempt.

Special Events

Many nonprofit organizations have special events. Art galleries and museums have exhibits. Performing art troupes have productions. Community theatres have plays. Activist organizations have rallies and demonstrations. Other organizations have auctions and annual fund-raising galas.

Are the events publicized on the organization's Web site? Is there an activities calendar that individuals can subscribe to by giving their e-mail address? Shared Adventures (www.sharedadventures.org/activities.htm) does a great job with its activities calendar. Can people purchase or reserve tickets online? Can they easily invite their friends to an event? These capabilities would provide supporters with greater value from the organization's Web site. It would give them an additional reason to visit the Web site regularly. It would automate some of the event activities of the organization.

The study examined some of the special event capabilities of U.S. nonprofit organizational Web sites. There were some organizations, because of the type of organization they were, for which special events did not seem likely (about 13 percent of the sample). Of the remaining Web sites, 53 percent publicized at least one upcoming event; 34 percent did not. Of the Web sites which publicized at least one upcoming event, only 12 percent of these Web sites allowed interested persons to purchase tickets online. From a marketing perspective, it is unfortunate not to allow an individual to buy something you have to sell. Of the Web sites which publicized at least one upcoming event, only 13 percent of this group provided a convenient way for interested persons to invite a friend to the event. From a marketing perspective, this is a missed opportunity to have favorable word-of-mouth advertising.

Since, in our study, we examined the Web sites but did not interview the organizations, we really do not know why these organizations do not publicize events, allow individuals to purchase tickets, or allow individuals to invite a friend. Clearly, the organization benefits by having these capabilities. It is possible that some nonprofit managers do not realize they should be doing these things. It is also possible that some organizations, especially smaller organizations, may not feel it is possible to have this functionality on their Web sites.

There are vendors that offer these capabilities to nonprofit organizations. TicketOps (www.ticket-ops.com), for example, will help a nonprofit organization develop some of these functions. It is usually up to the organization to publicize its own events on its Web site, maintain an events calendar, and allow individuals to subscribe to the calendar which is typically e-mailed to subscribers monthly.

Staff Contact Information

It is generally a good practice to provide staff contact information on an organization's Web site. When Web site visitors can easily find the names and contact information for staff members, they can direct their inquiries to the person in the organization with whom they are most interested in communicating. A section of the Web site devoted to introducing the staff, especially when including a photo and brief professional biography, personalizes the organization, making it feel less institutional to the visitor.

In the study, 62 percent of the Web sites analyzed did identify *some* staff members and allow visitors to send these staff members an e-mail message. Therefore, 38 percent of Web sites did not. Organizations did provide their postal address and primary telephone number on their Web sites. We found that 93 percent of the Web sites in our study showed a mailing address and telephone number.

In conducting workshops on Internet marketing for nonprofit organizations, the authors have found two objections to providing staff identification and contact information on their organizations' Web sites. First, some individuals feel they need to protect their privacy and not identifying themselves on their organization's Web site allows them privacy protection. We certainly agree that, when it comes to individuals' *private* lives, they have the right to be as anonymous as possible in a modern society. However, we would add that, when it comes to individuals' roles as representatives of a nonprofit organization, they should be expected to be identified in their professional roles. Indeed, anonymity in a professional setting is counterproductive.

The second objection we hear is that staff members are sometimes concerned about receiving too many e-mail messages or telephone calls, which may disturb their work. This is a reasonable concern for a busy manager. In this case, inbound communications can be screened in a variety of ways. For example, the executive director of an organization can list a telephone number that is routed to a receptionist. A busy administrator can be issued two e-mail addresses. One is listed on the Web site and can easily be routed to a specific folder in the manager's e-mail software. This mail can be perused at the manager's convenience. The manager's e-mail address that is listed on the Web site can also be forwarded to an assistant who can respond to common questions, reducing the quantity of e-mail requiring the manager's attention. A manager can have an alternate e-mail address for use by organizational members, large donors, board members, and other individuals with whom the manager would want to communicate more responsively.

Online Press Room

The online press room is a location on the Web site in which the organization's press releases and similar content (for example, media interviews of organization staff) are archived. Individuals can visit this section of the Web site and perform a key word search to identify and access documents of specific interest. Many organizations feature their most recent press releases, articles, and interviews at the top of the online press room page. Others allow interested persons to be added to an e-mail list to receive future press releases.

The United Way (www.unitedway.org), for example, has a media center link on its front page. The media center provides press releases, media kits, and executive speeches. The United Way's media center also allows visitors to sign up for RSS feeds.[17]

The Web site study found that 57 percent of Web sites had press rooms, while 43 percent did not. We can only speculate regarding why many organizations do not have an online press room. It could be that managers in smaller organizations do not feel they have sufficient time or staff to develop and maintain the content on the Web site. However, establishing this capability in an organization's Web site is relatively simple. An individual with some experience in developing Web sites and inexpensive off-the-shelf Web development software is all that is needed. The time commitment to save the organization's press releases and media coverage to the online press room is not excessive.

Online Advocacy

Many organizations advocate causes and issues that are consistent with their values and missions. Do these organizations use their Web sites to help further these issues and causes? The study assessed whether or not the Web sites analyzed allowed for online advocacy. Specifically, the study looked to see if there was an advocacy campaign which allowed supporters to add their names to a petition or provided a letter draft that could be downloaded or sent electronically to a public official. The study found that 33 percent did have this capability; 65 percent did not.

Activist organizations generally try to influence other organizations, institutions, or policy-makers to change their practices or policies. The source of activist organizations' influence typically comes from grassroots[18] support and media attention (which is often a byproduct of grassroots support). Therefore, online tools which enable supporters to help advocate for change help activist organizations further their goals.

For example, the Web site for the Center for American Progress, a liberal political activist organization (www.americanprogressaction.org), has an "Actions" tab on the navigation bar on its front page. In this section of its Web site, visitors are given the opportunity to take some action on one or more issues. Visitors may be able to send a notice to an elected official or sign a petition.

Advocacy techniques may also benefit other types of nonprofit organizations. Advocacy of issues that are clearly consistent with a nonprofit organization's values helps to define the organization to the Web site's visitors. Online advocacy helps to define the personality of the organization (what the organization values and how the organization differs from other organizations). Visitors can see for themselves which issues the organization cares about. People prefer to support an organization that stands for something, that has similar values to them, and that does something good for other people.

Volunteer Recruitment

Many nonprofit organizations rely on volunteers. Some struggle with recruiting sufficient numbers of motivated, qualified individuals willing to volunteer. In today's information age, the first place many people will go to in order to learn about volunteering for an organization is its Web site. This allows individuals to learn about volunteer opportunities without feeling any sense of obligation or social pressure that they may feel when talking with a staff member. Gathering information online is also more convenient and requires less effort for many individuals.

The study assessed whether or not the Web site provided content that allowed individuals to learn about volunteer opportunities. About 69 percent of Web sites did present some information on volunteer opportunities; 31 percent did not. For those organizations that need volunteers, it seems reasonable to include online content that would describe the various volunteer positions, expected time commitment, any required training, a description of the duties, and a staff person to contact. It would be a good marketing practice to include volunteer testimonials and photographs of volunteers in action to help interested prospects obtain a sense of what it would be like to volunteer for the organization and what kind of people volunteer for that organization.[19]

Volunteer Retention

Retaining volunteers is important. It reduces the need to recruit new volunteers. Retaining these supporters helps provide a community of experienced, knowledgeable volunteers to help the organization further its cause and mission. One simple tool is simply adding volunteer recognition pages to the organization's Web site. For example, the Community Service Learning Center at Grand Valley State University features a "Volunteer of the Month" page on its Web site.[20]

Community-building is a term that has become popular in recent years. Applied to volunteers, it refers to activities that help new volunteers integrate into the social network of existing volunteers, and it refers to activities that strengthen social ties among members of the volunteer community. One Web site capability that may facilitate volunteer community-building is an online discussion group dedicated for volunteer use. Can volunteers visit the organization's Web site, log in with their user names and passwords, and join in an ongoing conversation among members of the volunteer community? Such a forum, which is not accessible to non-volunteers, enhances communication, interaction, and, thus, community-building.

The study assessed this capability. It reported that only 14 percent of Web sites provided this community-building function for volunteers. These findings indicate that there is an opportunity for many nonprofit organizations to add this function to their Web sites. A number of vendors offer software solutions to add this capability to a nonprofit organization's Web site. One such vendor is Yazd Forum Software (www.forumsoftware.ca).

Other online content can be helpful to both volunteers and volunteer program managers. Volunteer manuals, guidelines, and policies that are available online allow volunteers easy access to this information and save the organization printing, handling, and storage costs. It would also be helpful to have any useful statistics or other related information on volunteering available. For example, volunteers might find it interesting to see the numbers of volunteers who serve in the organization, the average amount of time volunteered on a weekly or monthly basis, the longest serving volunteer, volunteer service for a recent event, and so forth. Testimonials, volunteer biographies, and anecdotes may be of interest to other volunteers and can provide a sense of shared values and experiences.

The study found that only 39 percent of nonprofit organizations had volunteer manuals, guidelines, statistics, or other information helpful to volunteers on their Web sites. This represents an easily correctable missed opportunity for many organizations.

Another Web site tool that can benefit volunteers and volunteer program managers alike is an online calendar. This allows volunteers to learn when they are scheduled to work. WhenToHelp (whentohelp.com) offers an online volunteer scheduling tool free for approved charities. A volunteer calendar can also be used to notify volunteers of an upcoming meeting, training workshop, social event, or to announce an immediate need for volunteers. For example, United Way of King County provides a training calendar on its Web site.[21] Our study assessed whether or not a Web site included an online calendar to assist volunteers. We found that only 33 percent of Web sites offered a calendar for volunteers.

Privacy Policy

It is a good practice for all organizations to publicize their privacy policies on their Web sites. This is done for public-relations purposes and for liability protection. Organizations have an obligation to inform Web site visitors if personal information is being collected and, if so, the protection given to that information. Can supporters obtain access to information collected on them to verify the information's accuracy? Does the organization promise not to disclose this information to outside organizations? In the case in which the organization collects no information, it should inform visitors of this policy.

The study found that less than half of the Web sites we analyzed published the organizations' privacy policies online. To be more precise, 42 percent of organizations put their privacy policies online, and the majority, 58 percent, did not. This is an easily correctable oversight, and there are many examples of privacy policies online to examine to assist an organization in developing its own policy. Privacy Rights Clearinghouse offers useful information to nonprofits regarding their online privacy policies.[22] Other resources to assist in developing a privacy policy are listed at the end of this chapter.

Online Purchases

Some organizations allow for online product purchases. For example, a museum could sell its gift shop items on its Web site. Other organizations have periodic auctions as fund-raising events. These auctions could be placed online. Some organizations allow volunteers, contributors and other supporters the opportunity to purchase shirts, coffee mugs, pens, and other products with their logos.

Many organizations have educational programs. Free literature and brochures can be downloaded from the Web site. Books and reports can be purchased online. Books that organizations do not sell, but still relate to programs of interest can be linked on the Web site. For example, a political organization can have pictures of books it would like to promote on its Web site with links to an online bookseller. The political organization can have an affiliate agreement, if it chooses, with an online bookseller, in which a commission (usually 5 percent) is paid for book sales originating from the nonprofit organization's Web site. The affiliate agreement does not increase the price of the book for the buyer. Online booksellers usually have their affiliate programs listed on their Web sites.

Best of the Left Podcast (www.bestoftheleftpodcast.com) encourages its supporters to use its Web site when shopping for books. The Web site has a search box for Amazon.com. If shoppers' Amazon.com purchases originate from Best of the Left Podcast's Web site, then it receives a small commission from Amazon.com. Best of the Left Podcast encourages its listeners to use this feature as a free way of supporting the organization.

In our study, 21 percent of Web sites had a retail section or an auction section. We also examined whether or not items offered for sale appeared to be related to the organization or its mission. The study found that among the Web sites offering items for sale, 70 percent of those Web sites offered items that were somehow related to the organization's mission.

Offering appropriate items for sale can be an additional revenue input to the organization. The Metropolitan Museum of Art (www.metmuseum.org/store) offers a sophisticated online gift store. Offering items for sale that feature the organization's logo allows supporters to show their support for the organization to others and it helps to promote the organization. Offering books and educational materials helps the organization to further its mission and support its causes. Goodstorm.com is an example of a vendor that offers online shopping capabilities for nonprofit organizations.

Web Site Address

An organization's Web site address, or uniform resource locator (URL), is something that is in the manager's control and should be given some thought. It is to the organization's advantage to make it intuitive for visitors to guess the Web site address from the organization's name. For example, the Web site address of Boy Scouts of America is www.scouting.org. While this is a simple Web site address, and seems intuitive, some visitors might have difficulty finding the correct Web site.

The study found that in 83 percent of cases, the Web site address was easy to remember. For example, scouting.org is easy to remember. It would be preferable for the organization's Web site address to be boyscouts.org or boyscouts.com. Since, an organization can register multiple Web site addresses, the organization could have used both .com or .org Web site address domain names. Therefore, it would be possible for Boy Scouts of America to use scouting.org, scouting.com, boyscouts.com, boyscouts.org, boyscoutsofamerica.com, or boyscountsofamerica.org. If all of these addresses were registered by the organization, then visitors could type any of the examples and find the organization's Web site. Registering a Web site address costs only $10/year (prices may vary a bit depending on which registering service a manager uses) for each address and it is a good investment to register all addresses that people are likely to attempt when finding an organization's Web site. (See www.godaddy.com for information on registering your Web site addresses.)

This section has presented an array of functions and capabilities that nonprofit organization Web sites can offer their online visitors. By combining the capabilities presented in this section with design concepts, a nonprofit organization is in a strong position to improve the effectiveness of its Web site.

USABILITY TESTS: DOING IT YOURSELF

Usability testing is important to do. It helps managers understand how users will navigate through the Web site and also helps them trouble-shoot areas that are not quite working. While usability tests from a professional can be costly ($5,000 to $15,000), your organization can conduct its own tests. Steve Krug, author of *Don't Make Me Think: A Common Sense Approach to Usability Testing*[23] emphasizes that focus groups are not usability tests. Focus groups will allow a small group of people to sit around and discuss what they like and don't like about your site. While this information can be important, this is not a usability test. Focus groups are good for determining what your users need or want before the site is developed or when a site is undergoing a significant redesign. But Krug argues that a usability test is about one user at a time going through a Web site or prototype of a Web site to figure out what the site is all about (for example, is it clear what your organization does from the Web site) and try to use the site to accomplish certain tasks (for example, can a user locate volunteer opportunities and sign up).

Usability testing is important because oftentimes the organization is too close to the project. Consider that several people in the organization have been hashing out what appears on each page or what needs to be eliminated for weeks or even months. By then, there is no perspective left. So testing allows managers to see new perspectives from actual Web site users. Krug argues that even conducting one test is better than testing none at all. Indeed, he feels that recruiting representative samples of users is a little overrated and argues that anyone can serve as a respondent. He suggests testing early in the process rather than after the site is completed so that your organization does not waste precious time and resources developing a site that scores low on usability. Indeed, Krug argues that multiple phases of testing are superior to ensure that the fixes actually work. So how does this work and what do you need?

As stated earlier, you will need to conduct a few rounds of tests (more if your site is very complicated or if you are making substantial changes). You need three to four users per round. Later in the process, you may want to get people from certain backgrounds or people from various stages in the visitor engagement cycle if you feel that you need that perspective. Set up computers in a conference room or office. If you can get a PC *and* Mac, that is better since the two platforms do vary. In order to capture the information on the screen, you have a few options. First, you can use a camcorder and television and set up a second facilitator in order to observe. You don't need to record the information because chances are you won't ever refer to it as long as you have an observer. One other option is to screen recording software that records all of the things on your computer screen. Some to consider include Cam Studio, My Screen Recorder Pro, BB Flashback, Camtasia, Adobe Captiva, and FRAPS.

Essentially, you will develop a list of questions and tasks that you want to test. Almost anything is possible. For example, let's say you have redesigned your organization's site to emphasize a new literacy program. Can the user can locate the program information and is it written in a way that is comprehensible? Suppose you just added an online donation feature. Can users locate it,

Table 3.3: Some Usability Questions to Consider

Do visitors enjoy using the site?
Do they understand the purpose of the site?
Are they able to accomplish specific tasks?
Does the site have the right tools for sharing?
Is there any incentive to return to the site after the first visit?
Is there a way to recover from errors when browsing?

understand it, and use it? Throughout the process, the facilitator (who needs no real special training) can ask the respondent follow-up questions throughout the process. You can get a copy of a good script from Steve Krug's site (www.sensible.com) that is especially helpful if you have never done this. You will also find a good consent form to adapt from the Web site. The main financial outlay (aside from purchasing any equipment) is a stipend for each respondent. This can vary; but you should offer something (typically $25 to $100 per respondent). The insight you will gain from this process is vital to your Web site's success.

After you have conducted the usability tests, what do you do with the information? It is likely that many people found the same problem, so you will need to find out the best way to fix that problem (especially if respondents offered different solutions). Some typical problems include that the concept that you are trying to get across simply is unclear. The words that users are looking for, especially with search functions, are not there. There could be too much clutter. That is a typical problem since most organizations try to put a lot of information on their site and don't know how best to organize it. Generally, you should resist the temptation to add things to the site, especially when respondents talk about new features. Krug recommends that rarely is it necessary to start over. Sometimes the biggest challenge is to fix things that don't work without messing up the things that do work.

> Conversation with the Pros: Denise Burchell, Interaction Design Director, R/GA
>
> Denise Burchell works for digital powerhouse R/GA in a relatively new, unstandardized position as an interaction designer. Burchell thinks that the fact that this is a new position and hard to articulate is a good thing—it leaves her plenty of room to experiment. Essentially an interaction designer works to define project objectives, help solve problems, and then test and validate the work. As such, she is an ethnographer, market researcher, strategist, consumer advocate, sociologist, information architect, interface designer, marketing consultant, brand consultant, content strategist, art director, and user-testing coordinator. "We are often the 'glue' in a project, making sure smaller issues aren't overlooked as new team members are added, and helping people with very different backgrounds communicate with each other," Burchell says. "Since we are in the middle of a lot of the small processes that make up a project, we end up learning at least a little bit about a wide variety of topics, and being influenced by many different perspectives. That's one reason why it's so interesting."
>
> The biggest mistake she sees small companies and nonprofits make is organizing their Web sites in a way that reflects the organization's internal structure. Instead, they should try to organize it in the way their intended audience would think about it. By doing so, the online information and

resources are easy for people to find even if they aren't familiar with the company.

Similarly, many small companies and nonprofits often make the mistake of prioritizing the content they want people to want over the content their audience actually prefers. The Web site does not come with a guaranteed captive audience, so there should be a balance of "push" and "pull" messaging to keep people interested.

She cautions nonprofits not to set the goal of building a "cool" site with lots of bells and whistles. Those extras aren't likely to age gracefully, and unless the Web site is the business, there are better things to do than redesign it to keep up with trends. A better goal would be to satisfy business goals within a simple, straightforward site structure, with content that's useful and easy to find. Over time, this strategy will be more successful and sustainable. If you're going to use Flash or AJAX, motion or sound, consider making that a small part of your overall site experience so that you can update the bulk of your site easily, inexpensively, and, ideally, in-house.

Burchell says that there are several general trends emerging on Web sites. First is the use of social networks. Everyone seems to be using Twitter (almost without regard to whether or not they have something meaningful to say). And most sites that distribute content feature a "social block," a collection of icons belonging to social bookmarking, social networking, and social news and media sites. This makes it easy for readers to further syndicate content and drive more traffic to content sites. Another important trend, especially for nonprofits, is storytelling. It's long been a technique used in traditional marketing and advertising, but organizations are starting to use video, animation, and slideshows to tell stories online. Some examples include The Story of Stuff (www.storyofstuff.com), and Boone Oakley's agency portfolio (www.youtube.com/watch?v=Elo7WeIydh8).

Another trend is the use of application-inspired navigation and tools. Online user experiences and desktop application user experiences are becoming more similar. Web sites are using interactive metaphors that people have learned and become comfortable with by interacting with applications. We're just starting to see the impact of this crossover in early adopters like Getty Images Moodstream (http://moodstream.gettyimages.com/) and Le Coq Sportif (www.lecoqsportif.com/search/#/us/all/).

Lastly, the use of mobile applications is finally reaching popularity in the U.S. With the release of the iPhone, a new model for online interaction was born. In this new medium, the user's location can be used to go beyond a personalized experience to a context-specific experience. Companies can insert their brand into their customers' lives in new and meaningful ways. In addition to the iPhone, Google's Android, the Palm Pre, and other smartphones can take advantage of add-on applications.

Burchell advises small- to medium-sized nonprofits to speak in an approachable tone and avoid an academic writing style. Be clear and succinct, provide teasers or summaries for longer articles, and facilitate skimming by pulling out the most poignant points and treating them differently in visual design like pull quotes in a magazine. While people do read a lot on the Web, most don't spend a lot of time reading a single long article on-screen. Provide a podcast or PDF that users can download, and make sure that the PDF has your URL in the header or footer of each page.

"And I can't stress enough how important it is to listen to your users and find out what they're most interested in hearing about," she says. "Ask early and often. If you let your audience guide you, you'll be much more effective in satisfying them, and in return they'll be more receptive to hearing what you have to say."

WEB SITE ANALYSIS WORKSHEET

Managers can use the following worksheet as a guide in conducting a self-analysis of their Web sites.

1. Would you say that the primary purpose of the Web site is fund-raising or communicating with supporters?
2. Can the visitor enroll in an e-newsletter or action alert?
3. Rate the Web site on the following criteria:

	Excellent	Good	Fair	Poor
a. Access to information about the organization's mission and services.	❏	❏	❏	❏
b. Convenience of making philanthropic transactions (making a donation, volunteering, or advocacy).	❏	❏	❏	❏
c. Ability to expand support to others through use of online tools that aid in supporting the mission (making it possible for family, friends, and colleagues to be informed about the nonprofit).	❏	❏	❏	❏
d. Online stewardship and information on accountability.	❏	❏	❏	❏

4. Special Events

	Yes	No	Not Applicable
a. Is there an upcoming event identified on the Web site?	❏	❏	❏
b. Can supporters buy tickets online?	❏	❏	❏

c. Is there a tool to allow supporters to send their friends an e-invitation? ☐ ☐ ☐
5. Can supporters make a contribution online? Is it convenient? Are online donations secured?
6. Does the Web site allow visitors to identify nonprofit staff members and to send an e-mail message to them?
7. Does the site have an online press room? (Providing in downloadable format background information, press releases, photos, and other material of interest to the media.)
8. Can supporters sign up for an e-mail list for topics of interest or for general updates of the organization?
9. Can supporters learn about volunteer opportunities online?
10. Is there a "send-to-a-friend" option so that the visitor can send an article or link to a friend?
11. Does the nonprofit offer detailed information regarding planned giving?
12. Is there a gift-planning calculator on the Web site?
13. Is there an online discussion group for the nonprofit's volunteers?
14. Are there volunteer manuals, guidelines, statistics, and other information helpful to volunteers?
15. Is there an online calendar to help volunteers remember important assignments and deadlines?
16. Is the nonprofit's privacy policy published on its Web site?
17. Is there a shopping or auction site as part of the nonprofit's Web site?
18. If the nonprofit uses online shopping, are the items being sold somehow tied to the mission of the nonprofit or do the items feature the organization's logo?
19. Is there an online advocacy campaign (petition or letter to public official)?
20. Is the nonprofit's Web site address easy to guess and remember?
21. Is it easy to determine the organization's target group or audience?
22. It is easy to find the mailing address and telephone number of the organization?

LESSONS LEARNED

- Understand that visual design and information architecture is important to consider for Web site development.
- Simple is always better when developing the Web site. Good, clear navigation is one of the most important areas to consider. Don't add bells and whistles unless you have a clear purpose for its inclusion.

- All visitors are not created equally. Spend more time and money on the first-time visitors, trying to get them to become regular visitors, and then regular visitors, trying to get them to become advocates. Provide content to push them down the inverted pyramid.
- Take the time to plan. Even though the software and templates make it easier, don't jump right in without a clear understanding of what you want, why you want it, and how you will measure it.
- Consider conducting good usability tests before launching the Web site.

FURTHER READING AND RECOMMENDED SITES

Don't Make Me Think: A Common Sense Approach to Web Usability by Steve Krug
Designing for the Social Web by Joshua Porter
The Non-Designer's Web Book by Robin Williams and John Tollett
Jakob Nielsen's Web site, www.useit.com
The Web Designer's Idea Book: The Ultimate Guide to Themes, Trends & Styles in Web Site Design by Patrick McNeil
The Principles of Beautiful Web Design by Jason Beaird

Online donations: Click and Pledge (www.clickandpledge.com)
Volunteer management, online donations, e-advocacy: Network for Good (www.networkforgood.org/)
e-advocacy: E-advocates (www.e-advocates.com)
Online giving: Electronic Giving Solutions (www.egsnetwork.com)
Online planned giving: The Nonprofit Matrix (www.nonprofitmatrix.com/category.asp?Cat=Plannedgiving)
Discounted software for nonprofit organizations: Tech Soup (www.techsoup.org)
Online shopping: Goodstorm (www.goodstorm.com)
Online volunteer management: ServiceLeader.org, Nationalserviceresources.org, Servenet.org, Clubrunner.ca

Developing a privacy policy:

Colomar Group. 2007. "Developing a Privacy Policy for Your Web Site." Available online at http://colomar.com/PrivacyPolicy.php
Wuorio, J. 2007. "7 Steps to Developing a Privacy Policy with Teeth." Available online at www.microsoft.com/smallbusiness/resources/marketing/privacy_spam/7_steps_to_developing_a_privacy_policy_with_teeth.mspx

NOTES

1. Steve Krug, *Don't Make Me Think: A Common Sense Approach to Web Usability, 2nd Ed.* (Berkeley, CA: New Riders, 2006); Spool, Jared User Interface Engineering, www.uie.com.

2. Interview with Aria Finger, Chief Marketing Officer, Do Something, July 8, 2009.
3. Krug, *Don't Make Me Think*.
4. Joshua Porter, *Designing for the Social Web* (Berkeley, CA: New Riders Publishing, 2008), 5.
5. Tom Watson, *CauseWired: Plugging In, Getting Involved, Changing the World* (Hoboken, NJ: John Wiley & Sons, 2009).
6. Porter, *Designing for the Social Web*.
7. Adapted in part from Porter, *Designing for the Social Web*.
8. Watson, *CauseWired*.
9. www.wikipedia.com
10. Robin Williams and John Tollett, *The Non-Designer's Web Book: An Easy Guide to Creating, Designing, and Posting Your Own Web Site*, 3rd Ed. (Berkeley, CA: Peach Pit Press, 2006).
11. www.businesswire.com/portal/site/google/?ndmViewId=news_view&newsId=20090427005138&newsLang=en
12. ePhilanthropy, Code of Ethical Online Philanthropic Practices, www.ePhilanthropyFoundation.org.
13. www.paypal.com/cgi-bin/webscr?cmd=xpt/Marketing/merchant/NonProfits FAQ-outside
14. M. Johnson, "3rd Internet Survey of Australian Non Profits Released Saturday, April 15, 2006 (2006). Available online at www.ephilanthropy.org/site/News2?news_iv_ctrl=1107&page=NewsArticle&id=6146
15. A. Sargeant, T. Hilton and W. Wymer, "Bequest Motives and Barriers to Giving: The Case of Direct Mail Donors" *Nonprofit Management and Leadership*, 17(1), 49–66

    A. Sargeant, W. Wymer and T. Hilton T., "Marketing Bequest Club Membership: An Exploratory Study of Legacy Pledgers" *Nonprofit and Voluntary Sector Quarterly* 35 (3), 384–404.

    A. Sargeant and W. Wymer, "Making the Bequest: An Empirical Study of the Attitudes of Pledgers and Supporters" *International Journal of Educational Advancement* 5(3), 14.
16. www.energyoutreach.org/
17. See http://en.wikipedia.org/wiki/RSS for more information on RSS feeds.
18. See http://content.opportunityknocks.org/2008/09/22/a-definition-of-grass roots-fund-raising/ for more on grassroots organizing.
19. http://volunteer-management.suite101.com/article.cfm/how_to_find_volunteers
20. www.gvsu.edu/service/module-news-view.htm?newsId=4CD6A88E-E439-5A82-B5DC427EEC757FFC
21. http://volunteer-management.suite101.com/article.cfm/how_to_find_volunteers
22. http://www.privacyrights.org/fs/fs28-nonprofits.htm
23. Krug, *Don't Make Me Think*.

CHAPTER 4

Social Media Content Strategy

"Why is it happening now? The groundswell comes from the collision of three forces: people, technology, and economics. People have always depended on each other and drawn strength from each other. . . . Technology has changed everything as far as people's interactions go . . . and on the Internet, traffic means money."
—Charlene Li and Josh Bernoff, analysts at Forrester Research and authors of *Groundswell: Winning in a World Transformed by Social Technologies*[1]

CHAPTER OVERVIEW

The purpose of this chapter is to introduce managers to the world of social media and understand this movement and its implications for nonprofit organizations. As such, it is imperative to construct a strategy for social media tools related to an overall communications program. This chapter primarily deals with the strategic aspects of social media. This is important because many nonprofits jump onboard without a clear understanding of what they want to do with a social-media tool, and they typically have no idea what success looks like for their organization with this tool.

LIVESTRONG—THE LANCE ARMSTRONG FOUNDATION

Throughout this and the next chapter you will see many examples of organizations using specific social-media tools quite effectively. Larger organizations are able to leverage their time and energy to create a social media strategy that engages multiple stakeholders in different ways. Livestrong (www.livestrong.org) is one of the many organizations fighting cancer. Started by the 1999 through 2005 Tour de France winner Lance Armstrong, who fought and won his own battle with cancer, this organization teamed up with Nike to create the ubiquitous yellow bands encouraging people to "live strong." Livestrong has leveraged its message and its brand through Web sites, videos, Facebook, blogs, Twitter, and more. The purpose of the organization is to raise the awareness of cancer, to raise funds to help people with cancer, and to fund cancer research. The mission is to

Figure 4.1: Livestrong

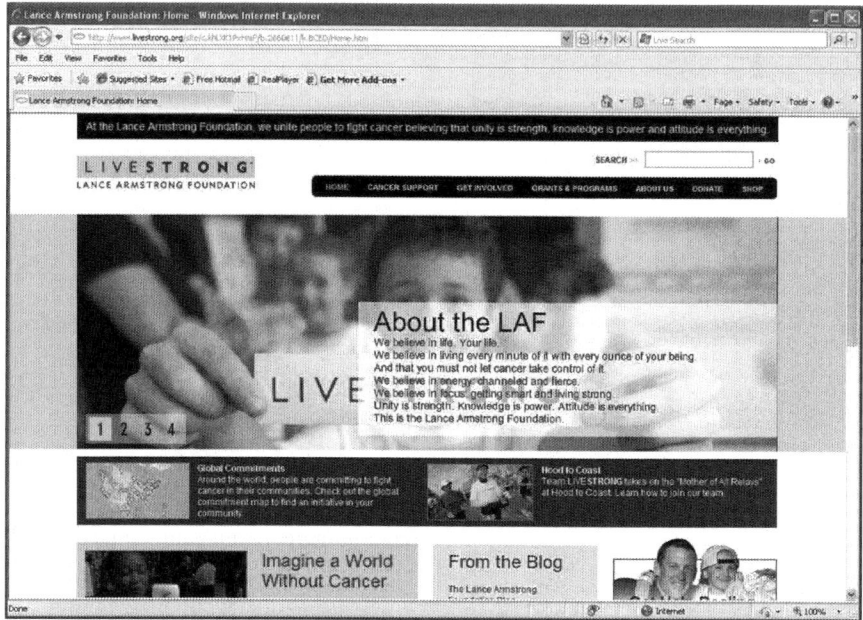

"unite people to fight cancer believing that unity is strength, knowledge is power, and attitude is everything." One suggestion for organizations just starting out with social media is to examine larger organizations as exemplars of strategy. Besides Livestrong, there are several others: Komen for the Cure, the American Red Cross, and the American Cancer Society are just a few good examples.

WHAT IS SOCIAL MEDIA?

Social media is the phenomenon of people using new tools (such as blogs, podcasts, and videos) and Web sites (like Facebook, Twitter, and LinkedIn) to share information, collaborate with each other, and have conversations—all online. This phenomenon is not new. For thousands of years, people have told stories and shared experiences primarily through face-to-face communication. As such, people were only able to build relationships with their family members, their neighbors, and people who lived in their immediate community. Today, that community is global. We talk with people overseas and across the street—all via smartphones, iPads, and computers.

According to the Pew Internet and American Life Report,[2] in January 2009, more than 35 percent of adults have a profile on a social network, with the fastest growing network being Facebook. To date, there are more than 500 million people on Facebook, and that number grows daily. And there is more than fifteen hours of video uploaded onto YouTube every single minute, with the average user spending sixty-two minutes with YouTube per month. More than sixty-four million people worldwide use Flickr to share photos, and more than three billion images are posted on that site. And everyday almost three million more photos are added to that. Amazingly, in December 2008, 4.5 million people visited Twitter, representing a 753 percent increase from the previous year. Now more than fifty-five million "tweets" are sent daily from more than 100 million people on Twitter as of mid-2010. More than 73 percent of active online users have read a blog, and more than half belong to at least one social network. More than half of active online users have uploaded photos, and almost one-quarter have uploaded videos. The bottom line, according to Universal McCann's Comparative Study on Social Media Trends in March 2008, "If you are online, you are using social media."[3] And John Haydon, marketing consultant, said that "the real value of social media is that it exponentially leverages word-of-mouth."[4]

What about nonprofit organizations? A recent survey conducted by Weber Shandwick (impact.webershandwick.com) in July 2009 asked 200 nonprofit communication executives their plans for social media. The survey provides some interesting insights:

- Nonprofits are neither ignoring social media nor are they putting all of their eggs in that basket; the survey found that most are experimenting with social media quite a bit. However, only 51 percent of respondents say that they are active users of social media. Larger organizations (with budgets greater than $25 million) are more likely to experiment with social media.

- Most (77 percent) agree that social media is worth the investment, and 85 percent see it as a priority for the future. In fact, 69 percent believe that their social media budget will increase in the next year.

- But most nonprofit organizations are finding that it is not a "cure all" to communication. Most (70 percent) believe that social media is useful for reaching external audiences but less effective at reaching donors, the media, and policy-makers or influencers. They also believe that the impact on external audiences is greater than other stakeholders.

- The primary goal for social media is awareness rather than for fundraising at this point.

- While many nonprofit organizations see the value, most struggle with the implementation of social media into communication platforms. Only 26 percent love it and believe they are good at it, while another 38 percent like it but are struggling with it. Interestingly, despite its widespread use and growing interest among nonprofit organizations, most respondents (64 percent) still don't have a stated social-media policy for employees, volunteers, and board members.

- Nonprofit organizations definitely see the potential for social media in advocacy; indeed, more effective than traditional media.

- Almost all (78 percent) feel that they need more training and a deeper expertise on how to effectively mobilize social media, and a majority (78 percent) believe that the value has yet to be determined for most organizations. But they generally (61 percent) agree that it is worth the risk.[5] This leads us to a discussion of developing a social-media strategy and how it integrates into the larger promotional plan.

Elizabeth Beachy, Co-Founder of Upleaf, recommends that nonprofits focus on two social networks, for example. Her favorites are Twitter and Facebook. She suggests spending some time each day communicating with supporters and updating information. Some of these social networks offer special applications for nonprofits. YouTube, for example, has a nonprofit channel with some features for nonprofits.[6]

THE IMPORTANCE OF A STRATEGY

Social media is exciting. It is tempting for an organization to jump right in. The costs are minimal (at least in terms of money) and the learning curve (for most tools) is relatively short. The potential for expanding your organization's impact could be enormous. But before your team puts up a Facebook page or posts a video on YouTube, start with a strategy. For most organizations, it is best to start with the marketing or communications plan. Remember the purpose of these plans is to set objectives and metrics and then to integrate all of the brand touchpoints—the various ways the organization engages with stakeholders—in order to achieve these objectives. These activities could include marketing, program development, fund-raising, public education, policy and advocacy efforts, and public relations. Laying out the long-term strategy allows an organization to be proactive rather than reactive.

There are major differences between traditional communication tactics and social-media tactics. The primary difference is that with social media, the audience is in control of the message, the medium, and the response. Communication is no longer mass or one-way but rather conversational. The focus is on the audience, and the brand has to adapt to this focus. The interaction is less about entertaining and more about listening, influencing, and engaging. But before beginning this engaging and long-term conversation with your stakeholders, make sure the foundation is secure—that the Web site is effectively designed, the e-mail marketing system has a solid database, and that you are maximizing the ability to be found through search-engine optimization. We have discussed these topics throughout the other chapters in this book. Once the foundation is solid, social media will simply serve as an integrated platform to engage with stakeholders.

START WITH A PLAN

Beth Kanter has developed a social-media strategy map that encourages nonprofits to develop a solid strategy for social media.[7] First, it is important to understand where social media fits into the broader communications plan. This plan could include fund-raising events and drives, events, issue awareness, advocacy, influencing policy makers, paid advertising, public relations, and media relations. Given the convergence of traditional media with digital media, some researchers have discussed ways that interactive marketers can categorize media types. Sean Corcoran at Forrester Research writes about the definitions of owned, earned, and paid media.[8] Owned media is essentially media that an organization creates and controls, such as blogs, Web sites, and social-media sites. The purpose of owned media is to develop deeper relationships with stakeholders. This is typically what we have been talking about in this book regarding social media. Earned media is an old public relations term meaning "free media" and includes television, newspaper, and magazine coverage. In an interactive space, earned media comes about as word-of-mouth about something the organization is doing. It can include when a video goes "viral," where word-of-mouth becomes the driver, and can also include any retweets or comments on blogs—essentially feedback from stakeholders. Paid media is more along the lines of traditional media like newspaper or magazine ads or television time. In an interactive space, it could include display advertising, paid search words, or other types of online advertising.

Ideally, you need all three types to effectively implement a communications plan. Forrester Research suggests that in order to leverage all three types, it is vital to understand a few key issues. First, maximize the owned media by reaching out beyond your existing Web site to create a portfolio of digital touchpoints. Be sure you are using your own Web site as well as other platforms like social networks, blogs, or Twitter to maximize your reach. This is especially true for tight budgets, since your organization may not be able to afford paid media. Second, recognize that simply being good at public and media relations will not translate into earned media. Those days are gone. Learning how to listen to stakeholders and respond to them will stimulate word-of-mouth. Last, paid media is not dead but rather serves as a catalyst to drive more engagement.[9] That said, once you have figured out the bigger picture, consider a few more steps in developing a social-media strategy.

OBJECTIVES

After determining the overall plan, the next step to developing strategy is to begin with an idea of what the organization wants to accomplish. Set these objectives with a clear understanding of how social media changes the communication dynamic with stakeholders. It is not about reaching a mass audience but more about influencing people through conversations. These objectives need to also be linked to other communication objectives dealing with fund-raising and event promotion as well as issue awareness. Objectives should be SMART: specific, measurable, action-oriented, realistic, and time-based. Some of the general goals include:

Listening and learning. Listening means monitoring what is being said about the organization, the cause, and competitor organizations as well as gleaning insights about audiences. Additionally, use these tools to gain information about best practices with social media. We talk more about listening systems later in this book.

Build relationships and issues awareness. Build relationships through conversations with stakeholders by giving them compelling content in a variety of media (e.g., blogs, podcasts, and video). Experiment with tools that are the best match for the organization and the objective.

Reputation management. Develop and improve your reputation by responding to comments and criticism that appear on blogs and forums. Additionally, organizations can position themselves as experts by participating in other forums and discussions.

Content generation and education. Content can come from the organization as well as stakeholders. Organizational content works to educate audiences on the cause and the impact that the organization has on its community. If this is a goal, it is important to make sure that content is updated regularly. Consider developing an editorial calendar.

Taking action and fund-raising. One of the areas with the some potential for specific audiences is using tools to raise funds and to solicit action from volunteers and advocates.

Building a community. It makes sense for some organizations to develop their own online communities (e.g., Nings) and keep them engaged with interesting content.

AUDIENCES

Once objectives have been determined, it is then important to understand the audience. Identify who is using social media and what types of social media they are using. For example, expect younger people to be on Facebook, but expect the Twitter audience tends to skew a little older.[10] Does this profile match your stakeholders? Why has this audience been selected? What key points do you want to make with these audiences? What do you want them to do with that information? These questions and more should be considered to determine not only what tools will be most effective, but also whether social media even makes sense for your organization.

There are several tools to use to identify target audiences. Many of these are discussed in chapter 10 about insights and evaluation. Additionally, use secondary sources in order to develop a stakeholder profile. If this is still not possible or does not yield a complete picture, consider using primary research tactics such as surveys, interviews, or focus groups.

Social media will be one of many tools (including more traditional means) that your organization uses for communication. Therefore, it is important for everything to work together seamlessly. The "home base" is the Web site. For some organizations, a blog may become the primary home base, and they may consolidate the blog and the Web site. Next, examine the outbound communication tactics such as e-mail, customer relationship management programs, and search-engine optimization. Make sure that each area is tracked to maximize effectiveness.

INTERNAL BUY IN

Before you can use social media, you must convince your organization's board of directors and executives of its value. Most will want to know the return on investment. In other words, what do you get for what you are giving up? The good news is that in terms of money, the organization is not giving up much (if anything) since most tools are free. But they do take time and, after all, time is money. Organizations also get pretty trackable results, which are covered in the last chapter. Since many organizations are unfamiliar with social media, there is an underlying fear. These include:

- There is a loss of control over the branding and marketing message since the whole goal is to engage stakeholders in a conversation.
- With this loss of control, there will be negative comments. Some organizations don't understand how to deal with these comments.
- Of course, there is a fear of failure, and this failure can be public since it involves a conversation with stakeholders.
- Given the learning curve and lack of established metrics, there is a fear of wasted time and effort.

Some organizations are wary of social media for a variety of reasons. Here are a few that should be considered: it will cost. These costs are not necessarily in the tool itself but rather staff time, staff education and training, and possibly computer upgrades (including greater bandwidth). There are security risks. Many executives are worried about the potential for hacking and viruses. However, implementing firewalls, using quality partners (for donations for example) and enacting a strong social media policy can go a long way toward reducing risks. And social media could hurt a company's reputation by allowing people to post comments. Of course, there are risks of allowing stakeholders to voice their opinions. But this also allows for a forum to address any negative comments, as well. Indeed, not using social media could come off as not caring what people think.[11]

To be successful, social media does require a mix of authenticity and transparency that many nonprofit organizations are not used to. Internal education is key. One of the best ways to educate people is to identify best practices and successful case studies about nonprofits and their use of social media. These are especially meaningful if they also contain results and effectiveness numbers. In order to overcome the fear of wasted time, the idea of experimentation should be emphasized. Learning is an important part of the process. Last, one way to reduce fear is to implement some structure. For example, if the organization is developing a blog, then a blogging policy should be required. This outlines what should be included, who should write the blog, and so forth. The sheer process of developing guidelines can lead to a deeper understanding of the medium.[12]

Creating capacity deals with the implementation phase of strategy. The primary cost to the organization is time, which can be a few hours per week to as many as thirty hours per week, depending on the strategy and tools used. Remember to factor in the learning curve time, as well. Eventually, this area may be addressed through human resources and staffing if the organization determines that full-time expertise is required. Some organizations like to use interns or volunteers for social media. This can be problematic due to the transient nature of their time. Interns will typically be available for a semester or two; volunteers could be more long-term, but that would be dependent on a variety of issues. If regular staffers do not know how to maintain the Facebook page, what happens when the intern or volunteer moves on?

Internal Training for Social Media

Training should be mandatory for anyone who will engage using social media. This will serve two purposes: (1) it will ensure everyone knows the communication plan and the social-media tools and how to use each tool, and (2) it will ensure that everyone knows the organizational policies regarding social-media usage. A few things to consider in the training program:

- What is social media? Introduce the various tools your organization plans to use and clarify any terms of services. This should be presented within the context of how the organization plans to use social media.

- What are the organizational policies? Introduce any organizational social media policies, including what is allowed and what is not allowed; expectations and participation criteria; who can speak on the organization's behalf and how to disclose important information. Outline any ownership rights and responsibilities and talk about the consequences for breaking policy.

- What are the legal considerations for engaging in social media? Include any legal policies that are important to social media (e.g., defamation, privacy) and explain the ramifications for posting information online. Be sure to include any examples that will be relevant for the organization and confirm the process from a legal perspective if there are any questions about the information posted.

- What are the risks? Explain the security issues related to social media and how the organization plans to reduce that risk. Describe the process for trouble-shooting.
- What are the engagement policies? This section should explain what is appropriate and what is not appropriate for posting, how much posting there should be on a platform, tips for increasing engagement with stakeholders, and the importance of balance when dealing with professional and personal information.
- Who can they go to with issues? Outline the help features or internal experts that staff can tap into with any problems or concerns.[13]

And most of all, teach them how to use the tools and let them have fun.

TACTICS AND TOOLS

The next chapter describes social media and digital tools for stakeholder engagement. It is important to understand that all are not relevant to every organization. Again, it is important to link the objectives to the tools and then to the metrics. Brian Solis developed the Conversation Prism that brilliantly displays the ways that organizations can communicate with stakeholders. There are literally thousands of tools and others being added daily. It is hard to stay on top of it, but it is crucial. We Are Media (www.wearemedia.org) suggests that tools be selected based on the following issues:

- Listening. For newcomers, listening should be the objective for the first social-media experiment. There are several tools listed in this chapter and the next for listening. The key skill is pattern analysis.
- Participate. After listening, participate in the conversation. Again, there are several tools to support conversations.
- Share the story. Share the impact of the organization through the myriad tools for storytelling.
- Generate buzz. Once the story is told, use social media to allow people to pass it along to others. Focus on influencers and try to build trust and credibility.
- Community building and social networking. If you feel that your organization requires its own online community, use tools like Ning to create a site. If your organization is trying to engage the masses, consider Facebook, MySpace, or one of the more targeted social networks.

The secret to a successful social-media strategy is a low-risk experiment. Use it as a learning lab to gauge the successes and the failures. Establish some discovery questions and then use the tools to try it out. This will allow organizations to ensure that their entry into social media is more effective and likely accomplishes their initial objectives.

> **Chapter Insight: How Much Is a Friend Worth? Social Network Analysis and Public Relations**
>
> How much are the 1,267 friends on your executive director's Facebook worth to your nonprofit? It depends. Social network analysis has been around for years, but it is only within the past few years with the advent of social media platforms like Facebook, Twitter, LinkedIn, and MySpace that conducting analyses has been feasible. Social-network analysis plots formal and informal relationships among people and organizations and reveals who is important within the network. While the number of friends is indeed important, what really matters is how these people communicate with each other and how meaningful the dialogue happens to be.
>
> Early research has been conducted by companies like Microsoft, Google, Facebook, and IBM on the value of these friendships. Early results show that "digital friendships speak volumes about consumers and workers, and decoding the data can lead to profitable insights. Calculating the value of these relationships has become a defining challenge for businesses and individuals."[14] One early insight that is important to nonprofits is that, at a certain level, these "friends" are considered trusted sources. In other words, if a cause is important to someone who is well connected, there is a good chance that some of those connections will engage with that cause, as well. Especially if that connected person is an advocate for the cause. For example, if a friend from high school has breast cancer and becomes highly involved with Komen's Race for the Cure, then there is a high likelihood that other friends from high school will donate or participate with that same cause.
>
> It is important to understand the dynamics of these networks. Cameron Marlow, a research scientist at Facebook, shows that one early step is to separate users' friends into clusters—family, high school friends, fraternity, work friends, and so forth. Studying this data, researchers determined that the average Facebook user has 500 friends, but only actively follows forty of them, communicates with twenty of them, and keeps in close touch with ten of them.[15] But while the typical person is close to only a handful of friends, they may use other friends in the network for specific areas of advice (technology, financial, and professional) or for word-of-mouth recommendation (special events, concerts, and restaurants). And causes. So it is important for nonprofits to figure out the most effective way to use social networks. Currently, social-network analysis using social platforms is a specialty, but considering how fast technology is moving, this could prove to be a valuable tool for all organizations.

As stated earlier, it is crucial to link objectives to tools to metrics. Measurement is evolving; each section below includes measurement for the larger tools. Generally, measurement includes issues like number of fans, followers, or friends; number of video or content views; volume of user content on comments;

retweet or peer-sharing statistics; engagement in terms of the length of time spent with content; media coverage; media impressions; click-through rates for ads; Web site traffic statistics; quantity of new visitors and so forth.[16] We discuss issues regarding measurement and evaluation in chapter 10.

THE IMPORTANCE OF CONTENT STRATEGY

With all of this information, it is tempting to ask, "How in the world can I manage all of this?" True words. Most nonprofits don't have enough time to keep up with current tasks, much less add to that growing list of things to do. However, there are some simple things you can do that will make this experience more rewarding for you and your stakeholders. First, let's define content strategy. According to expert Kristina Halvorson, content strategy is "plans for the creation, publication, and governance of useful and usable content."[17] Beth Kanter says that there are essentially three aspects to content strategy. First, there is Web site content, which includes the information currently on the organization's Web site. It is edited and scheduled as part of your formal content strategy. Much of this can mirror information in printed form, as well.[18] Halvorson adds that content strategy includes an editorial strategy (e.g., what you are publishing and when), Web writing (this is different from other formats in that it must be scannable), metadata, search-engine optimization, content-management strategy, and content-channel distribution strategy.[19]

Nonprofit expert Kivi Leroux Miller adds that there are easy ways to make content strategy work.[20] She suggests that nonprofits get organized and think ahead. When developing ideas for articles, blogs, or newsletters, think about what other channels the organization should be using (e.g., Facebook, Twitter). She recommends creating an editorial calendar for a specific time period (weekly, monthly, quarterly—whatever makes sense for your organization). Then determine how to organize the calendar, whether by platform or audience. Prioritize the content so that it is clear what is absolutely necessary versus what is nice to do if you have the time. Organize your content using tags and folders with various tools such as Gmail, Delicious, WebNotes or something similar.

Once the core ideas are there, then take a few minutes to see how you can reuse, revise, or revamp content for additional platforms. For example, is there a way to take a piece of a blog posting and put in a Facebook feed? See if there are extensions to a good blogging story. Miller (and Darren Rowse at www.problogger.com) recommends using a mind-mapping exercise that visually displays your blog posts so that you can brainstorm ideas on where to extend the content. For example, a blog post about new services at your domestic abuse shelter can lead to a profile of a woman who has been successful in your transitional living program. Additionally, by using listening tools (discussed later in the book), you can get information on what is being discussed and add to it. This can include mainstream media news, trade news, and aggregators as well as comments and posts from stakeholders. Get other people involved in developing content, such as your board members, volunteers, and constituents. The information can take various formats: lists and how to's, tips, editorials, and profiles. Once you have content, find ways to extend things (expand tweets into blog posts) or shorten things (pull out a quote from a blog post and tweet it). Consider your various audiences and channels. This strategy will allow you to have more time to create great content if you can extend it into various platforms.[21]

> ### Conversation with the Pros: Kim Young, Founder, the forest & the trees
>
> Kim Young doesn't care much for the dated and limited label of marketer. She prefers social currency builder, community developer, and partnership architect. Young has worked with nonprofits and for-profits for more than thirty years and started her consultancy, the forest & the trees, so she could focus on facilitating engagement, education, enlightenment, and empowerment of individuals. In that role, she also instructs nonprofits through the Dallas-based Center for Nonprofit Management as well as the State of Texas' OneStar Foundation. She has also been a national speaker for Center for Nonprofit Success. As such, she finds herself talking with many nonprofits about their plans for social media.
> "First, most are completely overwhelmed with the tsunami of information that is out there," Young says. "But many still have a transactional mindset—they want to use social media for fund-raising. But right now that is not its main purpose. It is about relationships." She adds that most organizations are fearful of relinquishing control and are concerned about negative comments. "When I show them that there is real-time conversations happening about their organization (say in the new Facebook tools), they are stunned," she says. She recommends that since social media is completely different from traditional media—it is not about broadcasting—organizations should conduct an audit first to map out their relationships and make sure they have a grasp on the basics. But these tools come with a high expectation from stakeholders, so it is important that the basics are taken care of. She also recommends not jumping into tactics without a plan. "Organizations need to think about integration—content creation and management strategy. They need an editorial calendar," Young says.
> Young tries to get organizations to see the future, and she believes that is building engagement platforms where the organization has many ways to engage various audiences. She cites charity water, the American Red Cross, Nothing But Nets, and Earth Hour as great examples of engagement platforms. These run the gamut from major organizations to a two-person collaboration. Young also recommends social-action platforms, such as change.org and care2.org. "I try to live by one of my favorite sayings: 'Fail fast and live in beta,' to make sure that organizations know how important these changes are to their existence," she says.

The last type, engagement, is what Kanter calls co-created content in the sense that many times stakeholders will take your content and refashion it themselves. A good example is remix or mashup videos that show up on YouTube, where someone has taken content that is accessible and remixed it. This information also gets shared in various ways.

Overall, Halvorson makes a few recommendations when it comes to content strategy. First, do less and not more. Don't try to put everything out there. Make sure that the content you are creating is based on an objective and not simply to fill space. Less content is easier to manage and easier for people to find. Second, she recommends conducting a content audit—essentially figuring out what you have so you know what you can do with it. Third, learn how to listen. Fourth, make sure someone is in charge. Last, start asking "why"—examine the reasons for developing content on various topics. Her wise words: "When it comes to your business, just because you can doesn't always mean you should."[22]

LESSONS LEARNED

- Social media requires a good strategy that complements the communication plan. This plan should include objectives, audiences, tools, and measurement for each strategy.
- Make sure that your organization develops the proper guidelines and policies regarding social media and then properly trains staff members to engage with social media.
- Understanding and developing a good content strategy is key, given that the goal of social media is oftentimes to create and participate in a conversation. Content strategy ensures that you have valuable information to talk about on your Web site.

NOTES

1. Charlene Li and Josh Bernoff, *Groundswell: Winning in a World Transformed by Social Technologies* (Boston: Harvard Business Press, 2009).
2. Pew Internet & American Life Project, *Adults and Social Networks Report* (January 14, 2009), www.pewinternet.org/PPF/r/272/report_display.asp.
3. Universal McCann, "Power to the People—Wave3 Study on Social Media Trends" (March 2008), www.universalmccann.com/assets/wave 3 20080403093750.pdf.
4. Primalmedia, "Social Media for Nonprofits," primalmedia.com/blog.
5. Weber Shandwick and KRC Research, "Social Impact: Social Media in the Nonprofit Sector," impact.webershandwick.com.
6. http://upleaf.com/2009/07/10-tools-for-marketing-your-nonprofit-on-the-web/
7. We Are Media, "Creating your Organization's Social Media Strategy Map," www.wearemedia.org/social+Media+Strategy+Map.
8. Sean Corcoran, "Defining Earned, Owned and Paid Media" (Forrester Blogs, December 16, 2009), http://blogs.forrester.com; Brian Solis, "Why Brands are Becoming Media" (Mashable, February 11, 2010), http://mashable.com/2010/02/11/social-objects/.

9. Ibid.
10. http://social-media-optimization.com/2010/02/a-look-at-twitter-demographics/
11. MarketingProfs, A Step by Step Guide to a Successful Social Media Program (2009), www.marketingprofs.com.
12. We Are Media, "Strategy Track Module 3, The Social Media Ready Nonprofit: Dealing with Resistance," www.wearemedia.org/strategic+track+module+3+f=print.
13. MarketingProfs, www.marketingprofs.com.
14. Stephen Baker, "Learning, and Profiting, From Online Friendships" *Businessweek* (May 21, 2009), www.businessweek.com.
15. Ibid.
16. MarketingProfs, www.marketingprofs.com.
17. Kristina Halvorson, *Content Strategy for the Web* (Berkeley, CA: New Riders, 2010).
18. Beth Kanter, "WeAreMedia: What's Your Social Content Strategy," http://beth.typepad.com.
19. Ibid.
20. Kivi Leroux Miller, "Content Creation for Nonprofits: Making the Most of Your Writing, Photos, Etc." (Webinar, 2009), www.nonprofitmarketingguide.com.
21. Ibid.
22. Halvorson, *Content Strategy for the Web*.

CHAPTER 5

Social Media and Digital Technology Tools for Stakeholder Engagement

"This is the new paradigm in philanthropy. It's [texting's] no longer a niche product for twelve-year-olds."
—Jeffrey Nelson, Executive Director for Corporation Communications, Verizon Wireless

CHAPTER OVERVIEW

The previous chapter discussed the reasons for the growth of social media as well as how various nonprofit organizations are using these tools. This chapter outlines each of the major social media and technology tools and highlights what they are most effective at accomplishing. This should serve the reader as a menu. After determining the purpose and objectives of using social media, then nonprofit managers can determine what will be the most effective tools to reach those goals. A list of tools is provided at the end of the chapter.

TEXTING TO SAVE HAITI

For years, in the marketing field, mobile technology has been touted as the "next big thing." However, due to a variety of issues—privacy concerns, low opt-in rates, and so forth—marketers (and nonprofit organizations) have been slower to adopt mobile campaigns. That changed in January 2010, when a 7.0 earthquake destroyed the town of Port au Prince, Haiti and the surrounding areas. The death toll to date exceeds 200,000 people. Like when disasters occurred before it, Americans jumped to aid. This time texting was at the forefront.

The American Red Cross and other organizations, such as Yele, CARE, Oxfam, and Save the Children, were on the ground helping earthquake victims. American corporations jumped on board with millions of dollars in donations and supplies. But it was the $5 and $10 donations that ordinary people donated through texting—the charges were merely added to their cellular phone bills—

that would add up quickly. This effort showed that the mobile phone can be one of the most powerful fund-raising tools in history.[1] The Red Cross's texting campaign raised more than $36 million with its Text HAITI to 90999 campaign. This includes more than three million donors proving how effective mobile campaigns can be. The campaign saw spikes when a public service announcement from First Lady Michelle Obama urged people to make donations via text, and the Red Cross said it was seeing more than $700,000 per hour come in during the NFL playoff games whenever commentators were talking about the program.[2]

"This is bigger than anything that had occurred previously in terms of developing the mobile channel as an alternative to the conventional method of making donations," said David Diggs, vice president of wireless Internet development for CTIA—The Wireless Association.[3] Indeed, texting serves as an effective way to reach younger people who are more tech-savvy. This is a base that many organizations have found hard to reach.

However, the texting effort is not without its problems. For one, while they did not take a part of the donations, mobile companies did not typically distribute the donations to nonprofits until bills were paid (sometimes up to ninety days later). But many companies elected to bypass this rule for the Haiti disaster. Second, Red Cross studies showed that the average donation was smaller for the Haiti earthquake compared to other disasters. For example, while the total number of gifts was higher, the average size of donations to Haiti was $109 compared to $208 for the 2006 Asian tsunami. This fueled the concern that perhaps the small amounts were at the expense of larger donations. Third, it was hard to determine who to give to (at least before the Clinton Bush Haiti Fund and the Hope for Haiti telethon). Red Cross did receive the majority of donations, but some experts cite the British Disasters Emergency Committee, which acts as an umbrella organization for thirteen charities, as a more effective model.[4]

Despite the distractors, it is clear that mobile platforms have potential for nonprofits, especially in disasters. Here are a few things to consider from Red Cross's texting effort: first, keep it going. A texting campaign has a longer shelf life than traditional pitches due to the viral components of social media. Second, go where the crowds are; much of the world's population is mobile. Third, get with using mobile technology for business transactions. And fourth, choose the price points (e.g., $5 and $10 in the Haiti case) wisely. This allows donors to feel good about their donation but not give so little that the organization suffers.[5] For more information on mobile giving, check out the Mobile Giving Foundation (www.mobilegiving.org).

BLOGS AND WIKIS

Description: Blogs and wikis have become one of the staples of a social-media strategy. There are several "self-publishing tools" that are effective at communicating with multiple stakeholders. Blogs are essentially Web sites with dynamic content. Blogs allows authors to create content that then ideally builds trust with audience members. These are called posts. One of the most important ways to interact with audiences is through comments. Once a story (or post) is put on a blog, audience members can provide feedback through comments. Blogs can be used on a host service (like wordpress.org or blogger.com) or can be hosted on other independent servers (such as the organization's server or server provider). Audiences are built if the content is dynamic and consistent. While most blogs do not generate revenue, a few large and popular blogs utilize banner ads and Google Ad Sense.

Blogs are effective at developing thought leadership; forming better relationships with stakeholders; optimizing search-engine results; attracting new donors, volunteers, and advocates; telling stories; and providing an active forum for testing new ideas. There are a few issues to think about before beginning a blog. First, read a few blogs before starting one. Then comment on articles and posts. This starts the conversation, which is what social media is all about. It is important to understand the blogging culture. Links and attribution are important in the blogosphere (see the section on Creative Commons at the end of this chapter).

Second, determine the content of the blog and the author of the blog. The author should be someone who is passionate about the cause and is an engaging writer. This person should be able to speak in a human voice, not in jargon and corporate speak. The author does not have to be the executive director. The blog should have an editorial calendar or at least a schedule for posts in order to maintain consistency. Remember that consistency leads to an audience. Consider issues such as topics and the intended audiences. Generally, posts are three to ten paragraphs (depending on the topic), but the length should be determined by what is best for the author. Some authors are able to write longer posts and do it less often. Other authors are more effective by using shorter posts that are more frequent. Be sure to include links and to add some additional content where appropriate (such as videos or audios). Try to have a photo for each post. Remember, you can always use Flickr for photos (just make sure to adhere to the creative commons license) and use key words and phrases from posts to find links. Make sure to edit for grammar and structure.

Third, promote the blog by commenting on other blogs and using search engines (like Technorati and Ice Rocket). Be sure to include the blog's URL in correspondence and link to it from the Web site. If you are also on Twitter, cross-promote the blog, but be wary of blatant self-promotion. Last, as far as comments from others are concerned, make sure they are enabled on your blog and answer as many as you can. Keep the negative comments, too; pulling these down will catch the ire of the blogosphere.[6] This is the foundation for two-way conversation with stakeholders.

Wikis are a browser-based Web-collaboration platforms where people can add, revise, and otherwise edit content. While some are open source, others are used to collect knowledge for organizations. Wikis include "talk pages" that parallel each page, where contributors discuss what should be included on the pages. The best example of a wiki is Wikipedia, which is a collaboration on multiple topics whose accuracy is governed by the masses. It typically appears at the top of search results, so nonprofits can develop a page that includes the basic information and then provide links to the organization's main Web site, Facebook page, or blog. We Are Media is a wiki dedicated to teaching nonprofits about social media. Slideshare is a platform that allows organizations and people to post presentations (typically as a PowerPoint or Keynote deck) in order to share content with the public. Slideshare can be useful if the organization has developed a presentation for donors or other important stakeholders.

Objectives: Blogs are effective for generating awareness and engagement with multiple stakeholders, establishing expertise and thought leadership, and telling stories about problems faced by the cause and/or the accomplishments and social impacts achieved by the organization.

Tools: For blogs, the most popular are Blogger, Wordpress, Movable Type, Blogware, and TypePad. For wikis, Wikia, PBworks, Wikispaces, and Wetpaint are useful. Additionally, consider Slideshare for posting and searching for presentations. Blog search tools include Google Search, Technorati, IceRocket, MetaTube, and Yahoo! Search.[7]

Measurement: The interaction (or stickiness) of the blog is determined by the number of blog posts and then the number of comments made by visitors. It considers the amount of time spent on a site as well as how often visitors return to the site. The more time spent, the "stickier" it is. The greater the number of comments, the greater the impact of the blog post. Additionally, content can be reposted on other blogs, which is another factor in effectiveness. Consider this as word-of-mouth or viral marketing. Inbound links are also important to evaluation, so be sure to link to other blogs and allow them to link to yours. Rankings of blogs (such as the Power 150 for marketing and advertising blogs) are also indicators of content value. The ultimate effectiveness test of a blog post is whether it makes it into the mainstream media (such as a story on CNN or in a major newspaper).

Costs: Free (or a small fee depending on hosting) but can take a considerable time commitment if the organization aims for frequent postings.

In practice: The Red Cross is a well-known organization using many different types of social media, including blogs, wikis, podcasts, widgets, texting, mobile technology, and social-networking sites. One of its most important functions is to educate the public about disaster relief and what the Red Cross does for people living through a disaster. Two important tools are its wiki (http://redcrossfund-raisingtools.wikispaces.com) and its blogs. The wiki lists

Chapter Insight: Blogging Policy

A study conducted by the *Chronicle of Philanthropy* found that 79 percent of nonprofit hiring managers say that their organizations do not have a policy governing social media usage and blogging, despite that fact that 95 percent reported using Facebook, LinkedIn, and Twitter for various purposes. Having a policy to govern social media is important. "As more people jumped on the speeding bandwagon, friending and tweeting on behalf of their charities, they made mistakes, sometimes bringing uncomfortable exposure to themselves or their employers," says Kris Gallagher, internal consultant in marketing and communication at DePaul University.[8] She offers a few issues to consider in developing a policy for your organization:

- Be sure to enlist the help of legal advisers and other areas, such as marketing and communications, so that everyone has a say in the content. The size of this committee will also depend on what type of organization you are. Healthcare and medical may want to enlist the help of doctors and therapists.

- Make sure you decide what is important for the organization and be sure that you consider the tradeoff between privacy rights and free speech. Different organizations may need a tighter rein on speech than others (medical organizations compared to arts organizations).

- Take a look at other policies and adapt them rather than reinventing the wheel. Social Media Governance is a Web site that includes sample guidelines (www.socialmediagovernance.com), and Blogger's Legal Guide explains the law regarding intellectual property and copyrights (www.eff.org/issues/bloggers/legal/liability/IP).

- Be sure to consider disclosure issues for bloggers. Make sure that employees understand that it is important not to cross the line from personal opinions to opinions sanctioned by the organization.

- Be sure to think about issues regarding accountability and policy tone. Make sure that the policy reflects the values of the organization.

- Understand that the policy should be organic and should continue to be tweaked as social media tools arise.

Other information to consider includes protection of confidential information by not allowing discussion on social-media platforms; avoiding conflicts of interest; and knowledge of trademark or copyright issues, defamation, and personal responsibility. Beth Kanter posted the Easter Seals Blogging policy on her Web site as a example of an effective policy (http://beth.typepad.com/beths_blog/2008/04/nonprofit-blogg.html).

tools that can be used to generate awareness for the organization (including links to all of the social media tools listed above) and well as key messages that are important in fund-raising campaign development. Two blogs specifically talk about areas that are in trouble. The main blog (http://blog.redcross.org) includes podcasts emphasizing global issues as well as a disaster news portal that offers real-time information on disasters. There is a youth blog focusing on volunteer opportunities and scholarships (http://redcrossyouth.org). The Red Cross is effective at utilizing various types of social media to leverage the messages that are most appropriate for the audience.

MICROBLOGS

Description: Microblogs are blogs with shorter messaging capacity. Twitter, the most popular microblog, requires posts to be no more than 140 characters in length. Originally used for internal communication, Twitter has gained global popularity and is now used as a communication and research tool. Each person creates a profile on Twitter.com and can then search for and select people to follow. Once the profile is developed, other people can follow you, as well. This lays the foundation for two-way conversations. These text-based instant messages are called "tweets." It is also possible to "retweet," where users pass along information they have received in tweets (acting like a viral marketing campaign). Tweeting constitutes two-way communication and is considered effective for many purposes due to the short message length. Messages can be received on cell phones, Web sites, smartphones, iPads, the Twitter Web site, e-mail, or Facebook. Additionally, there are several Twitter-related tools that make sending and receiving tweets easier and more efficient. For example, hashtags are community-driven conventions for adding context and metadata to tweets in order categorize subject matter. This allows you to create groups on Twitter.

Before tweeting, there are a few things to think about regarding Twitter. First, make sure that the conversation is authentic. Don't send out marketing messages. Typically, the marketing and development approach does not work for Twitter (or any other social media, for that matter) like it does for events and capital campaigns. Using social media is about having a personality, inspiring conversation, and building community.[9] Second, make it a two-way conversation by following those who follow you; reply to tweets and retweet other's messages if they are compelling or relevant. While it is hard to follow everyone who follows your organization, it is best to include them all. You cannot have a conversation if you don't follow others; followers cannot message you if you don't follow them, and not following someone is considered a snub in cyberspace. People use Twitter because they want to be followed. Third, since following everyone can be overwhelming, use favorites for the most important tweets. Fourth, provide value in the message and remember that "less is more." Experts say to strike a balance between tweeting enough to maintain a conversation but not so much that it becomes annoying. Last, don't just talk about your organization's content; retweet other content to build relationships.[10] Remember, you can also use tools such as bit.ly to shorten your Twitter URLs. Indeed, a quick Google search shows several Twitter guides (e.g., Mashable). Additionally, table 5.1 includes several tools that can be quite useful for Twitter.

Table 5.1: Tools for Twitter

Tool	Description
TweetDeck	A desktop widget offering great functionality for posting tweets and sorting tweets. It also integrates with Facebook.
HootSuite	A free Web service for organizations with multiple Twitter profiles and users.
CoTweet	A tool where multiple people from the same organization can communicate through a single Twitter account.
FriendOrFollow	A tool to see which of the people you are following are also following you and which people are following you but you have yet to reciprocate.
Twitoria	An application that allows you to see which followers are active on Twitter.
WeFollow	A user-powered Twitter directory where you enter the hashtags you want to be known for on Twitter.
Twellow	The Twitter "yellow" pages.
TwitterCounter	Charts the number of followers over time.
bit.ly	A tool that shortens your URL and enables you to track metrics on the many people who click your links.
Twitalyzer	A tool that goes beyond the analytics to show the influence, signal-to-noise ratio, generosity, and other metrics related to your Twitter account.
Search.Twitter.com	An easy tool to monitor what people are saying about your brand or organization. This allows you to set up RSS feeds related to key terms.
TweetBeep	This is like Google Alerts for Twitter.
Monitter	This service provides a live streaming view of what people in your location are saying about your company or employees.
Radian6 and Techrigy	Two enterprise-class monitoring tools that help a company listen to conversations on Twitter.
TwitBacks and TwitterGallery	Designs for Twitter profiles.
TwitHawk	This tool connects you with people who are actively discussing your organization on Twitter.

Erik Bratt, "Twitter Success Stories" (MarketingProfs, 2008), www.marketingprofs.com.

Objectives: Objectives include creating awareness and engagement with stakeholders (but make sure to only send out relevant content and not trivial posts). Twitter is also great for promotions that require short messages and grassroots efforts.

Tools: Twitter is the most popular tool and is synonymous with microblogging. Jaiku, Plurk, Prologue, and Yammer are also microblogging sites. Search with Tweet Scan and Summize.

Measurement: A measure of popularity is how many people are following you. Another issue is to consider how many people are retweeting your content. You can use tools such as TweetBeep, TweetGrid, or Twilert to search key terms to see what is being said about the organization. Twitalyzer is a tool that calculates your influence on Twitter (see table 5.1). Other services include Google Analytics and Omniture for more sophisticated metrics.

Costs: Microblogging is free except for the time commitment (which can be less than other tools due to the short nature of messages, but can be long if the user follows many other users). It may take some time to learn the Twitter language and culture.

In practice: Twitter has been effective for fund-raising. Toronto resident Danny Brown's 12for12K had a simple mission: twelve months, twelve charities, and $12,000 per charity. Brown noticed that several charities were hurting as a result of the global recession and decided to help. His task was to convince people to donate to charity when they were losing their jobs. His campaign used two important concepts: instant communications and the power of the retweet. Brown and his supporters tweeted about the mission, created an avatar for supporters to include on their Twitter profiles, and included a hashtag (#) to help categorize their tweets, which generated buzz and interest. One supporter hosted a twelve-hour tweet-a-thon to generate as much money as possible for Share Our Strength.[11] Through Twitter, Brown was able to reach his goal.

There are several other high-profile Twitter charity events. Twestival was an event held in February 2009 in Washington where more than 200 Twitter fans met face to face with people they only knew by their online nicknames. They gathered to raise money for charity: water, an organization who provides clean drinking water in developing countries.[12] This same event was repeated in more than 200 cities globally, raising more than $250,000 in twenty-four hours. In Austin, Texas, the Blood and Tissue Center of Central Texas was the beneficiary of an experiment by the Social Media Club (www.socialmediaclub.org) called Social Media for Social Good. The objective was to use Twitter to increase the awareness about blood donation and to increase the number of blood donors. The Austin Tweet Up Blood Drive resulted in forty-five donors (double the daily amount), with many of them being first-time donors.[13] Tweetsgiving (http://tweetsgiving.org) was an effort in late 2008 by Epic Change to raise $10,000 for a new classroom in Tanzania. A huge success, Tweetsgiving resulted in $11,021 from 364 donors in forty-eight hours. Additionally, the campaign received more than 3,000 gratitude tweets, 15,830 page views from 7,563 unique visitors in 101 countries, was the top trend term on twitscoop (a trending tool), and garnered more than 100 press and blog mentions. Why did it work? It was a simple concept that was timely and well-integrated into social media that garnered many evangelists.[14]

SOCIAL NETWORKS

Description: Social-networking sites allow people to share things about themselves with a selected group of "friends" who join their network. Most sites are able to handle multiple types of content (such as photos, text, audio, and video), and users create their own profiles, where they keep their personal information and invite friends to join their networks. To date, Facebook has more than 500 million users; MySpace has more than 250 million users. The key to social networks is forming and maintaining networks. Causes are important to the social network (for example, Facebook has an application called Causes), but most people are there to socialize and communicate, not to be "pitched," so it is important to understand the social-networking culture before diving in. Ning (www.ning.com) allows users to create their own social-network sites, which are effective for community-building. Ning works well with other popular social-networking sites.

Facebook is the most popular of these sites in the U.S. Many nonprofits believe they need to be on Facebook and rush to create a profile. However, the creators of Facebook made a few design changes in early 2009 regarding profiles, groups, and pages. Nonprofits are sometimes confused as to which one of these they should use for their Facebook presence. But before examining the difference between these options, it is important to think about the following issues. First, make sure to understand the overall objective for Facebook. Will this replace your existing site or augment it? Does this align with your overall communication objectives? Second, make sure that Facebook is the right network for you. Remember, there are several social-networking sites, and some are quite targeted, which could be a better fit for your organization. Third, what is your current social-networking presence? Do you already have a group on Facebook? Will they work together? Fourth, consider your content plans. Once people are on the site, then what? Remember that while Facebook has many millions of members, some of the features are limited, and your organization must figure out how it fits into the bigger picture. Last, the issue of measurement is critical. While Facebook does have new and improved analytics, it is still important to understand what this means for your organization. How will your organization define success?[15]

That said, there are several reasons why your organization should consider a Facebook presence. Dave Rigotti on Search Engine Journal (www.searchenginejournal.com) outlined several arguments for developing a fan page. First, fan pages are public and thus subject to search-engine indexing. Facebook profiles require logging in to Facebook to access it. Second, fan pages include links and allow communication with fans through updates. This feature enables managers to build a database of interested stakeholders. Third, you control the content by developing the fan page before someone else does. Last, when a person decides to join your organization as a fan, that information goes out through their newsfeed, making this a mini viral marketing campaign.[16]

So which is better: profiles or fan pages? The answer for most nonprofit organizations is fan pages. Profiles are for individuals, while fan pages are for organizations (but they do require a person as an administrator). To create a fan page, go to facebook.com/pages.create.php. People can join pages and communicate by writing on the wall and adding and tagging photos. Groups are a little different from pages and profiles. Table 5.2 examines some of the differences between the two. Table 5.3 outlines some of the best practices for nonprofits on Facebook.

Objectives: Social-networking site objectives include generating awareness and fund-raising (although don't expect much), creating engagement with stakeholders through conversations, establishing relationships, and promotion of events and activities. Social networks are also great for grassroots efforts.

Table 5.2: Pages and Groups in Facebook

	Facebook Pages	Facebook Groups
Security Features	Allow for greater number of friends	Set up for personal interactions
Relationship to Real People	Does not list administrators and are considered entities unto themselves	Linked to the administrator(s)
Emails and Updates	New content is sent through updates and there is no limit	As long as there are less than 5,000 members, admin can send e-mail
Search-Engine Indexing	Indexed	Not indexed
Applications	Applications are included	Applications are not included
User Control	No real restrictions to joining	More control over who joins; must be invited and/or accepted by the administrator (like a club)

Howard Greenstein, "Facebook Pages vs. Facebook Groups: What's the Difference?" (Mashable, May 27, 2009), http://mashable.com.

Table 5.3: Best Practices for Nonprofits on Facebook

1. Configure settings to allow for more participation (under "settings" and "share")
2. Use your logo as your page picture
3. Add the http:// to all website URLs so that the link is automatically added and sharable
4. Add the "Links" app to get the organization to show up in "news feeds"
5. Ask questions to start a conversation as opposed to simply posting statements
6. Add the "Causes" app for fundraising; also add "Donate Now" buttons so as not to limit fundraising potential
7. Add the "Notes" app if you don't have a blog
8. Add the "Social RSS" app as a tab to automatically add blog posts to Facebook
9. Select a vanity URL that matches your organization's main website
10. Have more than one administrator for the page (in case someone leaves the organization)

Facebook Best Practices for Nonprofit Organizations DIOSA Communications, www.diosacommunications.com/facebookbestpractices.htm.

Tools: Facebook and MySpace are the two largest social networks (though many have migrated to Facebook since it was opened to the general public). LinkedIn is a professional network. Others include Bebo, Orkut, Gather, Moli, and Ning. Additionally, there are several other networks that are targeted to specific groups (Wikipedia has a great list), including social networks that are popular in other countries.

Measurement: Measurement includes the number of friends and other connections (including groups) and the number of wall postings or other areas of engagement. Some sites have internal analytics.

Facebook Insights allows information on user exposure, actions, and behaviors. It focuses on the quality of content in the stream, rather than the number connections. With the new Insights tool, you can track total interactions on your page, including media consumption and interactions per post. The total interactions metric captures all of the feedback received from Facebook users. This number measures the aggregate count of wall posts, likes, discussion posts, and comments on any content such as photos, videos, notes, or links in the past seven days. The goal of the metric is to provide an updated snapshot into how fans are engaging with your page's content. Also useful, the geographic breakdown and demographic information offers you access to detailed data about your fan base in an effective way that isn't available on any other site.[17]

Costs: Social-networking sites are free but time-consuming, depending on the level of interaction.

In practice: Dollars for Darfur raised $150,000 in 2007 through a high school challenge on Facebook. Like many successful Facebook campaigns, it

Figure 5.1: Facebook—Dollars for Darfur

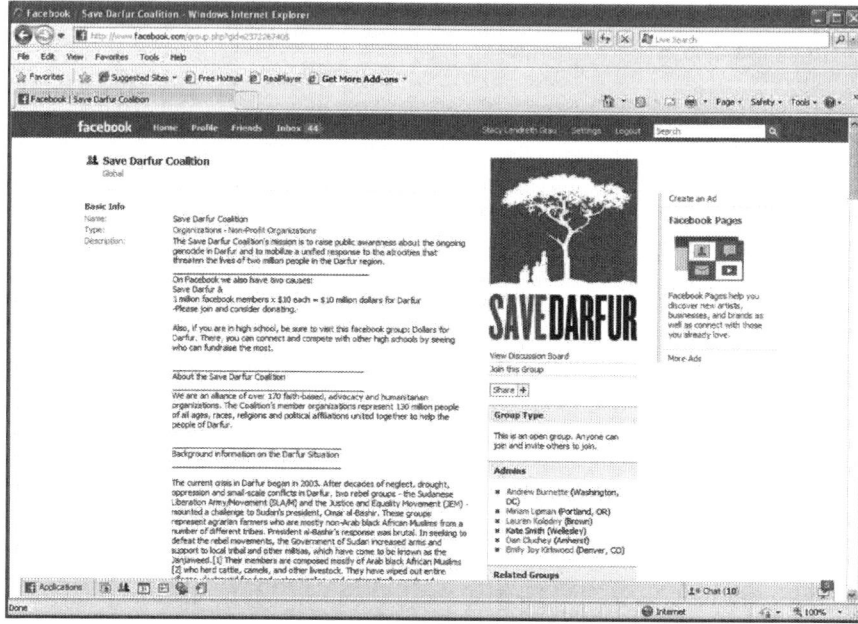

Figure 5.2: Stand Now

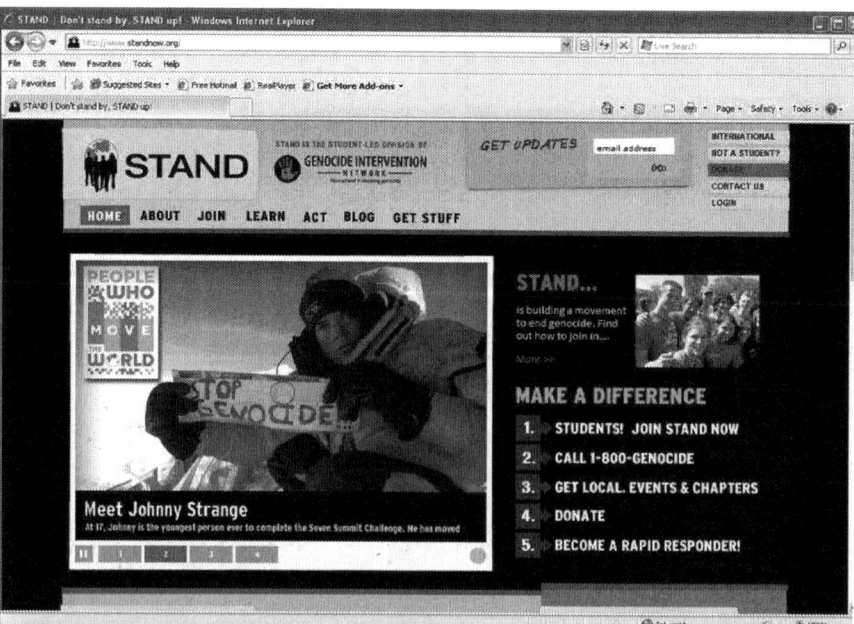

Tools for Stakeholder Engagement 103

Figure 5.3: Facebook—ONE

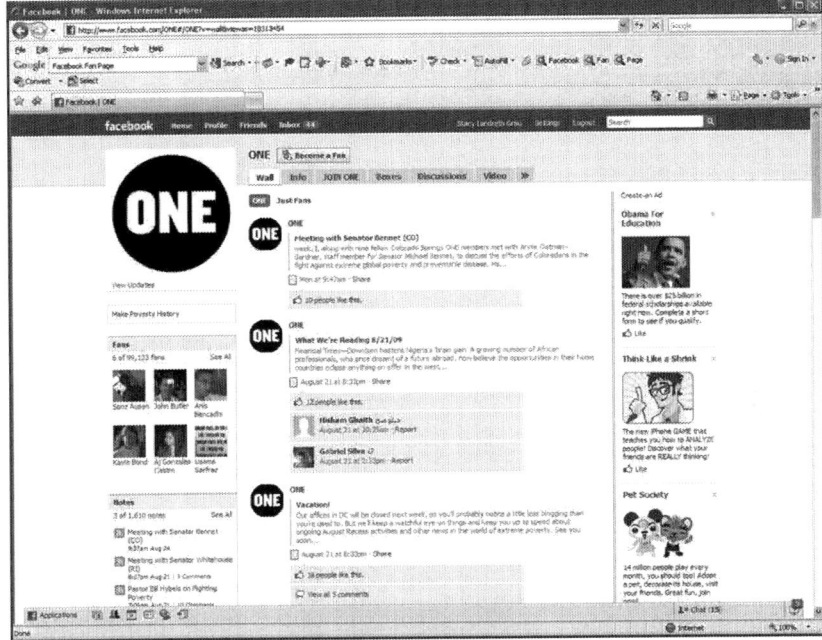

Figure 5.4: Facebook Causes

> ### Chapter Insight: Facebook Causes
>
> One unique feature of Facebook is Causes. Its aim is to present an "unprecedented opportunity to engage our generation, most of whom are on Facebook, in seizing the future and making a difference in the world around us." Causes provides the tools so that any Facebook user can leverage their network of real friends to effect positive change.
>
> The goal of all this is "equal opportunity activism." Causes attempts to level the playing field by empowering individuals to change the world. Any Facebook user can create a cause, recruit friends into that cause, keep everybody in the cause up-to-speed on issues and media related to the cause, and, most importantly, raise money directly through the cause for any U.S. registered 501(c)(3) nonprofit or Canadian registered charity.[18]
>
> While the Obama campaign used this tool effectively, many organizations are finding that typically they are seeing less than $1,000 in donations. Most see none. Only a few have raised more than $100,000 using this. While the application allows Facebook users to list themselves as supporters of a cause on their profile, fewer than 1 percent of those who have joined a cause have actually donated money through that application. The few who do donate do so through credit cards that are processed by Network for Good. The median gift is $25. The idea is to take advantage of the vast circles of online friends connected on Facebook (and other sites) to reach potential donors on a more personal level. In other words, the hope is that people will donate to causes that are important to their friends. Managers are finding that Causes can be useful for raising awareness but less so for raising cash. "I definitely think it's first and foremost a tool for brand and reputation," said Sue Citro, digital membership director for Nature Conservancy (one of the few in the $100K club). "It definitely does more for influence than for fund-raising."[19]

worked because it leveraged the power of young people by focusing on the right social-networking sites. The campaign was easy to use and provided recognition for top fund-raisers. The organization is now part of Stand Now and continues to leverage social-networking sites to increase awareness of genocide and raise funds to combat the problem.

PHOTO SHARING

Description: Photo sharing sites allows users the ability to archive and then share photos. These sites are particularly useful for nonprofits because photos are an effective way to tell stories. The process of sharing personal photos has grown in popularity due to the prevalence of digital cameras. Depending on the Web site used, once the photos are loaded, you can organize them into albums and tag them with captions.

Objectives: Photo sharing objectives include generating awareness, storytelling, fund-raising (displaying photos of auction items, for example), inspiring action, and advocating grassroots programs.

Tools: Flickr is the most widely used photo sharing site. Additionally, Photobucket, SmugMug, Shutterfly, KodakGallery, Snapfish, Phanfare, DropShots, Fotolog, MyPhotoAlbum, and many more are quite useful.[20] The best way to decide which is best is to explore the features of each site.

Measurement: There is no real measurement for Flickr other than the numbers downloads.

Costs: Costs include a digital camera ($100 and up—the image quality is important, so aim for a camera with at least three megapixels). Some digital cameras also come with photo editing software. Adobe Photoshop ($300) or similar editing software is professional software that can be used to clean up the photos. Google's Picasa is free and easy to use.

Oxfam is an organization dedicated to eliminating poverty and social injustice. While it uses many different types of social media, in 2007, it effectively used Flickr to start a photo petition to pressure Starbucks to give Ethiopian coffee farmers a chance to earn more money. The project asked people to upload photos in support of the effort. It was effective because it was a clear message and

Figure 5.5: Oxfam

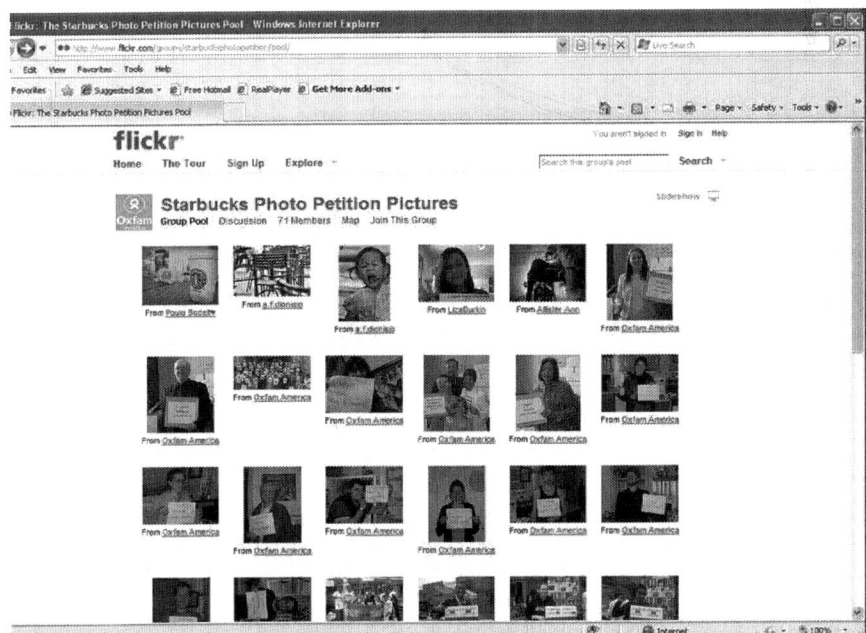

Figure 5.6: Oxfam

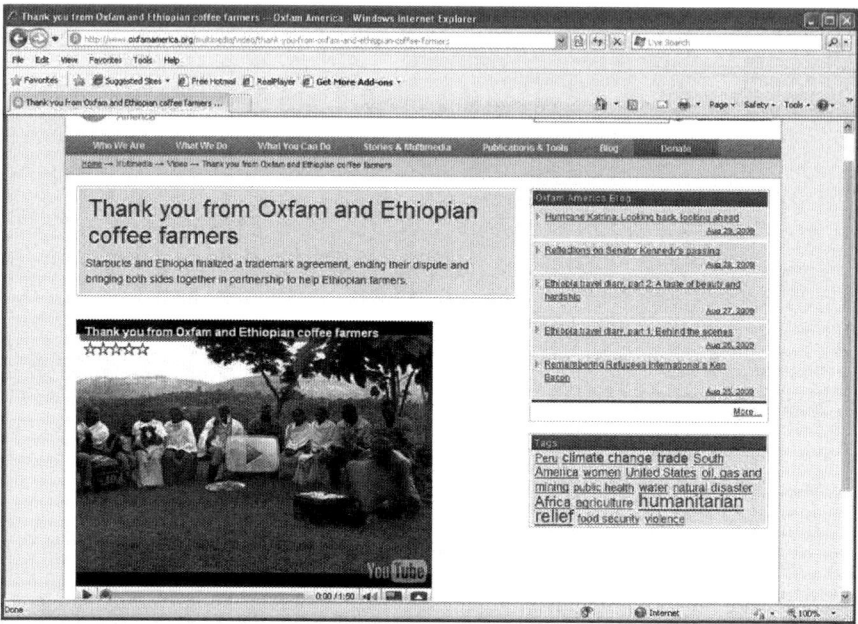

participation was easy. It leveraged existing relationships and used traditional public relations for added support.

VIDEO CREATION AND SHARING

Description: Video creation and sharing has also gained popularity from nonprofits because of its rich ability to aid in storytelling. Video creation and sharing can be used in two forms: videos that are posted on a Web site such as YouTube or using video within a blog. Both are important; however, understanding the channels for distribution will enable your organization to better understand the impact of video. YouTube, a combination of a medium and a community, is the largest video site and the sixth-largest Web site in the U.S.[21] Ramyan Raghavan, the nonprofits and activism manager for YouTube, suggests that nonprofits think about the audience and the objectives for their postings. He also recommends building a subscriber base who will receive new videos from the organization when available. YouTube is an interesting site. Not only is it large (in terms of visitors), but the demographics are pretty evenly split among age groups and gender. The average visitor spends sixty-two minutes per month, making it one of the "stickiest" Web sites of all. Additionally, a recent study by Convio, SeaChange Strategies, and Edge Research called "The Wired Wealthy: Using the Internet to Connect to Your Middle and Major Donors" found that more people were active on YouTube than Facebook or LinkedIn.[22]

YouTube recently launched the YouTube Nonprofit Program (www.youtube.com/nonprofit) that creates channels for eligible nonprofit organizations in the U.S. and U.K. It offers premium branding capabilities, including the ability to upload a banner or image to drive people to Web sites and other content from the video, the option to upload longer and larger video files (up to 1 GB), the option to embed a Google checkout feature to help with fund-raising, and an opportunity to develop a transparent overlay that encourages donors to take action.

To make an engaging video, Raghavan suggests that nonprofit begin with a clear understanding of two things: what the video should accomplish (such as raise awareness, or raise funds, or train volunteers) and who the video is targeting (such as donors, the general YouTube viewer, or volunteers). This is where many nonprofits get it wrong. They believe that by putting a video up, millions will come to see it. Next, she suggests that videos include a specific "ask" and give donors information about where the money is going. She cited the UN's Nothing But Nets campaign that asked donors to give $10 for a malaria net (www.nothingbutnets.net).

Next, make sure to include the stories and pictures of those who are being helped by your organization. People tend to donate and be engaged by videos that feature a face with the story. This increases the likelihood of a personal connection

Figure 5.7:   Nothing But Nets

Figure 5.8: charity: water

between the donor and the organization. Add a call to action overlay (the new feature for YouTube nonprofits). This is like an advertisement that appears thirty seconds into the video and then again at the end of the video to encourage action. One of the most successful videos has been one about clean water by charity: water. This video was professional, engaging, and provided a clear call to action. During World Water Day, the organization raised $12,000 in twenty-four hours with specific requests of $20.

Last, it is important to understand the numbers behind the video, so YouTube has created YouTube Insights that allow organizations to see who is watching and when they stop watching. This helps pinpoint if people are exiting the video before the "ask" and helps organizations design more effective fund-raising videos.[23]

Objectives: Video creation and sharing objectives include generating awareness, storytelling, and inspiring action. Video is especially effective due to the engaging attributes of the medium.

Tools: Video platforms include QuickTime from Apple, Windows Media Player from Microsoft, and RealVideo Player by RealNetworks. Google's YouTube allows video posting. BitTorrent is a peer-to-peer file-sharing site to distribute content. A few others include Hulu, Google Video, and MyVideo (there are several of these and you can find a complete list on Wikipedia).

> Chapter Insight: What Makes a Video Go Viral?
>
> The myth is that if you upload a video onto YouTube, viewers will come. And then they will pass it along to their friends and eventually millions of people will watch it. Well, not exactly. There is no guarantee that a video will go viral. And even if it does, so what? What does that mean for a nonprofit? Does it mean more awareness? More donations? Perhaps, but not necessarily. Michael Hoffman, CEO of See3 Communications, is an expert on online videos for nonprofits and gave a few tips on Beth's Blog: How Nonprofits Can Use Social Media (http://beth.typepad.com). Here are a few:
>
> - You cannot predict whether a video will go viral. And even if you could, the content of most viral videos (cute pets, people saying or doing something stupid, sex appeal) have nothing to do with most nonprofits.
> - YouTube does not translate into Web site traffic. Most users just watch more videos—they probably won't immediately jump to your Web site.
> - You need long-term supporters. YouTube videos don't necessarily translate into more donations or volunteers like a consumer product video translates into sales.
> - Don't be a one-hit wonder. Those who are most successful on YouTube are not single video makers but those making a series of videos with characters that bring people back.
>
> Overall, it is better to have a video strategy. The organization should make a commitment to the medium. And with some luck and hard work, the content will be compelling and people will share it.[24]

Measurement: Measurements include the number of viewings, number of subscribers, and video reviews. Additionally, YouTube Insights provides additional analytics.

Costs: The cost of a video camera (prices range depending on the features requested) for raw footage and software to edit (Apple's iMovie, Final Cut Express, or Adobe Premiere); use audio software like Apple's GarageBand for voiceover and background music. Some of this software (namely iMovie) comes pre-loaded on Apple computers.

PODCASTING AND AUDIO SHARING

Description: Podcasts are digital audio or video files that people listen to online, on the computer, or on an MP3 player (like an iPod). Think of podcasts as a radio show that is distributed through various means and not linked to a scheduled time period. The great thing about podcasts is that they are available for download at any time. While podcasts have not seen the exponential growth rate of social-networking sites and microblogging, it has seen recent growth. According to research by Arbitron/Edison Media Research, awareness of podcasting has increased from 22 percent to 37 percent, and the audience for audio podcasts grew 18 percent. By 2013, it is estimated that 37.6 million Americans will be downloading podcasts monthly. The core audience is males between eighteen and twenty-nine who are well-educated with a higher-than-average household income, which makes them an attractive donor target.[25] Most people listen to podcasts on their computers.

There are some things to consider when developing a podcast. First, determine whether the audience for podcasts matches the audience for your cause; otherwise, you may be wasting your time. Second, be sure that your content is valuable and engaging, which will typically determine the length of the broadcast. Most podcasts are ten minutes; longer is fine if the content is engaging, but longer than thirty minutes takes the risk that listeners will not have adequate time to complete it. Third, focusing on a single topic makes it a cohesive experience. Last, make sure that the podcast is promoted through various other touchpoints, and make responding to it easy.[26] Use RSS feeds and iTunes to share the content.

Objectives: Objectives for podcasts include increasing awareness and visibility online, establishing an ongoing communication channel with audiences, providing an avenue for unique and engaging content, establishing a position as a thought leader, and distributing information about the cause.

Tools: There are several tools to use to record and edit podcasts. Use Audacity, Sound Studio, GarageBand, WordPress's podPress Widget, Soundtrack Pro, Evoca, Gabcast, Hipcast, Podcast Station, or WebPod Studio to record and edit podcasts. There are several options that are either very inexpensive or free. Invest in a good microphone to make the recordings. Visit an electronics store to find inexpensive hardware. Additionally, it is important to market the podcasts. Post or search on iTunes, Podbean, Podcast, and Rhapsody. There are several providers that allow you to share podcasts.

Measurement: Measurement includes the number of subscriptions via RSS and downloads from iTunes and other Web sites.

Costs: Most recording and editing software is free or very inexpensive. Microphones can be purchased for less than $50. The rest of the expense is the time to develop, record, edit, and post the podcasts.

In practice: National Public Radio (NPR) is a radio station that is supported primarily through listener contributions and government support. As many of its listeners know, much of the content of NPR radio shows is more in-depth than other news channels. Shows include lengthy interviews that yield great content for podcasts. As such, NPR and many of its local affiliates have set up a system where listeners may download specific episodes as well as use RSS feeds to subscribe to regular programming.

VIRTUAL WORLDS

Description: Virtual Worlds are a growing aspect of the Web. Second Life (SL), developed by Linden Labs, is the one that has garnered the most attention and visitors with more than a million log-ins within a thirty-day period and more than ten million residents who appear in avatar form. It is the epitome of a trusted network and user-generated content. SL (www.secondlife.com) is the largest virtual world without a gaming foundation. SL contains a virtual economy, and several companies have a presence there, which presently is used for awareness. Most companies and nonprofits are still in the experimentation phase of SL. While it experienced an explosion of growth and attention in 2007, it has yet to gain mass acceptance like other tools.

Objectives: Second Life allows organizations to establish awareness with new audiences and experiment with completely new media sources.

Tools: Second Life is a virtual world that many organizations have used relatively effectively. There are several other virtual worlds, as well, such as World of Warcraft and Sims.

Measurement: The measurement depends on the activity (e.g., selling items, having events) in SL.

Costs: Second Life requires a time commitment to develop the avatar and interact in a completely virtual world. There is a large learning curve. Costs can also be added depending on the level of organizational commitment (through purchasing virtual real estate).

In practice: A few years ago, the Center for Disease Control (CDC) set out on a huge public health initiative. John Anderton, leader of Project Fulcrum, which is a new media initiative, developed an avatar named Hygeia Philo (Greek for "lover of health") to promote health policy in Second Life. The CDC set out to develop an agency outpost in Second Life to recruit new people into health professions, to advance public health, and to rebrand old public health brands. The CDC has experimented with other tools, such as YouTube and blogs, but decided to experiment with this completely new medium. The idea was to build a space to educate people about health and enable an ongoing and rich dialogue about important health issues. One experiment was the Second Life Health Fair, as events drive interest among the Second Life residents. "In the real world, this is a nice, local platform to display health information, to educate about specific issues while building community and establishing credibility of source," said Anderton. The attendance was reasonable, and the event garnered high-profile attention within the virtual world.

The American Cancer Society (ACS) has held a Relay for Life in Second Life for five years. This is a volunteer driven walk-a-thon in cyberspace where residents gather, camp out, donate money, and walk on the 96-acre custom-built track. Residents also sold items to raise money for the cause. The Relay for Life was the most successful fund-raising event in Second Life history. In 2007, the event raised $117,000 (real money) and attracted more than 1,700 avatars. ACS expanded their presence is the virtual world by purchasing an island in Second Life that fulfills a number of purposes, including serving as an interactive cancer information resource center, a venue for support groups, and headquarters for event planning.[27] Other nonprofits in Second Life include Live2Give, Global Kids, and March of Dimes. Most nonprofits are in the first stages of development. TechSoup is one organization experimenting with games in Second Life.[28]

Second Life has embraced nonprofit organizations by developing a learning community to share best practices. Nonprofit Commons is a nonprofit archipelago in Second Life, consisting of four virtual locations housing more than eighty social organizations. The Nonprofit Commons is managed by TechSoup Global. It was designed to lower the barriers of access to Second Life and to allow nonprofits to explore Second Life. It provides free office space to qualifying groups—to meet and network as well as create a cooperative learning environment and foster outreach, education, fund-raising, all in a virtual space.[29]

MOBILE AND SMARTPHONE TECHNOLOGY

Description: Mobile technology is increasingly being called the "fourth screen" due to the content being developed for cell phones and smartphones (like BlackBerry and iPhones). Mobile technology is considered the best in digital convergence and social media and is one reason why social media has gained in popularity. Cell phones allow people to do pretty much anything a computer can do—at least as far as communication is concerned. You can read a blog, post to Facebook, tweet, check e-mail, send a text message, play games, watch videos, take videos and photos, use a GPS, or surf the Internet. And cell phones are ubiquitous. More than 25 percent of the world's population has a cell phone, and more than 75 percent of the U.S. population owns one.[30] Especially for younger audiences, cell phones have become the preferred communication medium.

A new use for mobile technology is as a fund-raising tool. The best thing about mobile giving is immediacy. Alerted to a need either through a mobile device or traditional media, mobile users can quickly and easily respond. The time period from notification to contribution can be seconds rather than days, weeks, or months. This immediacy and ease of use empowers nonprofits to engage a new class of donors. As such, nonprofit organizations, such as the Mobile Giving Foundation, are working with several charities where text messages are sent out and donations are charged to phone bills. Keep A Child Alive (Alicia Keyes' charity) raised $50,000 in $5 gifts through texting. Greenpeace has used mobile technology effectively at increasing awareness as well as fund-raising.[31] UNICEF developed a TAP project where users could text and donate $5 that showed up on their cellular phone bill.

Objectives: Mobile objectives include increasing awareness and engagement with stakeholders, fund-raising, volunteer opportunities, and grassroots advocacy. Using mobile is especially effective at reaching Generation Y. Users vote for options (the BBC did a campaign about the war in Iraq), download content (like ringtones and games), and can receive alerts and education via text.

Tools: There are several organizations that can facilitate donations through text messages.

Measurement: Fund-raising campaigns through mobile texting and counting the number of volunteers as a result of communication through text is relatively easy; calculate conversion rate from text messages to action. Measurement will depend on the various objectives.

APPLICATIONS AND WIDGETS

Description: With the advent of iPads and smartphones, there are literally millions of applications for pretty much anything. These are developed and added to on a daily basis. Applications for iPhones and iPads essentially present content that is formatted for mobile technology. This is handy since organizations no longer have to worry about whether their content will be displayed correctly on these smaller screens. While many for-profits have started to use mobile as part of their promotion campaigns, nonprofits have started to use iPhone applications, as well. The Monterey Bay Aquarium's Seafood Guide helps consumers make sustainable seafood choices. The People Against a Violent Environment (PAVE) launched three domestic violence application that receives proceeds from downloads. The American Cancer Society has an app that augments the "official sponsor of birthdays" campaign theme. This app pulls information about friend's birthdays from Facebook so that it becomes easy to track. It also provides links to Web content and YouTube videos, which includes a fund-raising component. The American Heart Association has an app that is credited with saving the life of Dan Woolley during the Haiti earthquake. The AHA's Pocket First Aid and CPR app is used to look up instructions on how to treat excessive bleeding and compound fractures.[32] Additionally, there are several tools under development:[33] groups such as Miller Creative Edge in Chicago are developing a program called Campaign Edge. This is a program that can be customizable for nonprofits and is geared toward advocacy groups. Nonprofits would have a monthly fee and could send out rally notices, canvassing opportunities, and polls.[34]

Figure 5.9: iPhone App Example

A Web widget is a chunk of code that is installed and executed within an html-based Web platform without requiring additional compilation. These are similar to plugins and extensions to desktop applications. They are also known as gadgets, badges, capsules, snippets, and flakes. Essentially, it allows a nontechnical Web site publisher to pull in data and display that data from another Web site. Popular examples include weather widgets, news tickers, and horoscopes.

There are some questions to ask before developing a widget for your organization's blog or Web site:

- Does your organization publish compelling content on its Web site or blog?
- Does your content pose interesting questions that engage people in conversations?
- Do you have an existing strategy to facilitate conversation?
- Do your blog posts inspire many comments?

If you can answer yes to these questions, then a widget may be effective for your organization. Think of widgets as the bumper stickers of the Internet. The good thing about widgets is that they are easy to use, require no technical skill, can extend your reach and influence beyond existing platforms, can add to your listening system, and can make your organization easier to find.[35]

There are several examples of organizations using widgets. The organization can track where and how people are using them. Here are a few nonprofit examples presented by Peter Deitz of Social Actions.

- KaTREEna Plantometer: This is a widget that allows people to sponsor a tree, grove, thicket, or forest. The widget includes a slideshow of the type of trees as well as planting events.
- Every Human Has Rights: This organization is using a widget to encourage people to sign a petition regarding human rights.

Figure 5.10: The KaTREEna Plantometer

The KaTREEna Plantometer

"Page 1" "Page 2" "Page 3"

Figure 5.11: Every Human Has Rights

Every Human Has Rights

1) Find the widget

2) Read the request

3) Sign the petition

- $40 for 40 Years Fair Housing: This is a widget developed by move smart.org to foster vibrant neighborhoods by empowering housing seekers through technology to move to opportunity. This widget collects donations for the project.[36]

There are also specific widgets that facilitate fund-raising. Beth Kanter developed an "action learning experiment" using ChipIn to raise money for a

Figure 5.12: $40 for 40 Years Fair Housing

Homepage

About us

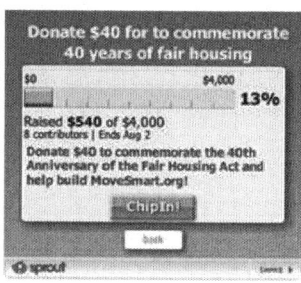

Donate

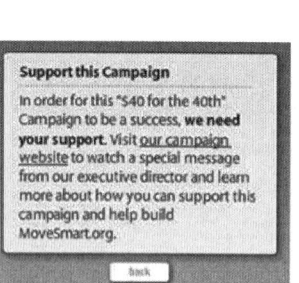

Support us

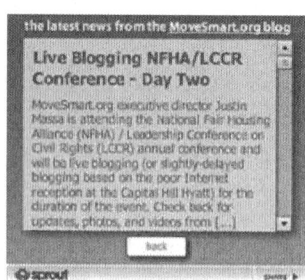

Blog

charity. She raised 117 percent of her goal for The Sharing Foundation to support an orphan, Leng Sopharath, and her education. She developed an entire strategy to raise the money through her various social networks, blogs, and personal contacts.[37] Network for Good offers a "Donate Now" button and charity badges for nonprofits (as well as many other fund-raising tools).

PRODUCTIVITY TOOLS

Description: There are several productivity tools that can be used effectively by nonprofit organizations. Many of them are inexpensive or free and provide an eclectic collection of tasks. Think of these as business productivity tools. We highlight a few here.

Acteva. Acteva (www.acteva.com) is a secure online event management solution for organizations focusing primarily on the event preparation as opposed to the event administration and attendance issues. It also allows an organization to run multiple events.

Basecamp. Basecamp (www.basecamphq.com) is an online project management tool that allows multiple parties to access data, charts, and graphs and collaborate on material. It enables organizations to assign tasks and deadlines, keep track of time, and share files while facilitating communication and collaboration. There are several pricing scales and several products available from Basecamp.

Google Docs. Google Docs (www.docs.google.com) allows users to upload documents so that they are available on the Internet for use, collaboration, and travel. It allows you to organize data, control access, and work in real time as opposed to carrying everything around on a portable drive. Google Docs can be used as a backup server (but there are some limits on size). Google Docs has many collaborative and publishing options, making this a very effective tool.

BitTorrent. BitTorrent (www.bittorrent.com) is an avenue for high-quality media downloads. This free software allows all sorts of downloads quickly and easily. It also allows users to publish your own films, videos, and other media content. It is compatible with any Web browser. This is primarily for digital distribution.

Google Alerts. Google Alerts (www.google.com/alerts) allows users to create alerts against Google searches and receive the results via RSS feed or e-mail. These are based on the six categories of Google information: news, Web, blogs, images, videos, and groups. It is primarily used to track information on the Internet.

AGGREGATORS, SOCIAL BOOKMARKS, AND REVIEW SITES

Description: There are several tools that enable organizations and people to organize information from social media. All of these are free and easy to use. They are all incredibly valuable as well. They include:

Aggregators allow users to gather and update information from the social Web in an easy-to-handle way. These can be through e-mail or through a dashboard such as iGoogle.

Social bookmarks are small icons found on blogs and Web sites that allow people to aggregate important sites and allow them to be shared with others.

Review sites and forums allow people to rate and comment on products, services, brands, and organizations. These reviews are seen as particularly useful and credible. Amazon was one of the first organizations to widely use reviews. Yelp is one site that allows people to rate almost anything. Angie's List is another good example of a review site.

Chapter Insight: Creative Commons License

Creative Commons (CC) is a nonprofit organization that is devoted to expanding the range of creative works that others can legally share and build upon. The organization has released copyright licenses known as the Creative Commons License, which allows the authors/creators of content to specify the rights they reserve and waive and how they want to be cited. The goal is to build a richer public domain by providing some alternatives to "all rights reserved" copyright. There are four license conditions:

Attribution: You let others copy, distribute, display, and perform your copyrighted work and derivative works based upon it, but only if they give credit the way you requested.

Share Alike: You allow others to distribute derivative works only under a license identical to the license that governs your work.

Noncommercial: You let others copy, distribute, display, and perform your work and derivatives based upon it, but for noncommercial purposes only.

No Derivative Works: You let others copy, distribute, display, and perform only verbatim copies of your work, not derivative works based upon it.

There are six major licenses of the Creative Commons:

Attribution (CC-BY): This license lets others distribute, remix, tweak, and build upon work, even commercially, as long as they credit the original creation. This is the most accommodating of all licenses offered in terms of what others can do with the work.

Attribution Share Alike (CC-BY-SA): This license lets others remix, tweak, and build upon work, even for commercial reasons, as long as they credit the originator and license their new creations under the identical terms. This is often compared to open-source software licenses. All new works based on the original carry the same license, so any derivatives will also allow commercial use.

> *Attribution No Derivatives (CC-BY-ND):* The license allows for redistribution, commercial and noncommercial, as long as it is passed along unchanged and in whole with credit to you.
> *Attribution Noncommercial (CC-BY-NC):* This license lets others remix, tweak, and build upon your work noncommercially, and although their new works must also acknowledge you and be noncommercial, they don't have to license their derivative works on the same terms.
> *Attribution Noncommercial Share Alike (CC-BY-NC-SA):* This license lets others remix, tweak, and build upon your work noncommercially as long as they credit you and license their new creations under the identical terms. Others can download and redistribute your work just like the attribution noncommercial, but they can also translate, make remixes, and produce new stories based on your work. All new work based on yours will carry the same license, so any derivatives will also be noncommercial in nature.
> *Attribution Noncommercial No Derivatives (CC-BY-NC-ND):* This license is the most restrictive of all that still allows redistribution. This license is often called the "free advertising" license because it allows others to download your works and share them with others as long as they mention you and link back to you. But they cannot change the content in any way or use them commercially.[38]

Tools: Atom, FeedBurner, PingShot, RSS 2.0, Digg, Delicious, Google Reader, iGoogle, Yelp, Reddit, and Yahoo! Pipes are just a few of the many resources available.

SOCIAL-MEDIA MEASUREMENT

It is easy to see that social media has the potential to revolutionize the way organizations communicate with stakeholders. And given the relative efficiency in which organizations can use social media, it is obvious that there is a positive return on investment for many, if not most, nonprofits. Indeed, in a research report by Forrester Research, 95 percent of for-profit marketers said they will continue to invest in social media or at least maintain the same level of investment. However, most marketers have not been able to figure out how to measure social media. Measurement and metrics are evolving with social media as different tools reach mass acceptance and usage.[39] Some marketers feel that social media is less about ROI than about conversations and deepening relationships with customers. However, just like with traditional advertising expenditures, marketers suffer from a lack of hard evidence of the relative effectiveness of social-media tools.

What are the benefits, whether tangible or intangible, that a social-media strategy might offer your nonprofit organization? Think about how this strategy may enhance programs or services or increase efficiencies through cost reductions or revenue increases. Beth Kanter encourages organizations to think of these benefits as two types: fundamental benefits and instrumental benefits. Fundamental benefits are those that reinforce the core mission of the organization. Instrumental benefits are more about behind-the-scenes effectiveness. For example, creating an organizational blog has the fundamental benefit of encouraging dialogue with the community and the instrumental benefit of reducing customer service calls. In this case, the staff time dedicated to developing a blog (as well as a blogging policy) is likely well spent. The idea is that many of these tools can have both types of benefits, and this translates into value.[40] That said, measurement can be divided into three areas:[41]

> ### Conversation with the Pros: Beth Kanter, Founder, Beth's Blog: How Nonprofits Can Use Social Media
>
> Beth Kanter is THE social-media guru for nonprofits. She is a frequent presenter on many technology Web sites, blogs, magazines, and book chapters, including *Psychology of Facebook Applications*, edited by BJ Fogg, and *Managing Technology to Meet your Mission: A Strategic Guide for Nonprofit Leaders*, edited by NTEN. Kanter was named one of the most influential women in technology by *Fast Company* in 2009 and one of *BusinessWeek*'s Voices of Innovation for Social Media. She consults, writes, researches, blogs, and trains organizations in social media. Kanter has been working with nonprofits for more than thirty years in fund-raising and marketing. In 1992, she was an early adopter of the Internet and started "Beth's Blog: How Nonprofits Can Use Social Media" (http://beth.typepad.com) in 2003 mostly to keep notes from all of her consulting and training projects with nonprofits. "I think my biggest impact has been as a thought leader in the space who shares all her mistakes, learnings, and secrets," Kanter says.
>
> One of the biggest problems that people find about social media is that it is difficult to keep up with new tools. "I don't try to keep up or feel like the information is crushing. It's a river of information, and I learn to dip in and look for patterns," says Kanter. As a result, she is interested in information coping skills and has written blog entries on how people can deal with the stress of too much information. She offers these tips:
>
> - Conduct an annual ROI on your blog using benchmarking and metrics and learn to use tools that help measure success.
> - Use tools that help streamline social media tasks such as RSS readers and TweetDeck as well as a social media dashboard.
> - Make time for reflections and determine how each tool works together to meet organizational goals.
> - Take breaks from the computer and cell phone. Try a hiatus from a specific tool and just take a day off from all social media.
> - Filter, simplify, and slow down.[42]

Social media measurement. Social media measurement is an area that is ever-changing. These metrics attempt to determine the ROI of each tool. This would answer, for example, the conversion rate of a Facebook friend to a donor.

Public relations measurement. Public relations measurement is also an area that has gained added attention. Since many PR campaigns involve social media, this area would include ways to measure the impact of social media on press coverage, for example.

Social-media monitoring. Social-media monitoring tools are being used less for campaign metrics and more for improving customer service, brand management, and prospecting. Nonprofits can use social-media monitoring for much the same issues; to improve programs and develop new programs and services for its constituents as well as to locate and engage with new and current donors.

Table 5.4: List of Tools

Type	Tools
Blogs	Blogger, WordPress, Movable Type, TypePad, Blogware
Blog Search	Technorati, Google Blog Search, IceRocket, BlogPulse, MetaTube, Yahoo! Search
Podcast	Podcast Pickle, Podcast Alley, The Podcast Network, World Podcast Forum, iTunes, Live365, Podcast
Podcast Hosting and Recording	Odeo, Hipcast, Audacity, Talkr, Podbean
Video Blogs	Google Video, Brightcove, YouTube, Photobucket, Dailymotion
Social Networks	MySpace, Facebook, LinkedIn, Hi5, Ning, BlackPlanet, Eons, Bebo, Orkut, Gather, Moli, Friendster, Skyrock, Netlog, Tagged, Badoo, Xanga, myYearbook, Classmates, SlideShare, Xing, Plaxo, ecademy, ryze, wallst, Networking For Professionals
Wikis	Wikia, PBworks, Boardhost, Wikispaces, Wetpaint,
Microblogging	Twitter, Tweet Scan, Pounce, Plurk, Prologue, Yammer, Summize, TweetBeep, TweetGrid, Twilert, TweetDeck, Twhirl, Twitpic, Twitxr, Twemes, MocoSpace, Tumblr, FriendFeed, Lifestream, Socialthing, 12seconds, Swurl, Utterli
Photo Sharing	Flickr, Photobucket, SmugMug, Shutterfly, Kodak Gallery, Snapfish, Phanfare, DropShots, Fotolog, MyPhotoAlbum, ImageShack, Multiply, Webshots, Fotki, Zoomr, Picasa, Zoto
Video Sharing	YouTube, Blip.tv, Hulu, Google Video, MSN Video, MySpace Videos, AOL Video, Dailymotion, Veoh, Metacafe, Break, Revver, Stickam, Viddler
Social Bookmarks	Digg, Technorati, Mixx, StumbleUpon, Kadoodle, Propeller, Delicious, Newsvine, Boing Boing, Fark, Slashdot, Reddit, Bloglines, BlinkList, Furl, Sphinn

LESSONS LEARNED

- Always start with a strategy and make sure it links to your overall communication strategy.
- Tie social media tools to objectives and measurements.
- Don't try everything at once. Choose two tools and spend the time to make those most effective. Monitor the progress to determine where to expand.
- Understand that measurement is evolving; therefore, it is important to keep up with trends and new technology.

FURTHER READING

The Social Media Bible by Lon Safko and David K. Brake
The Networked Nonprofit by Beth Kanter and Allison Fine
Groundswell: Winning in a World Transformed by Social Media Technologies by Charlene Li and Josh Bernoff
Podcasting for Dummies by Tee Morris, Evo Terra, and Dawn Miceli
Digital Video Essentials: Shoot, Transfer, Edit, Share by Erica Sadun
Videoblogging for Dummies by Stephanie Cottrell Bryan
We Are Media (www.wearemedia.org)
Beth Kanter's Blog (http://beth.typepad.com)
Mashable (http://mashable.com)
Nonprofit Technology Network (www.nten.org)
The Second Life Grid: The Official Guide to Communication, Collaboration and Community Engagement by Kimberly Rufer-Bach
Media Rules! Mastering Today's Technology to Connect With and Keep your Audience by Brian Reich and Dan Soloman
Mobilizing Generation 2.0: A Practical Guide to Using Web 2.0: Technologies to Recruit, Organize and Engage Youth by Ben Rigby
The Nonprofit Guide to the Internet: How to Survive and Thrive by Michael Johnston
Nonprofit Internet Strategies: Best Practices for Marketing, Communications and Fundraising by Ted Hart, James M. Greenfield, and Michael Johnston
Managing Technology to Meet Your Mission: A Strategic Guide for Nonprofit Leaders by Holly Ross, Katrin Verclas, and Alison Levine
Digital Engagement: Internet Marketing that Captures Customers and Builds Brand Loyalty by Leland Harden and Bob Heyman

NOTES

1. Michael Bush, "Red Cross Delivers Real Mobile Results for a Real Emergency" *Advertising Age* (February 22, 2010), www.adage.com.
2. Bush, "Red Cross Delivers Real Mobile Results."

3. Emily Bryson York, "Marketers Rushing to Haiti's Aid Hit Twit-Storm of Misinformation" *Advertising Age* (January 18, 2010), www.adage.
4. Nicole Wallace and Ian Wilhelm, "Charities Text Messaging Success Shakes up the Fund-raising World" *Chronicle of Philanthropy* (February 11, 2010), 7.
5. Bush, "Red Cross Delivers Real Mobile Results."
6. Carrie Shearer, "Marketing How To Guide: Your Template for Creative Blog Marketing" (Marketing Profs, 2008), www.marketingprofs.com.
7. Lon Safko and David K. Brake, *The Social Media Bible: Tactics, Tools and Strategies for Business Success* (Hoboken, NJ: John Wiley & Sons, 2009).
8. Heather Joslyn, "Social Media Policies Can Help Charity Workers Navigate a New World" *The Chronicle of Philanthropy* (January 14, 2010), 21.
9. Heather Mansfield, "10 Twitter Tips for Nonprofit Organizations" on www.fundraising123.org (March 18, 2009).
10. Safko and Brake, *The Social Media Bible*.
11. Erik Bratt, "Twitter Success Stories: 12for12K" (MarketingProfs, 2008), www.marketingprofs.com.
12. Paula Wasley, "A Lesson in Character Development" *Chronicle of Philanthropy* (February 26, 2009), 13.
13. We Are Media, "Tactical Track Module 4: Spreading Awareness and Generating Social Media Buzz," www.wearemedia.org/tactical+track+module+4?f=print.
14. Meshug Avi, "The Story Beyond the Stats of Tweetsgiving," http://meshugavi.com.
15. Jeremiah Owyang, "Why You Need to Have a Strategy Before You Make a Facebook Fan Page Now!" (Web Strategist, November 17, 2007), http://www.web-strategist.com/blog/.
16. David Rigotti, "Why You Need to Make a Facebook Fan Page for Your Web Site Now" (Search Engine Journal, November 12, 2007), www.searchenginejournal.com.
17. Nonprofits on Facebook, www.facebook.com/note.php?_id=8684129163&ref=mf.
18. Causes on Facebook, http://apps.facebook.com/causes/about.
19. Kim Hart and Megan Greenwell, "To Nonprofits Seeking Cash, Facebook App Is So Green," *Washington Post* (April 22, 2009), www.washingtonpost.com.
20. Safko and Brake, *The Social Media Bible*.
21. Ramya Raghavan, "Using Video to Connect with Your Donors and Prospects" International Fund-raising eConference (May 12–14, 2009).
22. Convio, "The Wired Wealthy: Using the Internet to Connect to Your Middle and Major Donors" (March 14, 2008).
23. Ibid.
24. Michael Hoffman, "Viral Video for Nonprofits—A Rethinking" (Beth's Blog, July 16, 2009), http://beth.typepad.com.
25. Elisabeth Sullivan, "Radio Free Internet" *Marketing News* (July 30, 2009), 6.
26. Lisa Formica, "The Power of Podcasts" (MarketingProfs), www.marketingprofs.com.
27. Relay for Life in Second Life, www.cancer.org/docroot/GI?contentGI_1_8_Second_Life_Relay.asp.
28. Beth Kanter, "Nonprofits and Second Life and Other Games" (Beth's Blog), http://beth.typepad.com.

29. Second Life Nonprofit Commons, http://secondlife.techsoup.org.
30. Safko and Brake, *The Social Media Bible*.
31. Debra E. Blum, "Calling in Donations," *Chronicle of Philanthropy* (March 26, 2009), F-3.
32. Rupal Parekh, "iPhone App That Saved Life in Haiti Reaps Rewards" *Advertising Age* (February 1, 2010), www.adage.com.
33. Britt Bravo, "iPhone Apps for Nonprofits" (Have Fun—Do Good, January 21, 2009), http://havefundogood.blogspot.com/2009/01/iphone-apps-for-nonprofits.html.
34. Sue Hoye, "For More and More Charities, There's an App for That," *Chronicle of Philanthropy 2010 Techology Guide* (February 25, 2010), T-1.
35. Beth Kanter, "Screencast Program Notes and Resources," http://nonprofitwidget.wikispaces.cm/resources
36. Peter Dietz, "Using Sprout to Get Your Nonprofit's Message Out (In Tact)," NTEN Webinar, www.socialactions.com.
37. Beth's Blog: How Nonprofits Can Use Social Media, http://beth.typepad.com.
38. Creative Commons, http://creativecommons.org/about/what-is-cc.
39. Ann Handley, Sheely Ryan and Allen Weiss, "Social Media ROI Success Stories: MarketingProfs," www.marketingprofs.com.
40. We Are Media, "Module 6: ROI Benefits and Value," www.wearemedia.org.
41. Handley, Ryan and Weiss, "Social Media ROI Success Stories."
42. "Happy Information Overload Awareness Day!" (Beth's Blog, August 12, 2009), http://beth.typepad.com.

CHAPTER 6

Online Fund-raising

"Online fund-raising—specifically e-mail appeals—is successful when you manage to bundle the long list of fund-raising best practices into one package and send it on to your e-supporters."

—Jeff Patrick, President, Common Knowledge

CHAPTER OVERVIEW

In this chapter, we will discuss ways in which nonprofit managers can more effectively use their Web sites and other online tools for fund-raising. We will discuss the advantages and disadvantages of online fund-raising. We will discuss micro and mobile donations, an emerging trend that some organizations are using quite effectively. We will discuss how to use online tools to enhance the organization's efforts to attract major donations. Using online tools to attract new donors and to enhance community-building are important topics here. Managers will learn more about the importance of the organization's Web site and e-mail campaigns in improving online fund-raising. Other emerging topics related to online fund-raising are discussed. The chapter concludes with a discussion of ethical and privacy considerations pertaining to online fund-raising.

BREAST CANCER FUND

The Breast Cancer Fund (BCF), a nonprofit that focuses on breast-cancer prevention, has an annual budget of $3.5 million and twenty-two employees. The audience is 95 percent women, primarily twenty to sixty-five years of age, who have been touched by breast cancer in some way. Importantly, BCF's e-mail list consisted of just 7,000 e-subscribers.

The Heinz Company offered to make a matching gift of $10,000. That is, if BCF could raise $10,000 from individual donors in ten days, Heinz would match the $10,000 from individual donors with a $10,000 donation of its own, effectively doubling individual donors' contributions. This led to the first important campaign decision: to inject urgency into the effort by setting a concrete, measurable goal of raising $10,000 in ten days.

When setting a goal like this, it's important to establish a baseline. With just 7,000 prospect e-donors, BCF could expect, realistically, $1,750 to $3,500 from the campaign. Given a 0.5 percent to 1 percent donor conversion rate, typical of online fund-raising appeals for an organization like BCF, you can do some quick math:

Average Gift = $50 (figure $35 to $75 for this type of campaign)
E-mail List Size = 7,000
Minimum: 7,000 x 0.5% x $50 = $1,750
Maximum: 7,000 x 1.0% x $50 = $3,500

BCF achieved their $10,000 goal, however, with just two e-mails sent four days apart—by doing many things right. According to Jeff Patrick, President, Common Knowledge, they got the online fund-raising fundamentals correct.

Political campaigns have been prime innovators of online fund-raising. One watershed event was Howard Dean's 2004 U.S. presidential campaign, in which Dean raised half of his campaign contributions online, an amount unheard of at that time. Prior to Dean's campaign, political fundraisers sought out major donors (wealthy individuals and organizations) with traditional offline techniques. Dean's campaign proved that substantial funding could be raised online when a large number of people gave in small amounts, providing a tool to allow the campaign to target a large audience inexpensively. Although Dean did not win the Democratic presidential nomination, the nominee, John Kerry, was able to raise $56 million online.[1] While online donations now represent about seven percent of all donations, by the year 2020, the majority of political campaign contributions are expected to be online donations.[2]

Political consultants discovered (as a result of the Dean Campaign's experience) that the online technology was readily available to facilitate online giving, and that the technology made online giving secure, quick, and easy. Potential donors could be targeted with messages that had the most relevance to them. Since then, political marketers have been further developing online fund-raising capabilities. In the 2008 U.S. presidential campaign, Barack Obama raised more than $500 million from three million individual donors (with average donation being $80).[3]

ADVANTAGES OF ONLINE FUND-RAISING

The Internet is part of a system that allows potential donors to find your organization. In traditional offline methods, organizations purchase mailing lists for direct marketing. They advertise in the media. In the online environment, Internet users find the organizations in which they are interested. Through Web site links, Google searches, or recommendations from friends, Internet users find nonprofits in which they are interested, even though the organizations may not have contacted them.

Another advantage is the widespread availability of the Internet to individuals. In Europe, 48.9 percent of individuals have Internet access. That percentage increases to 50.4 percent in Australia and the Pacific Rim, and 74.4 percent in North America.[4] Although there are differences in Internet accessibility among ethnic groups and between urban and rural areas, overall, Internet usage continues to rise in the population.[5] Those who may not have Internet access at home may have access at work, school, in public libraries, or in area Wi-Fi hotspots.[6]

Additionally, free or inexpensive software has given nonprofit organizations the ability to accept online donations all the time, from anywhere, with a major credit card or PayPal account.[7] Online donations are less expensive for organizations to process and more convenient for donors than traditional methods, such as direct mail and writing checks. Donors have the choice of making a one-time online donation or making modest automatic monthly withdrawals from their bank accounts. For example, Best of the Left podcast and blog (www.bestoftheleftpodcast.com) encourages members to become supporting members, which involves agreeing to have $5 each month withdrawn from the visitor's bank account. Visitors also have the option of making one-time donations using a credit card or PayPal.

Figure 6.1: Making It Easy to Donate

The "Donate Now" button to the right is an example of one element of making it easy to donate. This button should be placed on the first, and perhaps every, page on the Web site.	

The Internet is a great way to provide information to supporters and to communicate with donors on a regular basis. This allows the organization more opportunities for establishing bonds with supporters and building relationships.

Molly Schar, a donor communications expert, recommends that nonprofit organizations give more attention to attracting bequests from supporters. She recommends that nonprofits can develop brochures on bequest giving and post them on their Web sites. Schar recommends that nonprofits put articles, relevant to bequest giving, on their Web sites, in their e-mails, and in their newsletters. She also recommends that nonprofits use donor testimonials.[8]

DISADVANTAGES OF ONLINE FUND-RAISING

The online format lacks the person-to-person experience that fund-raising professionals find most helpful in communicating with major donors. Practitioners have found that an in-person request for a contribution, especially when soliciting large donations, is the most effective method. Compared to in-person exchanges, online fund-raising can seem impersonal. While online methods may not be as effective as in-person appeals, as described in the opening vignette, online fund-raising can attract a large number of small donations.

Another disadvantage of online fund-raising is that sometimes nonprofits need to rely on third-party vendors. If an organization is unable to develop its own capability to process online donations, it may contract with online solution providers. The organization must trust the vendor to behave ethically with donor information and with the nonprofit's logo and brand.

Most nonprofit organizations have found that the advantages of online fund-raising far exceed the disadvantages. Most major charities have reported raising substantial sums online.[9] Therefore, it is useful for nonprofit managers to learn how to effectively use online resources and tactics to increase contributions.

MICRO-DONATIONS

Micro-donations are small donations, usually less than $10. Micro-donation fund-raising targets a large audience. It began in the past by charities that collected spare change at registers and checkouts. Micro-donations have become more popular with the advent and popularity of online fund-raising and mobile donating.[10]

Nonprofit managers used to question the practicality of soliciting micro-donations because one large donation from a corporation or wealthy individual could far exceed a large number of micro-donations. Recently, however, with online and mobile technologies, micro-donations have become very attractive. Online micro-giving has proven its potential.

Mobile giving is a type of micro-donating that is enabled by using a mobile phone to access an organization's Web site. Mobile phone users can also make a micro-donation by sending a specific text message to a designated keyword and receiving a link to the page in response, or by navigating to the page from a referring site. Upon reaching the donation Web page, users are prompted to enter their mobile phone numbers. Donations are confirmed with a text message sent to the donor's mobile phone, and the donation is added to the donor's monthly phone bill.[11] PayPal gives mobile phone users the ability to establish an account through which they can make a micro-donation to a charity with a "Text to Give" feature.[12] In addition, Twitter has added an application called Twitjoy, in which users can click a button to make a small donation (25¢ to $10) to the charity of their choice.[13]

MAJOR DONATIONS

As online fund-raising has evolved, professionals have assumed that online tools would only be effective in attracting small- to modest-sized donations. Large donations from wealthy individuals could not be attracted online, and the most productive means of attracting large donations was through relationship-building and personal contact. Why do wealthy people require personal contact from the organization and small donors do not? Are wealthy people more important stakeholders with their larger contributions, and, therefore, demand greater personal attention? Can online fund-raising tactics be developed to attract large donations? The following discussion will explore this possibility.

CDR Fundraising Group has published a report that argues that online information technologies are particularly well-suited to engage major donors because (1) online communications can be personalized, (2) the organization can share information in real time, and (3) donors can easily interact with each other and the organization.[14] The Make-A-Wish Foundation (www.wish.org) has created a unique Web site for large donors. On the site, each donor is taken through a personalized experience of how his or her donation has made a difference in a child's life. The Make-A-Wish Foundation uses this tool to recognize large donors, and also to show large donors how their gifts are actually used.[15]

It is likely that people who make or might make large donations to their favorite cause use the Internet to learn about potential target organizations. This allows for an opportunity to connect with these people. While people who make major donations may not give the actual donation online, most will either have an existing relationship with the nonprofit or investigate the nonprofit from the information on its Web site. One study found that two-thirds of donors who contributed more than $1,000 to charities in the prior year visit the charities' Web sites before making their donation. More than half go to a third-party charity rating Web site before donating.[16]

In time, practitioners will probably find that a combination of online and offline tactics are needed to attract and retain major donors. A personal visit from the nonprofit's top executive will continue to be effective. The Web site can be used to complement traditional methods. For example, on the organization's Web site, supporters have the opportunity to view video testimonials of how the organization has impacted people's lives. Supporters can read and react to blogs on the Web site and can register to receive e-mails, e-newsletters, and action alerts. They can network online with others who also care about the cause, becoming part of the community of supporters.

DEVELOPING ONLINE COMMUNITIES

Nonprofit organizations thrive when their supporters build relationships and form a community that works together to further the nonprofit's mission. A nonprofit organization forms an online community when its Web site attracts people who are interested in the cause and allows them to contribute content or discussions on the Web site. Web site functions that facilitate user-generated content, discussion, and other contributions (such as real-time chats, forums, message boards, member directories, instant messaging, and blogging) help maintain a vibrant community of supporters. In an online community, supporters contribute much of the content, which may or may not be moderated. We recommend that nonprofit managers establish a means of monitoring user-generated content to screen out unwanted commercial messages or other inappropriate content. Several organizations, such as Team in Training (Leukemia and Lymphoma) and Komen for the Cure, have developed online communities for fund-raising.

Before an organization launches an online community, it should carefully consider whether or not it has the resources and commitment to ensure its success. Developing and maintaining an online community requires considerable time and effort. Is the nonprofit willing to make the necessary investment in time? Also, in an online community, some members will contribute content that is inappropriate, profane, or libelous. Members may contribute content that violates someone's privacy or copyright law. The nonprofit organization needs to anticipate these issues and develop an enforceable conduct code. It is helpful to have all online community members register, receiving a username and password. Members who violate the conduct code can be removed or warned, depending on the magnitude of the violation. An effective conduct code and its enforcement will help to maintain respectful communications among community members and will help reduce the potential for legal liability to the organization.[17]

ATTRACTING NEW DONORS

Attracting new donors is important for nonprofits. New donor recruitment is probably most effectively the result of an integrated marketing approach. Online activities complement offline activities, working together more productively than if either existed alone without the support of the other. The benefits of face-to-face interactions are supported by information on the organization's Web site. Individuals receive viral messages from friends, then click to your organization's site to learn more about your issue and your organization. This provides your organization an opportunity to make its case for support to someone who has chosen to visit your site to learn more.

The organization should always work toward moving its mission agenda further. New donor recruitment is a means to that end, furthering the organization's mission. While recruiting new donors is a vital activity, it should always occur within the context of supporting the organization's mission objective.

If an organization is currently using offline tactics, like direct marketing, paid advertisements, and so on, online activities can offer some advantages. Online tactics can personalize the new donor recruitment process. The organization can use online tools to present an effective case for the cause. Online, potential donors can easily make donations without taking additional steps like making a telephone call or mailing a check. The organization's Web site can direct potential donors to the donation page. Online communications have the major advantage of being inexpensive, too. For example, SmileTrain (www.smiletrain.org) makes a compelling case on its Web site's front page. It shows the children donors help, the importance of the cause, the amount of contribution needed to help a single child, and how to donate.

It is important to recognize that individuals are unlikely to visit the organization's Web site specifically to make a donation. They are more likely to visit the site because they are interested in learning more about the organization or the issue it supports. The interest that is demonstrated by the Web site visit is a major opportunity to educate the visitor about the importance of the organization's mission and how the individual can help further the cause. Individuals often are interested in helping others, and donate for this purpose, rather than simply giving to support an organization. The Web site has the capability to offer compelling testimonials about the importance of the organization's work.

For political organizations, Web site video segments of inspiring moments can evoke emotional connections among supporters. For example, many Democrats recall the effective use of testimonials from ordinary Americans during the 2008 Democratic National Convention or particularly inspiring speeches, both types of which can be found on YouTube. For human service organizations, images, videos, and other media can be used to take an abstract issue and make it real and human. For example, Operation Smile's (www.operationsmile.org) mission is to perform restorative surgery (using volunteer surgeons) for underprivileged children with cleft-palate deformities. Operation Smile's Web site offers before-and-after pictures of children who have been helped. The images are emotionally compelling. Potential contributors understand that their contributions are not helping the organization, but are helping children. Operation Smile wisely puts a bright "Donate Now" button on the upper right of its home page.

The case the organization makes on its Web site, coupled with compelling human stories, provides visitors with the reason *why* they should donate. The next task is to communicate to visitors *when* they should give. Visitors need to understand that their help is needed now. Give visitors reasons for why they should donate now.

Organizations will have a number of supporters who have subscribed to e-mail lists, e-newsletters, and action alerts but have not yet donated. In its communication to subscribers, a donation appeal should also be included in an appropriate manner. Do not solicit a donation in each communication; subscribers will begin to believe that raising money is more important to the organization than its mission. Instead, request a donation in about every other message (e.g., e-mails) or about once every two months.

Practitioners appear to agree that the best time to send fund-raising e-mails, or any non-urgent e-mails, to supporters or potential donors is in the afternoon on a Tuesday, Wednesday, or Thursday. When people log on to their e-mail accounts in the morning, they usually efficiently and quickly clear out non-essential messages. Many people do not check their e-mail from home on weekends, but wait until they return to work on Monday morning. On Monday morning, there is an accumulation of spam and other e-mail that must be quickly dealt with so the individual can begin the workday. Mondays and Fridays tend to be busier work days.

> Chapter Insight: Learning from the Obama Campaign
>
> The Obama campaign's ability to raise $500 million online from three million donors forced many practitioners to reevaluate prior beliefs about the potential for online fund-raising. Andrea Wood,[18] senior consultant for M+R Strategic Services, has the following recommendations for e-mail messages to attract contributions:
>
> - Make the e-mail feel more personal by avoiding the use of a heading in the body of the e-mail. Share information with the recipient that feels like inside information instead of canned press releases. Embedded video clips can make the message feel more personal.
> - Include a big red "Donate" button at the bottom of the message.
> - It is okay to send a fund-raising appeal soon after the previous fund-raising appeal if there is a compelling need for funding. If something is truly urgent, supporters will be more likely to want to help.
> - Create a link between a regular donor and a new donor. Recruit a pool of donors who are willing to match the contribution of first-time donors. This will help motivate the first-time donor to give because it multiplies the value of their donation. Once the first-time donor has given, ask the donor who has matched the contribution to send a thank you and a "welcome to our community" e-mail.
> - As mentioned previously, include an emotionally evocative video clip. People are emotional decision makers.
> - Include a deadline. Direct marketers have known for a long time that donors are more likely to make a donation when a deadline for action is included. Some people, when receiving a request for a donation, will put the message aside for later consideration. However, postponing consideration often results in no donation. People forget about the request, or the request is separated from the other information that makes the message more compelling.

E-MAIL CAMPAIGNS

One of the organization's Web site's functions is to compile an e-mail list that the organization can use for fund-raising. A good e-mail list is one of the fund-raiser's most important resources, and there are several good organizations (like Constant Contact) that allow an organization a variety of tools for their e-mail programs. The organization's reputation and its goodwill with supporters are important assets. Therefore, activities and practices related to the collection of e-mail addresses and the manner in which the e-mail addresses are used must be done in the most ethical way possible, always respecting the privacy of e-mail list members.

Supporters who are added to the organization's e-mail list should only be added if they ask to be added—this is known as an opt-in process. However, the organization's Web site should ask individuals if they would like to be added to the list of people who receive future updates and information. Large organizations may deal with multiple issues. In this case, it is best to allow people to sign up for specific future mailings that pertain only to the issues they care about.

On most of the Web site's pages, there should be a link to a form where individuals can provide their names and e-mail addresses. Some organization's have a simple "put your e-mail address in the box" configuration in the navigation pane that remains on the Web site's pages. Most organizations have a double opt-in process, in which the individual giving her e-mail address to the organization is sent a verification e-mail message to confirm the individual's desire to sign up to future messages from the organization. This prevents third parties from signing up others by giving their e-mail addresses. Opt-in procedures ensure that the organization's e-mail messages are not unwanted messages that annoy recipients.

The list of supporter e-mail addresses is called a house list. The organization will want to add to the house list and maintain its accuracy over time. Allowing Web site visitors to sign up for the organization's e-newsletter is one of the most effective means of attracting individuals to the house list. In the organization's communications, both online and offline, it should encourage individuals to visit its Web site and add their e-mail addresses to the community of supporters. Also, encourage current supporters to ask their friends to join the list. One tool for list maintenance is to remove undelivered e-mail messages from the list. Also, make it easy for people to remove their names from the house list if they no longer want to receive messages. Most e-mail messages have a link at the bottom for individuals to use if they want to remove their names from the list.

When organizations begin to send out e-mail messages to supporters, they invariably make mistakes. The Internet is a great medium for learning. It provides for quick feedback and the ability to make changes to determine what works best. The organization can experiment with a number of variables. The subject line can be changed along with different aspects of the body of the message. The organization can determine the best use of video clips and pictures. It can experiment with the most effective mix of factual information and emotional appeals, including testimonials and celebrity endorsements. The point is that it is useful to experiment in order to learn what works best for a specific organization. For example, during the 2008 campaign, the Obama team experimented with several subject lines, photos, videos, and links to see which would lead to the largest "lift" or increase in fund-raising.

When sending e-mail messages, the first objective is to get the recipient to open the message in her e-mail in-box. Does the subject line make the message interesting to the recipient? In general, individuals open e-mail from organizations they know. An individual is more likely to read an organization's e-mail if (1) the individual knows the organization, (2) the individual likes the organization, and especially (3) if the individual is part of the community of organization supporters.

At the most basic level, the recipient has to see the message in her in-box. Most e-mail software now have junk-mail filters to remove spam (unwanted e-mail) from the in-box automatically. When the individual adds her e-mail address to the organization's e-mail list, she should be directed to add the organization to either the safe sender list or address book of her e-mail software. This will ensure that the organization's messages do not get removed as junk mail.

VIRAL FUND-RAISING

Viral fund-raising refers to peer-to-peer fund-raising using social media. Viral fund-raising is new and will develop further in the future. Essentially, viral fund-raising involves individual supporters who raise money for their causes without the active involvement of the organization.[19] For example, an individual who is an enthusiastic supporter of a cause might develop a compelling video about it, post it to her Facebook page, and ask her friends to view the video. Some of them might choose to support the cause first with a donation and second by forwarding the video link to a group of their own friends. Thus, if the video and cause are compelling, a chain reaction through social networks can occur, raising relatively small sums from a large number of people. Individuals can also participate in an event like a walk-a-thon and ask friends to make their pledges on their personal fund-raising pages. Team in Training (and other race organizations) allow participants to develop their own fund-raising pages so that donors can see why they are participating and how much they have raised (and how much they have left to raise). Participants in these events typically have to raise several thousands of dollars in order to participate in half-marathon, marathon, or triathlon events.

Firstgiving (www.firstgiving.com) is a third-party or intermediary Web site that facilitates viral fund-raising by helping to process donations. Firstgiving has helped more than 1.9 million contributors to donate more than $103 million to approximately 28,000 nonprofit organizations. For example, an individual sets up an account on Firstgiving's Web site. Firstgiving provides an application on the individual's Facebook profile page (or through Causes on Facebook), which allows friends to click on a button and go to the individual's donation page that is located on Firstgiving's Web site. There, friends can make a secure credit card donation to the individual's cause. Firstgiving processes the donation, and then passes the funds to the cause, less a 7.5 percent fee. The nonprofit, therefore, receives 92.5 percent of the donation. Firstgiving, for its fee, provides:

- a Web site to host individuals' donation pages,
- a secure process for accepting credit card donations,
- verification of the target nonprofit organization through GuideStar, and
- the transfer of donations to the target nonprofit.

Viral fund-raising allows individuals to mobilize their friends to support their favorite causes and enables supporters to take action to help the organization. While having individuals in cyberspace fund-raising for the organization will make some managers apprehensive about giving up some control, viral fund-raising allows individuals to raise much more money for the cause than they could possibly donate on their own.

The nonprofit can help facilitate viral fund-raising in several ways. It can educate its supporters about viral fund-raising and encourage them to take action. It also can provide resources on its Web site that would include compelling, emotionally engaging video clips and fact sheets that may help supporters develop their own fund-raising e-mails.

ONLINE ADVERTISING

Online advertising can be useful in supporting the Web site and e-mail campaigns. Online advertising can reach people who might not have previously thought much about the organization and its cause or issue. Thus, it can serve an educational function (teaching people about your cause) and a brand-building function (building people's perceptions of your organization). Online advertising can also serve to remind people that your organization is still working vigilantly on an important issue. These functions—education, brand-building, and reminding—all help support the mission and fund-raising activities of the organization.

One major benefit of online advertising is the immediate publishing of information and content that is not limited by geography or time.[20] We will discuss three types of online advertising: interruptive advertising, banners advertising, and contextual advertising. Interruptive advertising refers to online advertising that attempts to gain the attention of the individual who is browsing online by intruding with an unwanted advertisement. Interruptive ads, also known as pop-up ads, tend to annoy people. Nonprofit organizations should refrain from the use of pop-ups ads unless they find a special context in which a pop-up ad will enhance the individual's information search.

Most people are familiar with banner ads, the small horizontal or vertical rectangular advertisements on Web pages. Some banner ads are active. Individuals click on them, and they are taken to the advertiser's Web site. Other banner ads are passive, having no linking function. The Internet Advertising Bureau (IAB) specifies eight different banner ad sizes.[21] Most Web sites will want to keep the file size of the banner ad relatively small (12K to 16K) to keep the time it takes for a browser to load the Web page reasonably fast.[22] Banner ads typically have three levels of complexity. At the lowest level are static banner ads featuring one image. Next, there are animated banner ads that show images in motion. Finally, there are rich media banner ads that contain an audio or video file—or they may use Java or Shockwave programming to increase the ads' interactivity.

The third type of online advertising is contextual advertising. This means that advertisements are shown to an individual if they fit within the context or subject expressed by the individual's interests. The most typical example of contextual advertising are search-engine advertisements. One needs to recall that Google became the dominant search engine not only because it returned search results quickly, but also because people were not presented with interruptive ads and banner ads that were prevalent in the early search engines. Originally, Google did not expose Web surfers to ads. After becoming a popular search engine, Google found that people did not mind simple test ads, as long as they were related to the subject of their searches, limited in number, and not distracting to the search. Thus, with the Ad Words program, contextual ads were developed in which an advertiser would pay Google for presenting its ad to a Web surfer when a specific keyword was used in the search. For example, a simple Google search using the keyword "poodle" resulted in a presentation of three ads (sponsored links) on the right column. The ads are simple text with names, a brief description, and a link. Nonprofit organizations could pay Google to present the organization as a sponsored link when keywords relating to their causes or issues are used in a search.

Another technique used on contextual advertising is to include linked keywords in an article sponsored by the nonprofit. For example, a nonprofit organization concerned with childhood obesity may produce various articles that are disseminated on a variety of Web sites. In the articles, certain keywords are hyperlinked, so that if the reader wants more information on that topic, she can click on the link. The link should take her to the section of the nonprofit's Web site that deals with the topic related to the linked keyword.

Both banner and contextual advertising can be useful in supporting the organization and its fund-raising activities. Banner ads are best used at a Web site that attracts a group of people whom the nonprofit organization is also interested in attracting. For example, a nonprofit that protects unwanted pets, like the Humane Society, may want to put a banner ad on Web sites that attract pet owners or animal lovers, such as justdogbreeds.com, terrificpets.com, pet-lovers.com, or pawsperouspets.com. While banner ads are good for targeting a specific group of people who visit special-interest Web sites, contextual ads are good tools for reaching individuals who have an interest in a topic related to your organization's issue.

ONLINE EVENTS

Organizations that have offline events can promote their events on their Web sites and send e-mail messages about the event to their supporters. Organizations will want to have a page on their Web sites that promotes and describes their events. Many organizations allow online event registrations and ticket purchases. Organizations not wanting to perform these functions in-house can hire an online solutions vendor. For example, ActiveEvents (www.activeevents.com) offers a variety of services to help organizations with their events. In this section, however, we are emphasizing online events, which we refer to as events designed to bring people together over the Internet for a particular purpose.

Online events are not limited by geographic constraints. They cost far less than equivalent offline events, making fund-raising with online events much more cost-effective. There are many different types of online events, such as contests, petition drives, fund-raisers, film viewings, debates, major speeches, and webinars. There are application vendors who can provide the technology and expertise for various event formats. It is usually simple to find one of these vendors with a Google search using the simple keywords "online events."

One of the most important determinants of success of an online event is the quality of the nonprofit organization's house list, the list of individuals who have supported the organization previously. The quality of the list must be good, meaning that the list should contain core supporters and volunteers. It is simple for organizations to use an Excel spreadsheet for organizing the house list. Some organizations use dedicated software to help them manage their donor list and integrate it with fund-raising and accounting functions. DonorPerfect (www.donorperfect.com) is one example. Other similar software can be identified with a Google search using the keywords "donor management software."

One common type of online event is a fund-raising event. They tend to be centrally controlled by the organization, decentralized, or a hybrid of both. An organization that manages its own fund-raising activities, encouraging people to donate directly to their organizations, is an example of a centrally controlled type of nonprofit event strategy.

A decentralized fund-raising event is typically demonstrated through participant-led, peer-to-peer fund-raising. The viral fund-raising example previously discussed is an example. Some large organizations are using a hybrid strategy, in which the organization creates a campaign theme (e.g., Race for the Cure), promotes the campaign, and seeks corporate donations, then coordinates regional and local volunteer-led events in which participants seek donations from their friends and work colleagues (e.g., Multiple Sclerosis Society Walk-a-thons). Typically, health organizations do a good job with this type of fund-raising (e.g., Komen 3-Day for the Cure walk for breast cancer).

Convio (www.convio.com) surveyed successful fund-raisers who used viral fund-raising successfully.[23] They concluded that there are six success factors for peer-to-peer fundraisers:

1. Start early.
2. Contact everyone you know.
3. Personalize your e-mails.

4. Create a schedule for sending donation requests and reminders.
5. Be persistent. Ask often.
6. Customize your personal fund-raising Web page.

It is also worth noting, from the Convio survey, that 75 percent of successful peer-to-peer fund-raisers had served previously as fund-raisers in the past and were, therefore, experienced. The managerial implication is that organizations should maintain contact and continue to develop relationships with former fund-raisers.

FUND-RAISING CAMPAIGN PROMOTIONS

Before the online tools previously discussed can have a significant fund-raising impact, the online campaign must first be effectively promoted.[24] Online fund-raising effectiveness increases as offline and online promotional activities are cohesive and coordinated. Cohesiveness in promoting the organization's mission is essential to fund-raising effectiveness. People want to give money to support a *cause* they care about, not an *organization*. Fund-raising campaign events should be promoted on both online and offline sources. The Web site, e-mails, and blogs should include information about the organization's offline events (like auctions and rallies). Offline events should encourage people to visit the organization's Web site and sign up as an online supporter.

Motivate the organization's donor/supporter base. Communicate regularly to supporters about the organization's upcoming events, fund-raising goals, and challenges. Enlist their help in publicizing the event by encouraging them to e-mail their friends; to put a notice on their Facebook, MySpace, or Twitter profile pages; to get the information distributed in blogs in which they participate; or to send press releases to their local newspapers. Then, provide supporters with feedback regarding how their efforts have made a meaningful difference to the campaign. Allow supporters to feel like part of a team, sharing in the organization's successes and achievements.

Keep e-mail messages and alerts to supporters brief and on point. Let supporters know how their fund-raising efforts have allowed the organization to further its mission. If fund-raising has allowed the organization to buy ad space in order to have a voice in a public debate, send them electronic copies of the ads and media coverage of the ad campaign. If a group of volunteers work together to raise funds, let them know how much was raised, the number of new donors added to the supporter base, and how the money was used to further the organization's mission.

The popularity of the organization's Web site is an important element of fund-raising campaign promotion. The more people who visit the Web site, the greater number of people who will be exposed to the fund-raising campaign's message. There are two key dimensions to making the Web site popular. First, you want as many people as possible who have some interest in your cause or issue to visit your Web site. Second, you want your Web site to be the top site listed in a search engine query. To accomplish this, the Web site must (1) have current content that is updated regularly, (2) be the best Web site available for information on your cause or issue, and (3) be part of an ongoing search-engine placement strategy. Search-engine placement refers to a set of tactics to ensure that your organization is listed at the top or near the top of a Google search for keyword searches related to your issue. Search-engine placement companies can be contracted to prepare your Web site for optimum search-engine placement.

OTHER TOOLS

Now we will discuss other tools which can sometimes be useful in online fund-raising. While these tools typically supplement the effectiveness of tools we have discussed previously, their use can be very helpful.

Web Video

Web video can use used to carry live proceedings of an event. Video can be a powerful part of the organization's Web site resource archive. Animated video can be used to demonstrate ideas or to satirically lampoon an organization's opponent. The cost of creating a Web video is modest and within reach of all but the smallest nonprofit organizations.

E-newsletters

Electronic newsletters, or e-newsletters, are sent by e-mail to individuals who have requested to receive them. Good e-newsletters have pass-along value, meaning e-newsletter recipients may forward a copy to an interested friend. Although the format will differ, the content of an e-newsletter is similar to a print newsletter. There are, however, some advantages of e-newsletters over print newsletters.

E-newsletters are less expensive than print newsletters. There are no printing or postage costs. No address labels have to be printed and attached. As soon as the e-newsletter is ready, it can be immediately sent to list subscribers, ensuring the most current content.

E-newsletters are very flexible. Stories, articles, and reports can be headlined and summarized in a paragraph. Then, if interested in the full story, readers can click on a link for the full article. There can also be links to interviews, commentaries, or speeches. The e-newsletter can contain fund-raising appeals, advocacy alerts, success stories, upcoming events, information for current and prospective volunteers, job openings, and updates on the organization's progress in furthering its mission.

Regular communication from the organization is valuable to supporters. It keeps them up-to-date with the organization's activities. It keeps the organization's work in their thoughts. It helps supporters to feel connected with the organization and its other supporters.

Celebrity Endorsers

A celebrity who supports a cause can be effective in bringing attention to that cause. Nonprofit organizations have found that celebrities can be very effective supporters. For example, pop singer Sarah McLachlan supported the Society for the Prevention of Cruelty to Animals (SPCA) by appearing in a fund-raising and awareness commercial for the nonprofit organization. She sings and speaks to the audience in the emotionally powerful two-minute video. The ad has been uploaded to YouTube and has been viewed more than 230,000 times.[25]

The power of using celebrities as endorsers of a cause is that they can bring a great deal of public attention to the cause.[26] The nonprofit organization, however, must manage the endorsement relationship effectively to gain the most value. The organization needs to avoid overusing the celebrity. You do not want the cause and the celebrity to be too tightly connected in the public's mind.

In selecting a celebrity endorser, the organization should only use a celebrity who is likeable and who truly cares about the cause. The more well-known the celebrity is, the more attention the celebrity will bring. To be an effective endorser, the celebrity should have some connection with the cause in the public's mind. Michael J. Fox was obviously a natural fit to endorse Parkinson's disease (see www.michaeljfox.org) research because it is widely known that the talented and likeable actor has the disease. A connection between the celebrity and the cause gives the endorser credibility with the audience. Angelina Jolie is connected to several charities that help refugee children in Africa—this is a good fit because it is widely known that she cares for these children and has actually adopted several of them.[27] The more the audience believes the celebrity cares about a cause, the more they will listen to what she has to say.

Online Auctions

Online auctions avoid the barriers of time and geography in allowing nonprofit organizations the ability to raise funds offering goods and services to supporters and the public. Online auction software is available for nonprofit organizations to use, or they can contract with a service provider.[28]

Nonprofit organizations typically receive donated items from individual and business supporters. Before hosting an online auction, the nonprofit has some questions to consider: should the work be done in-house or by an online auction service provider such as Bidding For Good (www.biddingforgood.com)? Who will volunteer to obtain items for the auction, take digital pictures of the items, and ship the items to the highest bidders? How will the online auction be promoted? Who will administer the accounting? Who will write thank you notes to donors and buyers?

PRIVACY AND ETHICAL ISSUES

The most important assets for most nonprofit organizations are their supporters and their good reputations. Violating the privacy of supporters or getting publicity for unethical behavior can do great harm to a nonprofit organization. By creating and strictly adhering to both a code of ethical conduct and an online privacy policy, the nonprofit organization can avoid many problems.[29]

By following some simple rules, the nonprofit can avoid stepping over most ethical boundaries related to its online activities. (It is assumed that your nonprofit organization is complying with all relevant laws.)

Rule 1: Make sure that the Web site is using current security technology so that donor information is protected.

Rule 2: Never release donor information to outside organizations unless legally required to do so.

Rule 3: Be a transparent and accountable organization. Make sure your organization has the highest ratings from rating organizations like Guidestar or Charity Guide. Show the public that your organization is a good steward of its funding by posting the appropriate information online. Show how much funding you receive, and show how you use that funding.

Rule 4: Never be deceptive. Always be completely honest in your fund-raising appeals.

Rule 5: Individuals outside your organization to whom you communicate should give you permission to send them communications.[30] Make it easy for individuals to remove themselves from your house list if so desired.

Rule 6: Inform Web site visitors, in a privacy policy page, what information you collect, if any, on individuals. Describe how you use that information. Make it simple for individuals to verify the accuracy of their information and to have the option of removing or correcting their information.

Rule 7: Designate an ombudsman who can receive and resolve complaints made against your organization, a staff member, or a supporter. Provide a means of lodging such a complaint on the Web site.

MONITORING YOUR ORGANIZATION'S IMAGE AND REPUTATION

The nonprofit organization needs to have a process for monitoring its ratings with watchdog organizations that advise donors. Examples are Guidestar, Charity Navigator, and the Better Business Bureau's Wise Giving Alliance. The organization should make sure it is complying with best reporting practices.[31]

The organization should also monitor what is said about it on the Internet. If there is a negative or untrue statement made about the organization online, it should detect it in order to respond appropriately. Google has a free service called

"Google Alerts" which the organization can use.[32] Google will periodically perform a search based on keywords the individual has established in setting up the alerts. If the Google search identifies a news story or a blog posting, for example, it will send an alert with a link to the individual's e-mail address.[33] There is also software designed to monitor what is said about the organization online.[34]

In addition to avoiding negative information about your organization, it should also actively promote and enhance its good reputation. The organization should have an active public relations program and it should actively strive to have its cause better known to the public.

LESSONS LEARNED

- It is important to understand that there are advantages and disadvantages to online fund-raising. It should be used in tandem with traditional face-to-face fund-raising (especially for large donors) but it can be a great way to gain smaller, regular donations.
- Building an online community is one of the foundations of online fund-raising because donors and supporters create a sense of community to further the mission of the organization.
- E-mail campaigns are an important means of communicating with supporters, maintaining supporter relationships, and facilitating fund-raising. This can be one of the most effective tools due to the degree of experimentation involved.
- As the popularity of social media increases, so does the relatively new trend of viral, or peer-to-peer, fund-raising. Tools such as social networks, Twitter, and videos are important. Additionally, online advertising can be effective, as well as online events and campaign promotion.
- Other tools, such as Web videos, e-newsletters, podcasts, celebrity endorsements, and online auctions were all discussed as potential tools for effective online fund-raising. However, privacy and ethical issues are important, as well as the need to monitor the Internet and nonprofit watchdog groups.

FURTHER READING

E-newsletters:

The Mercifully Brief, Real Work Guide to . . . Raising More Money with Newsletters Than You Ever Thought Possible by Tom Ahern

Every Nonprofit's Guide to Publishing: Creating Newsletters, Magazines & Web Sites by Cheryl Woodard and Lucia Hwang

Legal, privacy, and ethical issues:

Privacy Makeover: The Essential Guide to Best Practices: How to Protect Assets and Foster Consumer Loyalty by Joseph Campana

The Law of Fund-raising, 3rd Ed. by Bruce R. Hopkins
Ethical Fund-Raising: A Guide for Nonprofit Boards and Fundraisers by Janice Gow Pettey

Major donors:

Major Donors: Finding Big Gifts in Your Database and Online by Ted Hart, et al.

Online advertising:

The Complete Guide to Google Advertising: Including Tips, Tricks, & Strategies to Create a Winning Advertising Plan by Bruce C. Brown
Advertising 2.0: Social Media Marketing in a Web 2.0 World by Tracy L. Tuten

Podcasting:

Podcasting: Do It Yourself Guide by Todd Cochrane
Podcasting for Dummies, 2nd Ed. by Tee Morris, et al.
Podcasting Bible by Mitch Ratcliffe and Steve Mack

Recruiting new donors:

Fund-raising on the Internet, 2nd Ed. by Mal Warwick, Ted Hart, and Nick Allen
People to People Fund-raising: Social Networking and Web 2.0 for Charities by Ted Hart, James M. Greenfield, and Sheeraz D. Haji

Web sites that support fund-raising:

Nonprofit Internet Strategies: Best Practices for Marketing, Communications, and Fund-raising Success by Ted Hart, James M. Greenfield, and Michael Johnston
96 Ways to Make Your Web Site More Donor, Member and Volunteer Friendly by Stevenson, Inc.

Web video:

Web Video: Making it Great, Getting it Noticed by Jennie Bourne and Dave Burstein
How to Do Everything with Online by Andrew Shalat

NOTES

1. *The Political Consultants' Online Fund-raising Primer* (Institute for Politics Democracy & The Internet, 2004).
2. www.justinvisionary.com/2009/06/01/micro-donation-generation/
3. www.huffingtonpost.com/2008/11/20/obama-raised-half-a-billi_n_145390.html
4. www.internetworldstats.com/stats.htm
5. www.census.gov/compendia/statab/cats/information_communications/internet_publishing_and_broadcasting_and_internet_usage.html
6. http://en.wikipedia.org/wiki/Hotspot_%28Wi-Fi%29
7. https://www.paypal.com/cgi-bin/webscr?cmd=p/xcl/rec/donate-intro-outside
8. http://nonprofitfund-raising.suite101.com/article.cfm/fund-raising_in_a_recession_with_bequests
9. Gary Grobman and Gary Grant. *Fund-raising Online.* (Harrisburg, PA: White Hat Communications, 2006).

10. www.givingspace.org/papers/microphilanthropy.htm
11. www.ideablob.com/ideas/4130-iGive-Micro-donating-made-eas?tab=advice&oc=4232
12. https://www.paypal.com/cgi-bin/webscr?cmd=xpt/cps/mobile/Text2Give-outside
13. http://watercharity.org/node/74
14. www.npcdivision.com/downloads/WP_Engaging_MD_online.pdf
15. www.dmnews.com/make-a-wish-sets-up-large-donor-site/article/138446/
16. Convio, Sea Change Strategies, and Edge Research, "The Wired Wealthy: Using the Internet to Connect with Your Middle and Major Donors," (Convio, Sea Change Strategies, and Edge Research), http://my.convio.com.
17. See http://www.microsoft.com/communities/conduct/default.mspx for an example of the Conduct Code.
18. www.mrss.com/clients/fund-raising_tips_from_obama_campaign_1-9-2009.pdf
19. www.philanthropyjournal.org/resources/special-reports/nonprofit-tech/spread-viral-fund-raising
20. http://en.wikipedia.org/wiki/Online_advertising
21. http://www.iab.net/iab_products_and_industry_services/1421/1443/1452
22. http://computer.howstuffworks.com/banner-ad2.htm
23. http://eon.businesswire.com/portal/site/eon/permalink/?ndmViewId=news_view&newsId=20090714005180&newsLang=en
24. www.theoutsourcingcompany.com/blog/internet-marketing/how-to-promote-an-event-online/
25. www.youtube.com/watch?v=9gspElv1yvc
26. www.informaworld.com/smpp/content~content=a908659479~db=all~jumptype=rss
27. www.rightcelebrity.com/?p=1787
28. http://nonprofit.about.com/od/fund-raising/a/auctions.htm
29. www.fundraising123.org/article/ephilanthropy-code-ethics
30. www.onphilanthropy.com/site/News2?page=NewsArticle&id=5257
31. www.wcsr.com/resources/pdfs/_Tax11_2_07.pdf
32. www.google.com/support/alerts/
33. A more detailed discussion of using Google Alerts is available online at http://www.wildapricot.com/blogs/newsblog/archive/2009/07/07/get-started-with-google-alerts-part-1-how-to-set-up-news-alerts.aspx and http://www.wildapricot.com/blogs/newsblog/archive/2009/07/09/get-started-with-google-alerts-part-2-how-to-get-better-news-alerts.aspx
34. www.davechaffey.com/blog/online-pr/online-reputation-management-software/

CHAPTER 7

Volunteer Recruitment

"Thanks to our new, interactive, user-friendly Web site, Big Brothers Big Sisters has increased the number of volunteers and children served. Within four months, our new Web site has generated over 300 new volunteer inquiries, information requests, donations, and event registrations."
—Deborah Ortiz, President/CEO, Big Brothers Big Sisters of Southeast Texas

CHAPTER OVERVIEW

In this chapter, we will enhance the reader's understanding of the role of the nonprofit's Web site in complementing the organization's volunteer recruitment efforts. The reader will better understand how to more effectively use her organizations' Web site to improve volunteer recruitment efforts. Readers will gain a better understanding of the different types of volunteer efforts and how to capitalize on those efforts via online strategies.

IMPORTANCE OF ONLINE VOLUNTEER RECRUITMENT EFFORTS

Many nonprofits are finding their volunteer recruitment efforts improved by more effective use of their Web sites. River City Youth Foundation, in Austin, Texas, lacked sufficient staff members to effectively manage its volunteer recruitment process. However, it was able to use its Web site to expand its volunteer base by showcasing its volunteer needs among the variety of other volunteer choices available to individuals in its community. River City Youth Foundation added a YouTube video clip to its Web site that provides visitors with a testimonial about its mentoring program (http://rivercityyouth.com/volunteer). It allows supporters to receive information in a format of their choosing. For example, the nonprofit communicates using Twitter, Flickr, Facebook, and RSS feeds. River City Youth Foundation links its Web site to volunteermatch.org (www.volunteermatch.org/search/org14504.jsp), an online service that helps individuals interested in volunteering identify suitable positions. When the authors last checked the Web site, there were no available volunteer positions.

The nonprofit's effective use on online resources has allowed it to successfully satisfy all its volunteer recruitment needs.

THE IMPORTANCE OF VOLUNTEERS

A nonprofit organization's volunteers are individuals who willingly perform a service for the organization without pay. Volunteers allow a nonprofit organization to direct a greater proportion of its resources toward program objectives because the organization does not have to pay for their labor. Volunteers also attract resources to the organization because: (1) volunteers usually make financial donations to their organizations, and (2) they often recruit other volunteers and solicit donations.

The required skill sets of volunteers will differ, depending on the volunteer roles in which they serve. Volunteers who are effective in assisting with a direct-mail annual campaign may not be effective in assisting with planned-giving development efforts. Therefore, the right volunteers must be recruited for the roles in which they are needed.

TYPES OF VOLUNTEERING

Episodic vs. Ongoing Volunteering

Episodic volunteers are those who serve on an "as needed" basis, on special events, or on projects of a limited duration. An example might be the mother of a Girl Scout who participates in a bake sale to raise money. In contrast, ongoing volunteers work regularly. An example would be the Girl Scout troop leader who conducts weekly troop meetings.

Many nonprofit organizations rely upon their ongoing volunteers to maintain their programs and regular activities. Big Brothers and Big Sisters of America, for example, was established with the idea of matching adult ongoing volunteers with children in single-parent homes.

Family Volunteering

The most common reason given by people as to why they do not volunteer is lack of time. Some organizations, in response, have encouraged individuals to volunteer together as a family. Adults who feel they have insufficient time to volunteer individually because of time demands of work and family may feel that family volunteering is an opportunity to have quality family time and to demonstrate good parenting. Volunteering together is a creative way for families to enjoy each other's company while making a contribution to the community. Parents teach their children what they value and the importance of contributing to a valued cause. Organizations are recognizing the needs of families and are responding by creating family volunteering opportunities.

Student Volunteers and Interns

A growing number of high schools, colleges, and universities are encouraging or requiring their students to get involved in their communities by working with local nonprofit organizations. Educators often label student volunteering "community service learning."[1] Some institutions have offices to coordinate student volunteers, whereas other institutions lack a formal program.[2] Many schools, such as Trinity Valley School in Fort Worth, Texas, require their high school students to donate a specified number of hours in order to graduate, although most volunteer more than the minimum required number of hours by volunteering at the Presbyterian Night Shelter, Tarrant Area Food Bank, or tutoring youth in area schools. Many colleges and universities have embraced this idea and incorporate volunteering into their curricula.

Virtual Volunteering

Some individuals prefer volunteer opportunities that they can complete at home on the Internet.[3] Busy work schedules, congested city traffic, or disabilities can make virtual volunteering an appealing alternative. Nonprofit organizations are finding creative ways to use virtual volunteers. Some nonprofits are using online volunteers in a support role. Others are using online volunteers to communicate directly with clients using e-mail or chat rooms.[4] For example, the Web developer for a Texas nonprofit actually lives in Florida but is able to develop the organization's Web site through e-mail and text messaging.

Volunteers with Disabilities

People with disabilities are an underutilized source of volunteer talent. They are often not fully employed, yet want to engage in meaningful work. Many reasonable accommodations can be made with little effort and cost. The American Library Association has developed a useful document for libraries to use when recruiting people with disabilities for volunteer positions.[5] In a 2000 Harris poll, 48 percent of people with disabilities who have access to the Internet believe it has substantially improved the quality of their lives. This compares to 27 percent for people without disabilities.[6] People with disabilities value online communication and might be a good source of virtual volunteers.

VOLUNTEER ROLES

Nonprofit organizations have a variety of volunteer positions to staff. However, it is useful to think of volunteer roles as falling into one of the following categories: (1) board member or managerial, (2) fund-raising, (3) general support, and (4) direct service.[7] Understanding the various roles is important because each attracts different types of people. Each role will be discussed in turn.

Board members (or administrative volunteers) are those volunteers who serve on the board of directors or other leadership positions. These volunteers are responsible for developing the organization's strategy for fulfilling its mission and developing tactical plans for achieving strategic objectives. These volunteers are more likely than other types of volunteers to have higher levels of education, higher levels of income, and higher occupational status.

Fund-raising volunteers' primary tasks involve raising money by soliciting contributions. These volunteers may also be responsible for writing grants. For many organizations, fund-raisers may be the most difficult volunteers to recruit. Fund-raising involves setting challenging goals, working as part of a team, and feeling energized by a challenge. Fund-raisers also serve a public relations role because they represent the nonprofit to the community.

General support volunteers get the "behind-the-scenes" work done that is necessary, but less visible, for the day-to-day operations. They staff telephones, do clerical work, prepare mailings, help write newsletters, work on maintenance projects, clean, run errands, and so forth. General support volunteers do not seek positions of authority, but they feel a duty to help where they are needed and can be useful.

Direct service volunteers provide the organization's services directly to its clients or its members. A direct service volunteer may be a scout troop leader, a museum docent, a youth sports coach, a counselor, or a companion. Direct service volunteers want to make a meaningful contribution to the nonprofit. They want to feel what they are doing is significant, and that it improves the lives of the organization's clients.

Chapter Insight: Developing a Volunteer Program

Nonprofit managers should work out the purpose of the volunteer programs, the role of volunteers, and how the volunteer program furthers the mission of the nonprofit. The planning should include:

- Purpose statement: why does the volunteer program exist?
- Needs assessment: what needs will the volunteer program address?
- Outcomes: what will be the impact of the volunteer program?
- Budget: what is the budget for the volunteer program?
- Staff acceptance: how will paid staff be prepared to work with and manage volunteers?
- Position descriptions: what will volunteers do?

MOTIVATIONS FOR VOLUNTEERING

An individual may volunteer for a variety of reasons. One's decision to volunteer is guided by one's values, beliefs, and attitudes. The stage in a person's life can also play a role in volunteering.

Having experiences that brings individuals into contact with a nonprofit organization and its volunteers can also impact a person's decision to volunteer. People who have friends who volunteer are much more likely to become volunteers than people having no friends who volunteer. Being raised in a family with parents who volunteer influences children, who may themselves become volunteers when they become adults.

Situational factors also influence volunteer behavior. A person may decline a request to volunteer for a nonprofit if that person feels she does not have sufficient time for volunteering, if the volunteering occurs at a too distant location, or if her personal safety may be at risk. All these types of influences affect a person's intention to volunteer.

Values/Beliefs

People care about some issues more than others. The issues people care about most mesh with their core values. Values vary in importance. People are defined by their values, especially their core values. People act in ways that are consistent with their self-image. People avoid acting in ways inconsistent with the values that are important to them.

Life Stage

The basic determinants of the traditional life stage are marital status, the presence or absence of children in the home, and the age of the youngest child. Our life stage influences our values and priorities.

Entering retirement is a major transition that influences volunteering. Our occupations are important. They provide us with a means of feeling useful and productive, of making accomplishments. Our jobs partially define who we are. When we retire, we often search for new ways to meet needs that were formally met through our occupations. Studies of senior volunteers consistently find that they volunteer in order to feel useful and productive and to be around other people.

Managers should take life stage into account when identifying prospective volunteers. Parents are good prospects for nonprofits offering youth services in their children's age group. Older adults whose children have matured into adulthood and left home have more freedom and may be good prospects. Middle-aged adults approaching retirement often desire to "give back" to their communities and are planning for a good quality of life after retirement.

Personal Experiences

Personal experiences play a role in helping people to identify, develop, and prioritize their values. Many nonprofit organizations have been created by individuals who found themselves in experiences in which they were witnesses to human privations and injustices.

FACILITATION

Facilitation is assisting the potential volunteer in becoming a new volunteer and assimilating the new volunteer into the organization by providing information and social support. Facilitation helps reduce the stress that potential volunteers may experience in anticipating a new role or in joining a new group. A facilitator, then, is a person who serves a boundary role between a potential or new volunteer and the organization, information and social support. A facilitator is usually a friend, family member, or associate of the person being asked to volunteer. When the person who is recruiting is known by the person being recruited, the recruitment effectiveness can increase as much as fivefold.

ATTITUDES

In addition to personal and interpersonal influences on volunteering, a person's attitudes will affect her motivation to volunteer. A person's motivation to volunteer can be satisfied in many ways. A person's values influence the *type* of volunteering that would be of interest. A person's attitudes influence the selection of the organization. If someone would like to volunteer for an organization that helps animals (values choice), her attitudes towards the various animal welfare organizations that are available will determine her choice of organization (attitude choice).

BENEFITS OF VOLUNTEERING

The most important reason for someone to volunteer is because they believe in the importance of the cause or organization and its mission. Individuals are motivated to volunteer when they perceive a congruency between the organization's mission and their own core values. For example, if the organization helps underprivileged children, and helping such children is an important value for an individual, that individual can express this value by volunteering for the organization. Activities that allow an individual to express important values are inherently rewarding. If you were to ask one of these volunteers why she volunteers, she would probably tell you she does so because it allows her to help children in need.

There are other benefits. According to the 2000 National Survey of Giving, Volunteering, and Participating (NSGVP), 79 percent of survey respondents reported that volunteering helped them with their interpersonal skills, such as understanding people better, motivating others, and dealing with difficult situations. About 68 percent of respondents said volunteering helped them to develop better communication skills. About 63 percent said volunteering helped them to increase their knowledge about issues related to their volunteering.

Volunteering can help an individual develop new knowledge and skills. It allows individuals to become part of a larger community, providing social benefits. One can derive motivation and a sense of achievement from volunteering. It allows one to explore new fields of potential job opportunities, and many employers prefer hiring individuals with volunteer experience. It allows one to develop new interests, have new experiences, and meet a diverse range of people.[8]

VOLUNTEER RECRUITMENT TACTICS

Targeted vs. Non-Targeted

One way to classify volunteer recruitment techniques is by targeted versus non-targeted methods. Non-targeted (or warm body recruitment) techniques refers to recruiting people when the qualifications needed are minimal. Recruitment tactics may include distribution of brochures, posters, speaking to groups, notices in appropriate media, and word-of-mouth. Obviously, the organization's Web site is an important communications channel.

Targeted recruitment techniques involve identifying people with specific skills or characteristics. Targeted recruitment requires a carefully planned appeal to a small audience. Targeted approaches require managers to identify and locate the volunteers they need, and then to deliver a customized recruitment message.

Concentric Circles Recruitment

Concentric circles recruitment refers to identifying groups who are already in direct or indirect contact with the nonprofit and then presenting them with recruitment messages. The most easily recruited prospects will be individuals who (1) care about your organization and its mission, and (2) know others who are part of your organization's community.

Individual staff members and volunteers, including board members, can provide a list of individuals they know who might have an interest in volunteering. Staff and volunteers are in a good position to better understand the potential match between people they know and the organization. Therefore, a good prospect list could be developed within the organization. Referrals from staff and volunteers are valuable prospects because (1) they are more likely to accept an invitation to volunteer than people outside the social networks of your organization, and (2) since they are referred by your organizational community, they are less likely to be unsuitable to serve in your organization.

Managers can identify prospects who have an interest in the organization by looking for individuals who have demonstrated their interest through their prior support. Donors, members, clients, and patrons who have demonstrated an interest in the organization may volunteer if asked. If the organization has processes for keeping track of these groups, then a prospect list can be developed from the organization's internal records.

Personal vs. Nonpersonal Recruitment

All things being equal, personal appeals are typically more effective than nonpersonal appeals. Personal appeals are made person-to-person, between two people. Nonpersonal appeals are delivered in another manner. Nonpersonal appeals are often made to a mass audience, often broadcasted through advertising or news media. An appeal that is made on the organization's Web site is an example of a nonpersonal appeal.

The effectiveness of recruitment is greatly increased when individuals are personally asked to volunteer. Personal recruitment techniques, therefore, are generally more effective because individuals are personally being asked to volunteer rather than seeing an announcement for a volunteer need.

While personal recruitment methods tend to be most effective, this does not imply that there is no role for nonpersonal volunteer recruitment methods. Nonpersonal recruitment tactics may reach individuals outside of the social networks of the organization's supporters. Nonpersonal methods extend the organization's reach.

Chapter Insight: Volunteer Matching Sites

Although the purpose of this chapter is to help managers use their organization's Web sites to improve volunteer recruitment effectiveness, it is important to recognize that volunteer matching sites exist to help nonprofit organizations. Volunteer matching sites are Web sites developed for the purpose of helping individuals identify suitable volunteer opportunities. Some of the most widely used volunteer matching sites, which can be found through a simple Google search, are:

- Idealist
- Network for Good
- VolunteerSolutions
- Volunteers of America
- VolunteerMatch
- Points of Light

SUPPLEMENTING RECRUITMENT EFFORTS WITH ONLINE SUPPORT

Providing content related to volunteering on an organization's Web site enables people to learn about volunteering opportunities. There are several reasons for supplementing existing volunteer recruitment efforts with Web site support. Doing so is an effective, fast, low-cost way to provide information to interested persons. It is an excellent way to target nontraditional volunteers and individuals who are under-represented in an organization's current volunteer community, such as youth, seniors, ethnic minorities, or people with disabilities.

We refer to using online resources to recruit volunteers as supplementing the organization's other volunteer recruitment efforts because, as discussed earlier, personal recruitment tactics are typically more effective than nonpersonal tactics. While we present online recruitment tactics as supplemental, they are an important component of the organization's volunteer recruitment program.

It is important for managers to understand that many individuals who are curious about volunteering for their organizations will search the organization's Web site to improve their understanding of what volunteer positions are available and what the volunteering experience will be like. Managers have to understand what information individuals want and how to present this information in an appealing manner. Managers also need to understand that individuals visiting the Web site have varying levels of interest and understanding about the organization. The following discussion is intended to provide managers with practical insights to improve the use of their Web sites.

Providing Necessary Information

Although managers will want to tailor the information on their Web sites to meet the needs of their unique situations, there are some common types of information that most Web sites would do well to provide to prospective volunteers.

Recommended information includes descriptions for available positions. Each volunteer position should have a clearly defined description. Table 7.1 below lists information that is commonly included in a position description.

In addition to having position descriptions, Web sites should include information that helps prospective volunteers understand the scope of the organization's volunteer program. How many volunteers does the organization use over the period of a year? How many volunteers serve regularly? How many current openings are there? Are there special events in the near future that will require volunteers?

Lead Generation

Many businesses use their Web sites to generate sales leads, which are queries from Web site visitors to the business which, hopefully, will result in sales. This is analogous to nonprofits using their Web site to generate leads,

Table 7.1: Volunteer Position Description

Position Title	A descriptive title for this position
Duties and Working Environment	A paragraph or two that explains the various tasks required and the context within which this position will be performed
Training Requirements	Describe any training that is required of this volunteer
Number in Organization	The number of this type of volunteer in the organization if fully staffed
Number Available	Number of available volunteer positions of this type
Supervision	Identify to whom this volunteer reports
Commitment	Describe the average number of weekly or monthly hours required and specify any termination dates for this position
Qualifications	Describe the skill sets you desire from this volunteer and any personal characteristics that are helpful

queries from interested individuals that, hopefully, will lead to support for the organization in the form of volunteering.

When interested individuals obtain information from the organization's Web site and have questions or are ready to volunteer, the nonprofit must be prepared to respond promptly and effectively. Individuals may contact the nonprofit by telephone, e-mail, or from a Web site query form. Since the emphasis is on effectiveness in recruiting volunteers, it is preferable for the nonprofit to respond to a query by telephone or in person, if possible. Two-way communication is preferred. Many people have mobile phones and, therefore, can be contacted promptly after sending their query. This may not always be possible, however, and the organization should be prepared to respond appropriately via e-mail.

Applications

Most nonprofit organizations require prospective volunteers to complete applications. Applications provide contact information, qualifications, desired position, and permission for a background check (for liability protection). The nonprofit's Web site can make the application process more efficient. From the Web site, the prospective volunteer could download an application form and return it to the organization using the postal system, sending a fax, or in person. Also, the individual could complete and submit the application entirely online. Laws in most countries allow for digital signatures to facilitate online transactions. Managers developing application forms for the first time can view examples easily by performing a Google search using "volunteer application" as key words.

Staff Workload

In addition to improving the effectiveness of a nonprofit's volunteer recruitment program, online support can also reduce the staff workload. Individuals can

> Chapter Insight: Responding to Web Queries
>
> The immediacy of gathering information on the Internet has made individuals impatient. If individuals' queries are not answered promptly, they will obtain the impression that the nonprofit is inept or uncaring. Therefore, it is very important that the nonprofit is prepared to respond to online queries. The following is suggested:
>
> - The e-mail system should be set to automatically respond to e-mail queries. This enables the individual sending the message to receive an immediate reply that lets her know the nonprofit received the message, that the message will be responded to promptly, and when she can expect an answer.
> - Promptness is important. A delay of three or four days is unacceptable.
> - The nonprofit's personnel will learn, over time, that queries tend to be similar. It would be wise, therefore, to have prepared answers for common questions. Staff could use prepared answers to respond to inquiries.
>
> Answers to common questions can be included in a "frequently asked questions" section of the Web site or the information can be better communicated in the Web site's content.

obtain information online, reducing telephone and personal visits to the nonprofit location for the purpose of exchanging information or completing forms.

PRACTICAL TIPS FOR EFFECTIVE WEB SITE USE

Before managers begin changing tactics, however, it is important for the organization to understand what it wants its Web site to achieve from its volunteer recruitment efforts. Does the organization want Web site visitors to be able to search for current volunteer openings and needs or does the organization prefer to give visitors a more general understanding of the overall volunteer program in the organization? Does the organization want interested volunteers to complete and submit application forms online? Is the organization prepared to respond to this new pathway for volunteer inquiries?

Tip 1: Clear Paths

Make a clear pathway to information on volunteering on the Web site's front page. Web users are impatient and are unlikely to spend much time or effort to find the information they want. With the exception of highly motivated individuals, most people will give up if they cannot find information they want in a few seconds. If volunteer recruitment is important to the organization, there should be a link to volunteer information in a prominent position on the front page.

Tip 2: Simplicity

Keep information simple. Visitors to your Web site want to move quickly to get the information they want. They need the ability to navigate easily throughout the Web site. Many staff persons, who are very familiar with the operations and procedures of their organization, underestimate the difficulty people outside their organizations may have in understanding its various programs. It would be useful to get feedback from people outside the organization on how to improve the information provided on the Web site.

On your Web site, use language that is clear and self-explanatory. Allow searches directly from the homepage. Remove unnecessary information on the site in which visitors are not interested. Keep the navigation and structure of the Web site as simple as possible. Keep forms brief, allowing visitors to avoid filling out a new form for each position in which they are interested.

Tip 3: Accessibility

Develop a Web site that is accessible to people with disabilities. As mentioned earlier, people with disabilities represent a group that has been overlooked by many nonprofits. Advice on how to make your Web site more accessible is readily available online. A simple Google search of "how to make Web site more accessible" will provide many excellent resources. Also, the Web Accessibility Initiate (WAI), which is easily found online, provides many practical tips for improving the accessibility of a Web site.

Tip 4: Message Development

Develop a compelling recruitment message. Make sure your Web site presents a persuasive case for becoming a volunteer with your organization. Include the benefits and intrinsic rewards of volunteering. Help the Web site visitor derive a sense of the rewarding experience that volunteering for your organization provides. A list of items included in effective recruitment messages is presented in table 7.2.

The recruitment message should be inviting and encourage individuals to involve themselves in your organization. Nonprofit organizations may have a specific message for each volunteer position available, or they may have a general message for all prospective volunteers with additional information for various

Table 7.2: Message Content

Description of organization and its purpose

The volunteer role description

The importance of the volunteer role to the organization and its mission

Benefits of volunteering

A sense of the volunteer experience the prospect can anticipate (establishing realistic expectations)

A solicitation for questions or concerns

A request to volunteer

---

volunteer positions. The message should describe the organization's need for volunteers and why volunteers are important in meeting that need. Multiple messages should be tested to determine which is most effective.

From the point of view of the Web site visitor, the message should feel as if the organization is communicating directly to her. A speaker would use different language if speaking to elderly people than she would if speaking to teenagers. She would use different language if communicating with a female audience than a male audience. The point is that the more managers know about the type of people who are visiting the Web site, the more prepared they will be to develop an appropriate message for that audience. Staff can observe the characteristics of people who have supported the organization in the past to get insights into the type of people who might be visiting the Web site. Over time, staff can gather information about the audience of the nonprofit's Web site from paying attention to individuals making online inquiries.

> **Chapter Insight: Increasing Diversity Among Volunteers**
>
> Because volunteer recruitment often occurs within existing social networks, over time, the group of volunteers in an organization may not represent the diversity of the larger community. As more emphasis is placed on recruiting volunteers from the Web site, new volunteers will differ from existing volunteers in terms of race, ethnicity, age, gender, education, income levels, religious beliefs, and skills. While increasing diversity will ultimately help the organization in the long term, existing volunteers and staff may not be as friendly and helpful to new volunteers who are different from themselves. Therefore, managers will have to give special attention to facilitating the growing diversity among volunteers, helping them to feel wanted and welcomed.

Tip 5: Testimonials

Some nonprofits have placed compelling testimonials on their Web sites from people whose lives have been changed by the nonprofit's good work. Ashoka (www.ashoka.org/volunteer/testimonials) includes a section on its Web site that is dedicated to the thoughts of its volunteers. Philabundance, an organization that combats hunger in Philadelphia, also has an area on its Web site for volunteer testimonials (www.philabundance.org).

Effective managers understand that people want to volunteer in order to help others. In his recent book *The Hidden Brain*,[9] Shankar Vendantam discusses brain research that indicates the human brain is structured to focus on the plight of individuals rather than groups. Many aid organizations have found that fundraising is more effective when it features individuals who are in need rather than groups in need.

Take advantage of the multimedia capability of the Internet. Volunteer testimonials communicate the rewards and benefits of volunteering and give the audience a sense of the people who volunteer. The People for Puget Sound posts its volunteer testimonials on YouTube. Ask volunteers to participate in producing testimonials, though they may need to sign formal release forms, and make sure that the testimonials are of consistent quality.

LESSONS LEARNED

- Volunteers are important to nonprofit organizations. As more people use the Internet as their primary information source, nonprofits must adapt their tactics to accommodate this change. This is especially true for younger volunteers who are very familiar with using the Internet.
- There are different types of volunteer roles. Volunteering offers several benefits. Individual choices related to volunteering are influenced by individual values and attitudes. Knowledgeable managers are better equipped to provide appropriate information for prospective volunteers who visit their Web sites.
- Although recruiting from the Web site is a nonpersonal method of recruitment, it allows the inclusion of volunteer testimonials, which can increase recruitment effectiveness.
- The effectiveness of online recruiting is affected by an appropriate and prompt response and follow-up from the nonprofit.

FURTHER READING

Books

The Nonprofit Guide to the Internet: How to Survive and Thrive by M. Johnston
Public Relations Online: Lasting Concepts for Changing Media by T. Kelleher

Volunteers: How to Get Them, How to Keep Them by H. Little
To Lead Is to Serve: How to Attract Volunteers and Keep Them by S. McBee
The New Breed: Understanding and Equipping the 21st Century Volunteer by J. McKee
The (Help!) I-Don't-Have-Enough-Time Guide to Volunteer Management by K. Noyes and S. Ellis
Volunteers Wanted by J. Rusin

Articles

Dhebar, B. 2008. A nonprofit manager's guide to online volunteering. *Nonprofit Management & Leadership* 18(4): 497–506.

Harm, A. 2009. "Recruiting and retaining volunteers: How organizations can overcome the challenges of working with volunteers." Available online at http://scholar.simmons.edu/handle/10090/8217.

Haski-Leventhal, D. 2009. "Group processes and volunteering: Using groups to enhance volunteerism." *Administration in Social Work* 33(1): 61–80.

Karl, K. 2008. "Give them something to smile about: A marketing strategy for recruiting and retaining volunteers." *Journal of Nonprofit & Public Sector Marketing* 20(1): 71–96.

Merrill, M. 2006. "Global trends and the challenges for volunteering." *The International Journal of Volunteer Administration* 24(1): 9–14.

Shields, P. 2009. "Young adult volunteers: Recruitment appeals and other marketing considerations." *Journal of Nonprofit & Public Sector Marketing* 21(2): 139–159.

Tang, F. 2008. "Involvement in voluntary organizations: How older adults access volunteer roles?" *Journal of Gerontological Social Work* 51(3): 210–227.

NOTES

1. www.servicelearning.org/what-service-learning
2. www.communityservicelearning.ca/en/
3. www.do-it.org.uk/magazine/features/virtualvolunteering
4. www.aarpmagazine.org/lifestyle/virtual_volunteering_resource_guide.html
5. www.ala.org/ala/mgrps/divs/ascla/asclaprotools/accessibilitytipsheets/tipsheets/9%20Volunteers%20with%20di.pdf
6. www.utexas.edu/lbj/rgk/serviceleader/virtual/working.php
7. Katheryn Wiedman Heidrich, *Lifestyles of Volunteers: A Market Segmentation Study* (Ann Arbor, MI: UMI Dissertation Information Services, 1998).
8. For more details on the benefits and considerations of volunteers, see chapter 13 of Gary Grobman, *The Nonprofit Handbook: Everything You Need to Know to Start and Run Your Nonprofit Organization* (Harrisburg, PA: White Hat Communications, 2002).
9. S. Vendantam, *The Hidden Brain* (New York: Spiegel & Grau, 2010).

CHAPTER 8

Online Advocacy and Activism

"Compelling people to take action and decision-makers to take notice can be a long and difficult journey. The Internet changes some of the rules of traditional advocacy work, but a strong campaign plan and a complement of offline activities are still required to achieve long-term wins."

—www.communitybandwidth.ca

CHAPTER OVERVIEW

Online activism is a rapidly emerging area of activity and deserves a general description. Then we will discuss the appropriate role of e-advocacy in furthering an organization's mission. We will provide an overview of online tools that are frequently used by activists groups. A discussion will follow that adds to the reader's understanding of e-activism tactics. Our goal is to help the reader better understand how to use online activism tools more effectively. These concepts will prove useful to all nonprofit managers who desire to reach and engage individuals to take action.

ONLINE ACTIVISM IMPROVES TRANSPARENCY IN U.K. GOVERNMENT

Early in 2009, there was a controversy in U.K. politics that attracted great media attention. Members of Parliament (MPs) in the U.K. wanted to exempt their expenses from the Freedom of Information Act. This would effectively shield from public scrutiny how MPs used their allotted public funding.

MP's efforts to exempt themselves was countered and overcome by a massive public outcry developed largely from an e-advocacy group, mySociety.org, which generated grassroots support. Net-based activists, using online tools like social networks and e-mail, initiated an e-campaign that soon became viral, attracting coverage of traditional media, and grew into a tidal wave of citizen involvement directed at their MPs. After the storm of protests, the legislative attempt was withdrawn.

THE GROWTH OF ONLINE ADVOCACY

The development of the Internet and related technologies has been a catalyst for civic engagement in democratic societies. However, this trend may apply mostly to national political issues rather than local political issues. Historically, activist organizations had to wait for the traditional news media to cover their causes in order to spread their messages. Internet technologies, such as social media, help empower ordinary people to spread the message themselves. This has helped reduce the dependency of activist groups on the traditional news media.

We use the terms *online activism* and *online advocacy* interchangeably. When we use these terms, we are referring to online tactics individuals and organizations use to work toward social change or a change in public or government policy. These tactics are aimed at building grassroots support for a cause, media relations, and lobbying government officials.

The Internet offers several advantages. It's available to a good proportion of the population, especially when you consider the proportion of the population with mobile access. It's convenient and easy to use. It allows for rapid, inexpensive communication. It is pervasive, especially for younger people. It allows for individuals to network for collaboration. A few important tools of online activists are e-mail, Web sites, e-newsletters, and mobile telephone applications.

In the U.S., the volume of e-mail members of Congress receive has increased by nearly 300 percent in the last ten years to more than 200 million messages a year.[1] About 90 percent of communications sent to Congress is now in the form of e-mail. The proportion of Americans who are contacting Congress has increased 18 percent since 2004, representing 44 percent of the voting age population (approximately 100 million adults). More than 80 percent of individuals sending their Congressional representatives e-mail were prompted to do so by an interest group.[2]

Activists face challenges in furthering their causes. They must educate people, inspire them to take action, let them know what they can do to get active, and then give them the tools to make real, sustained change. Some examples of the tools they use are:

- Send e-mails to government officials
- Print out flyers and other online materials and distribute locally
- Provide resources for their members, such as having research available on issues and votes of legislators
- Administer online forums and Web chats
- Encourage members to use information to write articles, opinion editorials (op-eds), and letters to the editor in their local newspapers

AN INTEGRATED STRATEGY WORKS BEST

Activist groups will find that the most effective strategy is one that combines both the communication power of the Internet with the interpersonal influence of face-to-face discourse. For example, MoveOn.org has found that it is easy for politicians to ignore mass-generated e-mails, but difficult to ignore a petition when presented in person. MoveOn.org has found that a holistic, integrated approach works best.[3] For advocacy to be effective, it must be done in an integrated manner. In the online realm, this implies that tactics using e-mails, Web sites, and e-newsletters must work together using a focused message strategy. Integration also requires online tactics to reinforce offline tactics. Offline tactics include telephone calls to government officials, personal visits to their offices, editorials in newspapers, and so forth. The combined, integrated use of offline and online tactics has a greater effect than either could achieve alone.

Online activism should work in concert with real-life, on-the-ground activism. Facebook, WordPress, Twitter, and Flickr are useful in building relationships, helping essential resources to be found, and enabling news and ideas to be shared easily. Technology is a means of making traditional techniques more impactful.

It is important to understand that some technologies work better depending upon the objective. Net Action (www.netaction.org) is an organization that trains activists to use technology more effectively. In its Virtual Activist Training guide, it explains that Web sites are good to present an overall argument for the cause. It is like an "address" where the information resides. E-mail, however, is more like a phone call and is good for engaging people into action for a specific event. To that end, it is important to determine the objective to be accomplished and the best use of technology to achieve it.

ETHICS IN ONLINE ACTIVISM

The Independent Sector has developed a model code of ethics for nonprofit organizations.[4] Ethical codes typically include a statement of the organization's values, a description of how the organization is accountable to its stakeholders, and a statement of the professional conduct of its employees. Online activists have some special considerations in addition to those applicable by all nonprofits.

For example, online advocacy organizations should make sure that all their activities are related to their respective missions. Online activists will have opportunities to engage in tactics that help increase the number of individuals in their supporter networks or that help raise funds. However, if opportunities to increase the supporter base or increase fund-raising are not effective in helping citizens to more effectively work together for social change, then they should be reconsidered.

As an example, an organization could encourage people to be added to its list of supporters by encouraging them to send a politician a form e-mail message through the organization's Web site, knowing that this politician ignores bulk messages coming from activist groups. The problem is that the organization knows the tactic is ineffective, but does it anyway because it will help add to its list of supporters. This is unethical because supporters get the mistaken impression that their participation will reach the politician. The organization, instead, should inform supporters that the politician will only read personal letters sent from constituents within the politician's geographic district and, therefore, encourage supporters from the relevant districts to write letters.

The guiding principle for an activist organization is that, when it asks supporters to take action, that action must be connected to the mission in a meaningful way. The prior example violates this principle because the requested action is ineffective since the politician does not read the e-mails and because the organization knows this but requests the action in order to increase the numbers of individuals on its house list.[5]

If the organization has a mission-driven focus, it will be more effective and have greater integrity. Therefore, activities that are not specifically related to making the policy change or social change should be avoided.

DEVELOPING RELATIONSHIPS

Changing public policy is the result of coordinated citizen action. Advocacy groups must gain support for their causes from a variety of constituencies in order to be effective. However, they typically have fewer financial resources than corporations and corporate-funded organizations, and often find it challenging to disseminate their messages.[6] Developing relationships with like-minded individuals is one of the most important determinants of advocacy success.

Grassroots Activism

Grassroots activism consists of a group of people organizing for a cause in which they believe. Online grassroots activism helps to give citizens more power to work collaboratively in making social change.

Activists rely on growing grassroots support from citizens. Individual citizens have little power, but working together, they can change their society. Online technologies allow citizens to exchange information easily and find other, likeminded individuals.

By communicating with the organization's members regularly, advocacy groups learn as much as possible about members' motivations and interests. They use this knowledge to communicate to members in a meaningful and relevant manner, which increases participation and loyalty. One method of doing this is by soliciting e-mail addresses of Web site visitors in order to send them periodic updates on the organization's activities. Having an RSS feed to which visitors can subscribe is another effective way of staying in touch with supporters.

Successful advocacy campaigns are viral, meaning that the grassroots community is grown by member-to-member discourse. The organization should encourage its members to send messages to their friends. Many activist

> Chapter Insight: Grassroots in Politics
>
> In certain cases, the Internet can be used to have a transformative effect on grassroots advocacy. In the U.S., for example, Howard Dean managed a political campaign for the presidency of the U.S. In less than twelve months, the Dean Campaign built an online community of supporters numbering more than 650,000. Although he did not win the election, Dean was the first candidate to successfully use online advocacy tactics to build a major base of support and to raise substantial sums of money.
>
> Barack Obama's presidential campaign in 2008 was in part successful due to the masterful use of online activism tactics to build a grassroots base of support, and activating grassroots supporters to become on-the-ground volunteers. The Obama campaign was very successful in motivating and communicating with supporters through mass text messaging—major announcements were first sent to supporters through text messaging prior to press releases. This helped supporters to feel like insiders and part of the campaign rather than spectators. The Obama campaign was also very successful in reaching out to younger voters by communicating to them using online channels.

organizations that effectively encourage their members to recruit others find that about 10 percent of members taking action during a campaign are new members. New members are helpful in future campaigns, they help replace former members who have become inactive and are a resource for donations and volunteering.[7]

To become viral, an advocacy organization needs to successfully promote its cause. The first step in promotion is making sure that the organization is a resource for information on its central issue. The advocacy organization that has the best organized, most easily accessed, and most complete source of information on the issue will attract the vast majority of visitors interested in the issue. The Web site that becomes the definitive site for a specific issue will have its Web site's link placed on other related sites.

Once the organization has rich and meaningful content on its Web site, it should submit its site to the major search engines, like Google, Yahoo, and MSN. Although the search engines will eventually scan the site to index its content, submitting it instead of waiting on the search engines' software to find the site will allow this to happen much quicker. It is also useful to submit pages on the Web site that relate to specific issues. Finally, when making substantive updates on the organization's Web site, it is a good idea to submit it to the major search engines so that the Web site will be indexed with the new information.

In order to give visitors to the Web site an incentive to return, the content must be updated periodically in order to be current and dynamic. Developing podcasts and video segments are a good way to give visitors fresh content that can educate and that they can use. Be sure to let people know that the information on the site is being maintained. Highlight new material, perhaps by having a "What's New" section on the front page. It is also advisable to allow visitors to comment on content, perhaps using blogs. Visitors are interested in reading the comments of others, expressing their own views, and reading others' reactions to their own comments.

Experts who can write columns are useful in putting new content on the Web site. Online editions of major newspapers use this technique effectively by promoting their regular columnists and featuring their columns on regular days.

Government

Relationships with officials are important in helping the activist group further its cause. If a politician cares about a specific cause, she will want to have a relationship with the activist community. Politicians who care about the organization's issue can be important champions who can attract attention to the cause.

Most officials, whether or not they care about a cause, do care about their relationships with their own constituents and supporters. The area in which an activist organization can be most effective is in encouraging its members to communicate with their elected officials in support of the cause. Politicians may ignore communications from activist organizations or individuals who are not their constituents. However, they are less likely to ignore communication from individuals who are eligible to vote for them. This is especially true as the number of constituents supporting a cause increases.

Activist organizations can most effectively influence a politician by developing a grassroots movement within the politician's geographical constituency. Members in that area can send the politician messages that voice their advocacy of the cause, and, as previously stated, it is most effective for activists to send e-mails in their own words (instead of a form letter), although the organization can suggest talking points. The effectiveness of sending e-mail messages to political leaders is greatly enhanced by having members place phone calls with their government leaders, meeting with them in person, talking with them at events, or sending opinion articles to newspapers in the politicians' district.

Media

Gaining traditional media coverage is often a goal for many activist organizations. This includes coverage in newspapers and on network and cable television, as well as coverage in the major blogs. In order to be effective, an activist organization should use a variety of pathways for promoting its mission and attracting attention to its Web site. Communications from the organization should contain its Web site address. Disseminating press releases helps get the organization's message out and have maximum impact when sent directly to journalists. Additionally, online press releases can be distributed through gateway sites, such as PR Newswire or PRWeb, which can be captured by news aggregating sites like Google News. While dealing effectively with the media is covered in greater depth in chapter 9, some points are worth discussing below.

Journalists are bombarded with quantities of information. Therefore, it is important to write concisely and with facts. As mentioned previously, having the definitive Web site on a specific issue allows reporters a location to use for more detailed information with press releases, fact sheets, and reports organized by topic and date. There should be easy-to-find links to advocacy issues. The section should allow journalists to add their e-mail addresses to a list for future press releases. Because most busy journalists use smartphones, they receive much of their e-mail as text messages. Keep e-mail messages brief and direct recipients to the Web site for the complete version, if interested. Finally, make sure to provide contact information that reporters can use for follow-up questions.

When representatives of the activist organization give speeches and make presentations, they should be recorded as podcasts. If these speeches are properly sorted on the Web site, interested persons can find them easily. Links to recent speeches should be highlighted on the front page.

Media alerts are an excellent means of sending summary news releases to members of the media to allow them to efficiently determine if developing a story on your news release is of interest to their audiences. A media alert is a memo-style announcement that provides basic information to the press about an event and its details. Media alerts are written so that reporters can promptly understand the essentials. Only essential information is included in the alert, which ends with contact details for the person with whom to communicate for further information.[8]

InvisiblePeople.tv was an effort to get people to change their perceptions about homeless citizens in America. The movement started small and gained visibility on mainstream media platforms when Mark Horvath embarked upon a road trip (in a borrowed Ford) across the U.S., chronicling the plight of the homeless. His journey has been covered in the *Los Angeles Times* and on CNN, Seattle-NBC, Detroit-ABC, and Albuquerque-NBC, as well as several social-media sites. The Web site features these stories, along with links to other social-media connections like YouTube, Facebook, Flickr, MySpace, and Twitter.

Collaborating with Other Advocacy Groups

Building coalitions with other advocacy groups concerned with the same or a similar issue can bring greater public attention to the cause and help motivate action for change.[9] The "Stop AETA" campaign is a recent example of how a lack of coalition-building can impede the desired change. In October 2005, the U.S. Congress was considering the Animal Enterprise Terrorism Act (AETA). AETA was the result of successful industry lobbying attempting to prevent animal rights protestors from engaging in activism opposing industry.

Opponents of the proposed law worried that legal, non-violent activism would be categorized as terrorism and be punished severely. More than 250 different organizations opposed the proposed law. Unfortunately, their efforts failed and the law was passed with overwhelming support in Congress. Professors Richard Waters and Meredith Lord analyzed the activities of these organizations and concluded that their inability to stop this industry-protective law cloaked under the fear of terrorism was the result of the groups failing to work together as an effective coalition.[10]

Professors Waters and Lord recommend that activist organizations focus on building and maintaining relationships with similar organizations for collaboration and, ultimately, success. Based largely on the work of Professor Linda Childers Hon of the University of Florida and Professor James E. Grunig of the University of Maryland,[11] Waters and Lord's relationship strategies include access, assurances, networking, openness, positivity, and sharing of tasks. Each strategy will be discussed below.

Access refers to ensuring that collaborating groups have the ability to quickly contact key decision-makers in each collaborating organization. Partners must be willing to engage in dialog regarding complaints or questions. Promptly responding to e-mail messages or being easily reached for a telephone conversation enhances access among collaborating groups.

Assurances refers to building a culture among collaborating groups that communicates that each group's concerns are valid and that collaborating groups are committed to maintaining the collaborative relationship. Groups can allow members of theirs and partnering organizations to submit their concerns on their Web sites through feedback forms. Web sites should inform visitors that the organizations will not sell or spam their e-mail addresses.

For the efforts of collaborating activist groups to be productive, they must *network* effectively. Effective networking is established through the number and quality of contacts among members of the collaborating groups. Collaborating groups can feature their network on their Web sites by communicating that they are part of a network, working together for change, and featuring links of collaborating organizations.

Openness refers to collaborating organizations directly discussing their relationships, both the nature of the relationships and how to make them more productive. Openness also refers to the free disclosure of thoughts and feelings among members across the groups. Greater disclosure enhances trust.

Positivity refers to efforts of collaborating organizations to make their interactions pleasant for participants. This implies that the organizations are working toward making the relationships more enjoyable for collaborating partners. Organizations should aim for their interactions to be unconditionally constructive. One dimension of positivity is the ease of use of organizational Web sites. This can be achieved by ensuring that navigation is easy, including a sitemap, and making a search engine available. For more information on improving Web sites, please refer to chapter 3.

Sharing of tasks implies that when decisions are made that impact multiple organizations, responsibilities pertaining to those decisions are equally shared. Collaborating organizations jointly solve problems. Through the use of online technologies, collaborating organizations can encourage members to become involved in advancing their message.

A REVIEW OF TOOLS FOR ONLINE ACTIVISM

In this discussion, we will present the tools that are available for online activist to use. Colin Delany,[12] of epolitics.com, has written extensively on online tools for political campaigns and much of this information also applies to e-activism. The mix of tools online advocates use will vary, depending on their needs and expertise. The following information presents a brief description and examples of each tool. Chapter 5 presents in detail how nonprofit organizations can develop more effective tools. The following sections discuss how these tools might be specialized for online activism.

Action Alerts

The e-mail action alert is one of the primary tools for activist organizations. They are typically used in conjunction with issue campaigns with clear goals (e.g., repeal healthcare reform; save the Trinity project). For example, the American Civil Liberties Union (ACLU) sends out action alerts on many of their key topics. The effective action alert typically has dedicated e-mail address for action alerts, recipients in the blind-copy field, a subject line that identifies the alert, an expiration date for action, clear directions for action, contact information, talking points (if necessary), a brief background of the issue, Web site information, and subscription information.[13]

> **Chapter Insight: Building Action Alerts**
>
> Net Action describes several issues to consider regarding e-mail action alerts:[14]
>
> - Make sure readers know who sent the action alert (identify the organization early on)
> - Make sure readers know how to contact the organization through e-mail, Web site and social media
> - Make sure your subject line is compelling to get the e-mail opened
> - Make sure to include a date that the alert is distributed and when action is needed
> - Make sure to summarize key points and keep it short and simple
> - Make sure to outline what action is required of the reader (petition, calls, e-mails, attendance)

Because the organization's supporters are so important, it must consider the appropriate frequency of e-mail messages to its supporters. Sending too few messages lets supporters drift away. Too many messages annoy supporters and may motivate them to unsubscribe to the list. Two or three messages each month is about the right frequency. Regardless of the frequency, some list members will leave. The organization will want to track the number of defecting list members while implementing tactics to attract new list members. The organization should notice when the number of list members who leave increases and try to discern the cause.

Some online trends are of concern to online activists. Spam blockers on e-mail software may inadvertently filter an activist's message to a supporter. Many people subscribe to multiple groups and may be inundated with messages, ignoring many. Also, younger individuals are using e-mail less than their older counterparts, preferring instead instant messaging social networking sites like MySpace and Facebook or text messages sent to their mobile phones. This is important to consider if the activist organization wants to reach younger people.

Blogs and Microblogs

Online activist blogs work best for organizations with a strong policy side and a good stream of content or with a blogger having a strong personality. Online activists should also monitor other blog sites to detect when someone has posted a commentary on their key issues. Issue monitoring is easily performed through specialized search engines (like Technorati) that search user-generated media, link blogs, by tag or keyword. Online activists can use such a service to make sure they are participating in discussions on issues with which they are involved.

Online activist Web sites and blog sites may find that offering RSS feeds is an effective way to keep supporters informed. RSS feeds enable interested persons to receive notices of updated content, keeping current on information disseminated by the activist organization. If the activist organization is involved in more than one cause or issue, it ought to have separate RSS feeds for each issue in order to allow individuals to subscribe only to the issue of interest.

Social Networks

A social-networking site is a Web site on which individuals and organizations set up profile pages containing basic information about themselves, and then link to other people's pages on the social network site. Facebook, one of the more popular social networking sites has about 350 million people with profile pages.[15] MySpace, another popular site, has almost 264 million members.[16] Social networks provide a means for people to meet and communicate.

Social networking sites, like Facebook, allow visitors to search for people by name, keyword, location, and so forth. Once a visitor has found someone in whom she is interested, she can request that person to "become her friend," which is a request to link to that person's profile page. When an individual logs on to

> **Chapter Insight: Activists use Facebook in Egypt**
>
> Facebook is the third most visited Web site in Egypt, after the search engines Google and Yahoo. About one million Egyptians—about 11 percent of the population—use Facebook.
>
> Egyptians are using Facebook to find likeminded citizens, communicate, and coordinate activities. Although political protests are suppressed in Egypt, small groups are using Facebook to organize and protest corruption. For example, Facebook was used to coordinate a nationwide shopping boycott in April 2008 as a way to support striking workers who were protesting subsistence wages. The movement grew from an idea to 40,000 supporters in one month. The government was surprised by the large amount of support generated using Facebook and was unsure how to quell dissent. The government, shortly before a planned protest on May 4, agreed to a wage increase. Unfortunately, a few days later, price increases were announced by the government, which offset the benefits of wage increases.[17]

her profile page, she will see any postings made by individuals with whom she has linked (her friends). She can send a general message to all the individuals who have linked to her profile page or she can target individuals with messages.

Online activist groups can use social networking sites to raise funds, find and communicate with supporters, increase the number of supporters for their causes, encourage members to engage in their own actions, organize events, and to promote the organizations' blogs and Web sites. Setting up a profile page for a group is relatively simple.[18] A number of activist groups are using social-networking sites. It would be a good practice for groups to have separate profile pages for their separate campaigns or issues, linking them together. It is also a good practice to provide a link for people to join the group's e-mail list. Beth Kanter, who specializes in helping nonprofit organizations learn how to use social media, is a good resource for readers who want to learn more about this tool.

As a useful example, the reader is encouraged to go to Facebook and perform a search for "Friends of the Earth Scotland," which is a small environmental activist group. One interesting feature of its Facebook profile is that it has a "notes" section which allows viewers to scan postings. Also, viewers can subscribe to an RSS feed to receive future notices.

The effectiveness of using social-network sites like Facebook depends upon attracting a relatively large number of individuals linking to the organization's page. Therefore, friends of your Facebook profile should be encouraged to recruit others. The organization's Web site and other communications should encourage visitors and readers to visit its profile page. The activist organization will then have the ability to send an action alert to a mass audience. The organization's friends should be encouraged to post the organization's action alert on their own profile pages.

As with all use of online applications, it is important to keep the social-networking pages' content current. If the organization lacks the ability to regularly update its content, then it would be better to have basic information on the site that does not get dated. It is also important to view the social-networking element of the activist organization's tool set as being important and worthy of attention. The organization should avoid assigning an inexperienced person to manage the social-network profile. Also, make sure the information disseminated from the profile is consistent with the organization's overall communications program.

Social Media

Social media refers to content that is produced and shared by people using facilitating social media Web sites (like YouTube and Flickr), rather than content provided by an individual or single organization. It has transformed the public from consumers of information to producers of information.[19] YouTube, Flickr, and Wikipedia are a few of the most popular social-media sites. And social media can take various forms, such as Internet forums and podcasts.

Social media is a useful tool in various contexts. It is useful for quickly and efficiently disseminating the organization's message. Social media is useful for distributing the organization's message when barriers prevent other forms of communication. Some governments censor the media. Sometimes, corporate-owned media ignore messages not in the interests of owners or advertisers. In these cases, social media is useful for bypassing the mainstream media and still succeeding in propagating the message. Some authoritative governments filter undesired content from the Internet. In this case, the activist can use text messaging to bypass Internet barriers.[20]

Activist groups can encourage members to place content on YouTube, which can potentially attract a great deal of attention. Activist groups can also allow its Web site to support user-generated content. User-generated content allows supporters to take action. It also allows for creative individuals to produce more content than would be possible just using paid staff. Supporters can give testimonies of their own personal stories as online presentations and can give energy to the organization's campaign. As a cautionary note, however, the organization should monitor user-generated content that is added to its Web site. It is inevitable that someone will put inappropriate content, or malicious code, on the Web site, and the organization needs to be ready to detect unsuitable content and remove it.

Video and Animation

Because of the increasing availability of high-speed Internet connections and the growth of social-media Web sites that accept user-generated video clips, the use of video by individuals has soared in recent years. With inexpensive equipment and software readily available, it has become quite easy for individuals to produce and post their own videos online. Social-media Web sites like YouTube have made user-generated videos a more effective tool.

A video presentation can more effectively make an emotional connection with an audience that would be much more difficult with just static text and pictures on a Web site. Just take a look at a few of the compelling videos on InvisiblePeople.tv and it is easy to see the power of video and animation to tell stories. A good video can make a complex issue more easily understood. Green-Speak.tv is aware of the potential effectiveness of video and exists to help environmental groups to use Web videos.[21] Activist groups can post video clips on their own Web sites, blogs, or Facebook pages. It is useful to post a video on YouTube, and then give the organization's Web site the capability to embed the video on the Web site without leaving to visit the YouTube site.[22] Finally, the organization should promote its videos through its blog, e-mailing, and other communication channels in order to attract an audience to the videos.

Text Messaging

Text messaging is the most used data application on earth, with 2.4 billion active users. About 74 percent of all mobile phones send and receive text messages. Text messaging is useful for individual-to-individual communication, in which activists can contact each other. Test messaging can also be used in an organization-to-group format, in which the organization can send a common text message to its supporters for which it has mobile phone numbers (3Jam is an example of a company that offers this service).

In the 2008 U.S. presidential campaign, Barack Obama's campaign used text messaging to send major announcements to supporters (donors and volunteers) prior to press releases. For example, Obama sent a text message to his supporters to announce Joe Biden as his running mate. Since most elections are won by a relatively small margin, Obama's ability to connect with supporters was one advantage he used.

Text messaging technology allows the organization to communicate promptly with supporters. It also allows the organization to conduct simple surveys, send reminder notices to supporters by geographic or postal zones, and showcase special events. Twitter has become a very popular application that offers a social-networking or micro-blogging service using text messaging technology. Sending messages from the Web site to mobile phones may incur a charge to the mobile phone owner.

Twitter and similar tools must be used appropriately to be effective. For example, former U.S. vice-presidential nominee Sarah Palin attempted to bypass the media and communicate directly with supporters using Twitter. Ironically, her initial tweets were perceived to be incoherent, making her use of Twitter a non-flattering story in the mainstream media and on talk shows.[23]

One of the most widely reported examples of the effective use of mobile phones to manage protest demonstrations was the series of protests surrounding the 1999 World Trade Organization meetings in Seattle. Many protestors brought their mobile phones to the protest. The phones were used to coordinate demonstrations. Protestors could react to changes in the protest plan quickly, and police were not able to monitor conversations between protest leaders and protestors.[24]

LESSONS LEARNED

- Although activist organizations are a special category of nonprofit organizations, many of the techniques discussed in this chapter can and should be adopted by other types of nonprofit organizations.
- The goals of online activism are to build grassroots support for an issue and to mobilize supporters in order to effect social change.

FURTHER READING

Blogging

Blogging for Dummies, 2nd Ed. by Susannah Gardner and Shane Birley
The Huffington Post Complete Guide to Blogging by the Editors of the Huffington Post

Social Networking

Groundswell: Winning in a World Transformed by Social Technologies by Josh Bernoff
Here Comes Everybody: The Power of Organizing Without Organizations by Clay Shirky
Building Social Web Applications: Establishing Community at the Heart of Your Site by Gavin Bell
Facebook: The Missing Manual by E. Vander Veer

Text Messaging

Always On: Language in an Online and Mobile World by Naomi S. Baron
Text Messaging Survival Guide by Evie Shoeman and Jack Showman
Twitter for Dummies by Laura Fitton, Michael Gruen, and Leslie Poston
Everything Twitter—From Novice to Expert: The Unofficial Guide to Everything Twitter by Monica Jones and Steve Soho

Online Advertising

The Online Advertising Playbook: Proven Strategies and Tested Tactics from the Advertising Research Foundation by Joe Plummer, Steve Rappaport, Taddy Hall, and Robert Barocci
The Complete Guide to Google Advertising: Including Tips, Tricks, & Strategies to Create a Winning Advertising Plan by Bruce C. Brown

NOTES

1. www.cmfweb.org/index.php?Itemid=&id=59&option=com_content&task=view
2. Brad Fitch and Kathy Goldschmidt, *Communicating with Congress: How Capitol Hill Is Coping with the Surge in Citizen Advocacy* (Washington, D.C.: Congressional Management Foundation, 2005), www.cmfweb.org.
3. Charles Lenchner, *Mission Over Membership in Online Advocacy* (NTEN, 2008), www.nten.org.
4. www.independentsector.org/members/code_main.html
5. www2.democracyinaction.org/blog/90
6. Richard D. Waters and Meredith Lord, "Examining how advocacy groups build relationships on the Internet," *International Journal of Nonprofit & Voluntary Sector Marketing* 14(3) (2009): 231-241.
7. Vinay Bhagat, "Online advocacy: How online constituent relationship management is transforming the way nonprofits reach, motivate, and retain supporters" (On Philanthropy, May 6, 2005), www.onphilanthropy.com.
8. Sandra L. Beckwith, *Publicity for Nonprofits* (Chicago: Kaplan, 2006).
9. P.A. Sabatier, *Theories of the Policy Process*. (Boulder, CO: Westview Press, 2007).
10. See endnote 7.
11. Linda Childers Hon and James Grunig, "Conceptual differences in public relations and marketing: The case of health-care organizations," *Public Relations Review* 17(3): 257–278.
12. Colin Delany, "Online Politics 101," (2008), available online at www.epolitics.com.
13. Using the Internet for Outreach and Organizing: A Virtual Activist Training Reader, www.netaction.org.
14. The Virtual Activist: A Training Course, www.netaction.org.
15. http://blog.facebook.com/blog.php?post=106860717130
16. http://www.alexa.com/data/details/main/myspace.com
17. David Wolman, "Cairo activists use Facebook to rattle regime," *Wired Magazine* 16(11), (October 20, 2008), www.wired.com.
18. http://mashable.com/2009/09/22/facebook-pages-guide/
19. http://en.wikipedia.org/wiki/Social_media
20. New Tactics in Human Rights (2009), http://www.newtactics.org/en/blog/samirnassar/uses-social-media-activists.
21. http://greenspeaktv.blogspot.com/2009/06/awesome-activist-animation-campaign.html
22. See http://greenspeaktv.blogspot.com/2009/06/awesome-activist-animation-campaign.html for an example.
23. http://news.cnet.com/8301-17852_3-10299815-71.html
24. www.npaction.org/article/articleview/607/1/222

CHAPTER 9

Public Relations in a Digital World

"Social media refers back to the 'two-way' approach of PR that Ivy Lee discussed in his day. It's about listening and, in turn, engaging people on their level. It forces PR to stop broadcasting and start connecting. Monologue has given way to dialogue."
—Brian Solis, Principle of FutureWorks PR and blogger at PR 2.0[1]

CHAPTER OVERVIEW

The world of public relations has drastically changed in light of the Internet and Web 2.0. As such, PR practitioners (and those who handle PR internally for nonprofits) have many more tools in their arsenal to converse with stakeholders. In this chapter, we will work to understand how digital strategies help organizations build relationships with stakeholders. We will also focus on the roles of various stakeholders for nonprofit organizations and also develop a public relations audit to gauge how well an organization communicates with its stakeholders. This chapter also aims to understand the tools for media relations, employee and volunteer relations, community relations, donor and investor relations, regulators, and evaluators.

SAMARITAN'S FEET GETS MILEAGE FROM A STICKY IDEA

Lagos, Nigeria, native Emmanuel "Manny" Ohonme received his first pair of shoes at age nine and turned that inspiration into a humanitarian organization that has given shoes to kids who are too poor to buy their own. Samaritan's Feet (www.samaritansfeet.org) was founded in 2003 because of Ohonme's story. Years earlier, a Wisconsin stranger gave him his first pair of tennis shoes. As it turned out, Ohonme was a pretty good basketball player, and his talent earned him a scholarship at the University of North Dakota–Lake Region. As a result, he was determined to give kids the chance that he was given. "Manny wants to provide that voice for children who don't have a voice," said Samaritan's Feet director of marketing Todd Melloh.[2] There are more than 300 million kids worldwide who have no shoes because of poverty. Through partnerships with various corporations and individuals, Samaritan's Feet has started to turn that around.

In late 2007, Ohonme and Melloh hatched a unique idea after hearing poet Maya Angelou speak in New York. Melloh convinced basketball coach Ron Hunter to coach barefoot to honor the 40th anniversary of Dr. Martin Luther King Jr.'s death and collect 40,000 shoes for Samaritan's Feet. It worked. Not only did fans also go barefoot, but the event collected more than 110,000 pairs, including 15,000 pairs from Converse alone. News releases and media information was distributed with a nice dose of social media to get people talking. It was an effective strategy. The event was covered in the local and national press, and Hunter was interviewed on ESPN's *Mike and Mike in the Morning*. To date, the organization has been spotlighted on *USA Today*, CNN, and ESPN, to name a few—all because of the "stickiness" of a great idea.

PUBLIC RELATIONS AND THE IMPORTANCE OF RELATIONSHIPS

Public relations has always been important to nonprofit organizations. It is about developing effective, mutually beneficial relationships between organizations and their target audiences, including the media, customers, employees, investors, community leaders and members, activist groups, and government agencies.[3] Public relations consists of strategies and tactics aimed at building those relationships with various stakeholders. One of the primary issues that makes PR different from advertising is that advertising is always paid for by an identified sponsor. That is not necessarily the case with public relations, as some PR efforts do not require paid sponsorship. For example, organizations don't pay for positive press coverage; however, this coverage often comes as a result of relationship-building. As such, PR plays an even more important role to nonprofits.

New technology has made PR both easier and harder for organizations. While technology enables dissemination of information more effectively, it has also led to an explosion in the number of important outlets (e.g., news outlets, video services, and influential blogs).

While public relations has been around for more than a century, the shift toward relationship-building has occurred over the past twenty years. There are several roles for the public relations function within a nonprofit organization. The technician role of public relations includes writing, editing, taking photos and videos, handling communication production, running special events, and pitching stories to the media. These all focus on the implementation phase of the overall communication plan. The manager role of public relations focuses on the activities that help identify and solve problems. They advise other managers about communication needs and are responsible for broad organizational results. This includes defining the problem, suggesting options, and facilitating communication between organizations.[4] In some instances, a nonprofit organization will have someone on staff perform these functions. In other instances, organizations use outside consultants.

THE ROLE OF STAKEHOLDERS

Generally, audiences can be thought of as internal or external, although these are not mutually exclusive and will vary depending on the nonprofit organization. Typically, internal audiences are perceived to be more valuable since they include people who the organization serves (called end users or constituents), the employees and volunteers who keep the organization running, and the donors who provide resources for the nonprofit organization to carry out its mission. It is vital to understand how internal audience members perceive the organization for many reasons.

- End users or constituents must be aware of what the organization offers, buy in to their mission and vision, and know how to contact it when the need arises.
- Employees and volunteers must serve as advocates of the organization's brand image since in many cases they are the "face" of the brand and provide important brand touchpoints by doing what they do each and every day. Depending on the size of the organization, these employees and volunteers are the drivers of the mission.
- Donors need to be clear about the value that the nonprofit brand provides in order for them to feel they are getting a strong return on their investment.

Overall, internal audiences are typically more engaged with the nonprofit organization for some reason, typically a rather personal one. Because of this passion, it is important they are clear about the brand message.

External audiences, on the other hand, may or may not have any awareness of the nonprofit organization. Community members are the broadest external audience and are bombarded with thousands of marketing messages, including messages from other charities, each and every day. The media is considered one of the most important external audiences from a public relations perspective since they have the power to provide a forum for nonprofits to "tell their story" through television, print, and online. The government and foundations may also be key stakeholders if the nonprofit seeks funding through grants or governmental regulation. Obviously, good branding may be key to gaining access to foundation and government grant money and government partners.

Competitors and collaborators are important stakeholders who are also part of the external audience. Nonprofits are unique because, while there may be several organizations serving the same cause, there does tend to be a level of collaboration not seen in the for-profit world (which generally sees this dynamic as competitive). This means that competitive organizations may join together to benefit a shared mission. For example, if a large organization with a strong brand like Goodwill Industries moves into an area where a small community nonprofit also runs a donation center and resale shop, there is an opportunity and possible incentive to work together if both are perceived positively by the community (even though they are considered competitors for the same donations). Having a

Figure 9.1: The Role of Stakeholders

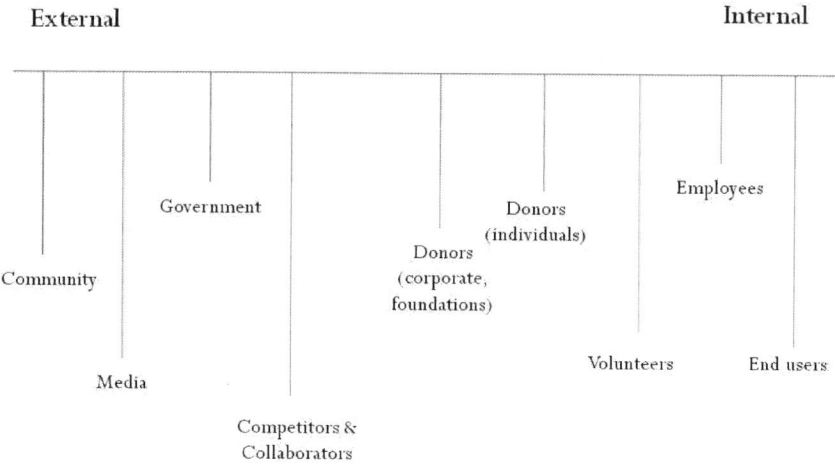

strong brand helps the nonprofit to attract strong partners for collaboration on programs and grants.

So while external audiences may not currently have the level of engagement of internal audiences, a good brand image and consistent brand message can serve as a roadmap for engagement.

DEVELOPING STAKEHOLDER INSIGHTS

One of the first things to understand regarding the importance of these various stakeholders is that they all have their own perceptions about the nonprofit brand, whether these perceptions are valid or not. In fact, the essence of the nonprofit brand is not the organization's view of itself but rather the stakeholders' response to and relationship with the organization. So it makes sense to gain a better understanding of what they think about the brand. It is important to understand each stakeholder's need and how to prioritize it within the larger mission. This research task can include questions regarding the awareness of the brand; perception of the brand from donors and non-donors, both in terms of objective and subjective measures; and how stakeholders view the nonprofit brand within the larger social sector of which it belongs.

Of course, marketers can use traditional research tools to gauge this awareness and perception. These include surveys (brand image surveys, donor satisfaction surveys, constituent satisfaction surveys, and general awareness surveys), focus groups, interviews with important groups (called key contacts or key informants), and comprehensive brand audits. Some of these can be facilitated online, which will be discussed in chapter 10. Managers can also use secondary research through the Internet, libraries, and databases, as well as specific organizations that house information for nonprofit organizations. However, as technology becomes more important to branding, it becomes clear that there are several ways to gain insights using digital tools, as well.

Listening counts for everything. Perhaps the most important thing that a nonprofit organization can do is to listen to its stakeholders. Luckily, burgeoning technology makes listening easy. Social networks, blogs, podcasts, and microblogs are excellent forums for conversations providing a cheaper and more reliable form of research. But culling these insights cannot be haphazard. Everything starts with systematic listening. Most of the tools to develop a systematic listening system are free (or relatively cheap), and many of these tools are highlighted in chapter 10.

According to Brian Solis, founder of FutureWorks and a blogger at PR 2.0, organizations who pay attention to the details—the dynamics and intricacies, the tone and nature of the dialogue—can realize a distinct difference between simply responding to a post and true engagement with stakeholders. He argues that the listening process needs to be more than searching keywords and responding to the conversations but rather attempting to engage in a true dialogue with key stakeholders. The goal should be higher than simply to communicate. "The type of listening I'm referring to here isn't simply identifying updates or threads tied to keywords in inject canned responses, generic questions, or disconnected updates based on the nature of the conversation," he says. "Listening requires a dedicated infrastructure and support system; essentially, the ability to not just hear something nor placate or acquiesce the emotions and concerns of real people, but the capacity and alacrity to adapt based on the information and insight that's absorbed."[5]

The PR Audit is essentially a broad-scale study that examines the internal and external audiences for a nonprofit organization and the relationship the organization has with these two segments. This is systematic and enables the organization to make decisions based on the results. Here are some major issues to consider when conducting a **PR audit**.

Important Stakeholders

One of the first actions is to determine who the important stakeholders are. Identify all of the internal and external audiences. While giving attention to them all is necessary, it is more important to pay careful attention to those engaged visitors who are advocates for the organization. One of the primary drivers of positive public relations is the power of word-of-mouth. Word-of-mouth is generated by "influentials."[6] These are people (typically one in ten) who influence what everyone else does, especially as related to music, fashion, politics, and pop culture. These influentials can be part of a formal evangelism program (like boards of advisors or volunteer groups) or they can be bloggers or others within the community who, for whatever reason, have a special place in their hearts for the organization and are willing to spread the word.

The Organization's Reputation with Stakeholders

Once these stakeholders are identified, it is important to assess the organization's reputation with them. After all, perception is reality, and thus it is important to find out what these perceptions are all about. Constituents may be unaware of new programs being offered by a nonprofit. Donors of an organization may be under the impression that a nonprofit is financially in good shape and are shocked to find out there are major gaps in the funding model. Organizations can use some of the research tools in this book to gain an understanding of relevant groups.

Issues of Concern to Stakeholders

Likewise, each of these stakeholders will have different issues of concern. Some may be constituents who are concerned about services and programs. The Samaritan House (www.samaritanhouse.org) is an organization that helps people who are HIV-positive. A cutback in services would be a major issue of concern to constituents who depend on these services. The Community Storehouse (www.communitystorehouse.org) is looking for a new location to house its resale shop and food pantry and the funding to get there. This would be a major issue of concern for board members. Overall, it is important to characterize these concerns and begin to develop a strategy on how to resolve these issues.

Power of Stakeholders

This is important and sometimes not as easy to research. The amount of power given to stakeholders depends on the organization. For example, health-related nonprofits that are heavily based on medical research, such as the American Heart Association, will have physicians and researchers as powerful stakeholders. The AHA relies (and funds) research on heart disease, and therefore this adherence to science does affect messaging to the larger public. On the other hand, many art museums and operas have artists and musicians as stakeholders, which influences their messaging, as well.

MEDIA RELATIONS

One of the most important external audiences is the media. While the influence of mass media has changed dramatically over the past few years, organizations still want to have a positive relationship with them. Local and regional media are especially important for small- and medium-sized nonprofit organizations. Traditional media outlets are still important players, despite waning viewership and readership. It is even more important to establish good relationships with local and regional reporters who can ultimately determine whether a nonprofit organization gets featured and influence how an organization is portrayed.

That said, the Internet has completely changed the way that organizations and consumers communicate. The same can be said for nonprofit organizations and their stakeholders. Indeed, the Internet (and social media) cannot even really be compared to television and print, which lack the ability for two-way communication. The Internet is far richer and more complex. Because of the ability for stakeholders to communicate with each other on social networks, blogs, and microblogs, organizations can lose control of the agenda. This makes most organizations uncomfortable, but it is a requirement given the popularity and ubiquity of social media. In order to influence the conversation—set the agenda—organizations will have to participate in the conversation.[7]

News Releases and Online Newsrooms

The primary staple for media relations professionals is the news release. This is essentially information written as a story that is sent out to the media. Most of the time, this has been the mainstream media, but that is changing. Regardless of whom you are talking to, whether the mainstream media or bloggers, there are a few things to keep in mind. Primarily, you want to make their job easier. Make sure that all necessary contact information is clear on the Web site so that reporters can reach the appropriate people. Additionally, some organizations have a special section on their Web site for the media (called a media room) that includes FAQs, fact sheets, company history, executive bios, important photos and video, links and news release archives. Also, consider getting information to journalists and bloggers through tweets or texts. Most professionals use these tools judiciously. But remember, not only journalists will visit your media room. Make sure that your information is updated, because the news release section is typically one of the most visited parts of any Web site.[8] And understand that when new releases are on your site, search-engine crawlers can find the content and index it so that it is easier to find. News releases are typically some of the first pages that are found in search results.

Media kits include a collection of news releases and advisories, fact sheets, brochures, photographs, contact information, and any other information important for media use. Putting this information online makes access by reporters that much easier. Make sure the kit is easy to download (such as a PDF format). Since news releases are a staple for media relations but now they are e-mailed, posted, or blogged about as opposed to faxed or mailed, it is vital to ensure that your news releases include tags for key words and social media tags in order to make it more accessible in digital formats. Ensure your sites are accessible on Technorati, Digg, and Delicious. Indeed, provide these links on the main Web site so that it is easy for any stakeholder to follow your organization.

Video news releases are short news packages that present the news item from the organization's viewpoint. Typically this lasts ninety seconds and is accompanied by B-roll material (background information). Multimedia news releases include an a little bit of everything—video, audio, photos, and text.

Indeed, the social-media release (SMR) is a relatively new tool pioneered by Edleman and SHIFT Communications.[9] According to Brian Solis, one of the main differences is that organizations don't e-mail a SMR to journalists; rather reporters discover it or are invited to view it. It is typically shared through social bookmarks or RSS. The standard template includes a headline, an introductory paragraph (and keywords), supporting facts, quotes, multimedia, RSS organization news, links to insert into multiple platforms (like Facebook, Twitter, or blog posts), links to news aggregators and communities in social bookmarks, and further information.[10] Last, some media relations professionals are using Twitter and other microblogging platforms to get their message out in a short format. Sometimes called the twitpitch, this does, at least for now, break through some of the press release clutter.

Rainforest Action Network (http://ran.org) has organized its press kit around the primary issues for which it advocates. Included is the contact information for the communications team. ASPCA (www.aspca.org) includes background information, facts, and programs in PDF format that make it easy for journalists (and other interested parties) to download quickly.

Consider distributing news releases through services to ensure that they are included on all major search engines. Some of these include Business Wire, Market Wire, GlobeNewswire, PR Newswire, and PRWeb. You can also purchase a basic news release coverage area in order to be included in online news services (including Google News). This is particularly useful for small- and medium-sized nonprofits that are geographically limited.

Chapter Insight: Journalists in the Online Press Room

The primary purpose of an online press room is to provide journalists with information. Many journalists go to an organization's Web site in order to find out how to reach the organization's public relations department. If the organization does not have a public relations department, then journalists need to know who to contact in the organization for information.

For a journalist on a deadline, not being able to quickly access the right person in an organization for information presents a problem. If an organization wants to make it easy for its information to be provided in the news media, being accessible is the first step.

Better online press rooms allow visitors to search for information using dates, keywords, and titles. Visitors should be able to search current documents as well as archived documents. Organizations should have position papers and statements to the press available in a variety of downloadable formats. The best online press rooms are designed with the needs of journalists in mind.

Table 9.1: Multimedia News Release Elements

Element	Details
News Release	Include all pertinent links; RSS enabled; search-engine optimized
Video	Broadcast quality (mpeg 2), Internet quality (Flash); post link on Web site
Mobile Content	Make sure it works with various platforms; consider developing iPhone apps
Podcast Release	Use RSS technology and search-engine optimization; include on iTunes
Photos	High-resolution (600 dpi) and low-resolution (72 dpi) at full size
Related Content (e.g., Twitter, Facebook, blogs)	Make sure content is sharable so that people can integrate social media

Leland Harden and Bob Heyman, *Digital Engagement* (New York: AMACOM, 2009).

With the explosion of outlets, media relations has taken on an added importance, especially by reaching smaller and more defined audiences. Some PR professionals believe that media relations will be done completely online in the future. The Internet allows an additional screen for a twenty-four-hour news cycle at networks like CNN, MSNBC, and Fox. Indeed, given that people catch up on the news at their desks or on their mobile devices, some of these Web sites can have more visitors than their television counterparts.

The New York City Coalition Against Hunger (www.nyccah.org) has a very well-organized and dynamic online news room that includes news releases with dates and titles, videos, public testimony and research among other issues. Another organization, Accion (www.accion.org), a microfinance organization dedicated to alleviating poverty, has included links to several major categories and made it easy to receive content from the organization.

Blogs

Technology has also added newer platforms such as blogs and podcasts. Some blogs are written by professional journalists, but most are written by "citizen journalists," or everyday people looking for a forum for their viewpoints. At this point, there are millions of blogs, according to Technorati, but most are not read. However, there are several blogs that have gained millions of followers. As such, it is important to locate influential bloggers from your community, in your sector, and in your region.

> ### Chapter Insight: Best Practices for Online Newsrooms
>
> In his book *The New Rules of Marketing and PR*, David Scott Meerman recommends some best practices for online newsrooms. Many of these principles are easily adapted to nonprofit organizations. First, start with a needs analysis to understand where an online newsroom fits into your overall digital strategy. Speak with journalists and bloggers to find out what types of information that they are looking for from nonprofit organizations. Second, optimize your news releases for browsing, since most visitors to the online newsroom will be browsing content. This includes everything from organizing news releases to designing easy and intuitive navigation. Additionally, make sure you optimize for search function by including key words. Third, include multimedia content, which is especially important for nonprofits since so much is told through visual stories. Fourth, include other background information, such as transformative stories to show how the nonprofit has helped people. Fifth, include valuable information—even if you are not sure it is valuable to journalists. For example, your organization may develop information on the return on investment for specific donors. Include that in your online media room, as well. Sixth, include information that is basic in case a writer is unfamiliar with your organization. Last, include a call to action by offering interviews.[11]

There are a few things to consider when courting bloggers. First, make sure you do your research about the blog content and the blogger. You can use Google Alerts or Google's Blog Search (or any other blog search engine) to find out what is being said about your organization or what is being said by bloggers in your area. An important issue to consider is that while the size of the audience does matter, the power of the blogger matters more. Second, don't jump right in. Take some time to read the posts (both good and bad) and find out more about who is commenting on the blogs. This will provide a good feel for

Table 9.2:   Top Blogs

1 Huffington Post	6 Lifehacker	11 Stuff White People Like	16 ReadWriteWeb	21 Joystiq
2 TechCrunch	7 Gizmodo	12 Official Google Blog	17 Seth's Blog	22 I Can Has Cheez Burger?
3 Engadget	8 Ars Technica	13 Gadling	18 Cinematical	23 TV Squad
4 Boing Boing	9 Smashing Magazine	14 TMZ	19 PostSecret	24 Daily Kos
5 Mashable!	10 BloggingStocks	15 ParentDish	20 Gawker	15 The Unofficial Apple Weblog

Technorati, www.technorati.com.

the blog content and positioning. Third, start small. Comment on a post first before embarking on a complete PR campaign with the blogger. Fourth, reach out to the blogger and provide quality content. Content is a key resource for all bloggers, and if your organization can be a good informational resource, it will provide more credibility. Last, consider developing a blog. This allows the organization to provide information on the cause (especially if you can get a larger perspective). For example, instead of concentrating on the school districts that your organization serves, instead act as a resource for all children in need in the area. This allows the organization to be a prime resource for information. Information on developing your own blog can be found in chapter 5. But be discerning about what you send to bloggers; they are not unbiased and may post their opinions with or without appropriately checking the facts.

CRISIS COMMUNICATION

A special subsection of media relations is crisis communication. Crisis communication involves using the media to preserve and strengthen the organization's long-term reputation when it is threatened.[12] With social-media tools, organizations can almost bypass the media and speak directly to stakeholders. But stakeholders can co-opt the conversation, as well. They can put up Web sites, blogs, and share their views on social networks. This affects search results, so it is important to engage with unhappy stakeholders. A few tips adapted from Rob Brown in his book *Public Relations and the Social Web* include: (1) identify and make contact with the unhappy stakeholder, (2) try to talk with them to resolve the problem, (3) try to assess the damage done to your image through blog alerts, or Google Analytics, and (4) determine how to participate with others. This last step is important to contain the damage to the nonprofit's brand image and allows one more way to engage with stakeholders.

Crisis can be anticipated and planned for by the organization. The key is to continue to build relationships with key stakeholders throughout a crisis situation. The crisis plan spells out how the entire organization will respond to a crisis (which can be scandal, management decision related, human errors, acts of God, or mechanical problems). Create the plan and make sure it is accessible by the crisis team. Technology can be useful here, as the plan can be stored on intranets. In addition, there are several tools, such as Basecamp and Google Docs, that can be used to communicate online in addition to e-mail and voice mail. Everything should be considered a crisis; think about the thousands of nonprofits that were forced to evacuate the Gulf Coast area during Hurricane Katrina. Determine who will speak for the organization. This will lead to a more cohesive and effective message as long as the spokesperson is credible.

Without going into detail regarding crisis communication, it is important to make sure to maintain trust and credibility, and social media can help with this. Talking directly to stakeholders through a variety of communication channels is important. Tailor each message to the audience—constituents, community leaders, donors, government—so there is less likelihood of confusion. Each stakeholder will require a different message. And opening up the lines of communication so that the public can ask questions and make comments is crucial. Blogs, Twitter, Facebook, and online communities all allow this two-way communication.[13]

COMMUNITY RELATIONS

The community at large is the broadest stakeholder and, as such, probably the hardest to reach. For some organizations, the sheer size of the geographical area makes this difficult (think of New York City, for example). The biggest issue about community relations is getting awareness for the nonprofit. Even in a small community, there are so many organizations competing for attention and donations. Let's consider just a few of the areas that require community support and attention.

The Mission

Creating awareness of who the nonprofit serves, the programs that are developed for constituents, and how to access these programs is paramount. However, it is equally important to understand that perhaps a vast majority of the community will never need the services that are provided. If this is the case, it is important to create a brand image that is credible. For example, if a nonprofit is serving kids in a particular community, that organization needs to become *the expert* on kids in that community. The United Way of Tarrant County conducts a community assessment regularly; as a result, they are seen as experts in research in the areas of healthcare and education for people living within Tarrant County. The organization then needs to demonstrate expertise through research (posted on the Web site), webinars, and other training and facts about the issue. This makes donating to a credible cause that much easier for people in the community.

The Financial Needs

Many organizations raise money through events such as runs or biking events, galas, auctions, and other parties. Organizations also raise money through annual giving and capital campaigns. These needs must be made apparent. As a result, nonprofits can develop microsites or special areas of the Web site to highlight events or projects.

Day-to-Day Communications

Some organizations need to be able to communicate with stakeholders quickly and effectively. Examples include schools that often need to get information out regarding anything from early dismissals to school lockdowns. Terry

Morawski is the assistant superintendent of communication and marketing for the Mansfield, Texas, independent school district (ISD). The ISD currently has more than 31,000 students in the cities of Arlington, Mansfield, and Grand Prairie. The fact that the district is spread out over three cities poses a major communication challenge. Traditional media does not have even coverage in this area. "Social media has allowed us to level the playing field," said Morawski. Having spent the last ten years in school public relations and stints with an arts nonprofit and a newspaper, Morawski and his team of five begin to dabble in social media after hearing a presentation from Geoff Livingston, a well-known social-media guru. "We had not wrapped our minds around the business applications of these tools yet," he said. But with a supportive superintendent and school board, Morawski's team has created some impactful uses of social media.

One tactic that is especially engaging is a blog for the school district. Superintendent Vernon Newsome and deputy superintendent Bob Morrison (now the current superintendent) traveled to China in the summer of 2008 on an educational trip and agreed to blog about the experience every day. Newsome added photos, and this enabled people in the community to get to know him on a new, more informal level. Morawski's team uses the blog to distribute information about the first day of school and new policies, to dispel rumors, and to create engagement (like when they asked parents to send in first-day-of-school photos to the Web site SmugMug). They don't have a regular blogging schedule but rather use the tool when it can be effective. They are open to positive and negative comments (although they do have to moderate some comments given the health, privacy, and legal requirements of a school district when it comes to protecting students and faculty). "We knew these conversations were going on . . . in the grocery stores, at the football fields. But now we can listen and participate in these conversations, as well," Morawski said. Right now, the Mansfield ISD is also using Twitter to announce weather-related school closings, for example, and is experimenting with Facebook. "It is a noninvasive way of talking to people that gets directly to them," Morawski said.

A NOTE ABOUT CREDIBILITY

Posting news stories and coverage on the Web site will build credibility. For example, the aforementioned Samaritan's Feet does a good job of posting video clips from the various news outlets that have covered the organization. This adds interest by using the principle of social proof. Visitors to the Web site can see that others have found out about the nonprofit and have found it interesting. This is great for gaining donors (one of the reasons why all good capital campaigns have a lead donor before going public). Additionally, there are several Web sites that evaluate nonprofits. These include the Better Business Bureau, Charity Navigator, and Guidestar to name just a few. If the organization has a positive review from any of these, post that information on the site. Whether nonprofits completely agree with the evaluation process, it does help new visitors since they have little background information. Last, there are ways to position the organization's executives and founders as experts in the field. Consider that Wendy Kopp (Teach for America) and Bill Milliken (Communities in Schools) are both positioned as experts in education. This can be achieved by providing a forum (through blogs, podcasts, and on-demand publishing) for nonprofit leaders to talk about the cause and the organization's programs.

Public relations in the digital world is not without its challenges. With the explosion of digital technology comes many new outlets and influencers. However, there is much more opportunity available, especially for nonprofit organizations. Most of these tools are free (or relatively inexpensive) and easy to use (except the time it takes to develop) and can be quite effective at increasing the involvement and engagement with relevant stakeholders.

> Conversation with the Pros: Emily Callahan, Vice President of Marketing, Susan G. Komen for the Cure
>
> Emily Callahan has rebranded an icon. As vice president of marketing at Susan G. Komen for the Cure (formerly the Susan G. Komen Breast Cancer Foundation), Callahan was instrumental in rebranding the leading breast cancer advocacy organization on its twenty-fifth birthday. On January 22, 2007, Susan G. Komen for the Cure was born with a new logo and new name with an ambitious pledge to invest another $1 billion in the next decade for breast cancer research—all aimed to realize the vision of eliminating breast cancer from the world.
>
> The idea began years ago with a charge to move from a well-respected breast cancer organization to *the icon* in the fight against breast cancer. A review of the brand images revealed a fragmented message: various fonts and colors, various programs—all without any unifying brand foundation. "Our brand research showed that the people who knew us, loved us," Callahan says. "But our research showed that even aided awareness of the Foundation was low. People did not understand if we were a race or a foundation or pink ribbons." This and the influx of competitors (many using similar colors and the pink ribbon) made for a cluttered competitive space. The goal of the new direction was to connect this fragmented branding into a compelling icon. However, given that the organization is divided into more than 100 local affiliates, all with their own marketing and branding efforts and local needs, the task was difficult.
>
> They have come a long way from the first Race for the Cure in the 1980s, when people were even uncomfortable saying the word "breast." But the organization needed to gain a greater awareness in order to get a bigger share of the donor wallet. Affiliates and other stakeholders were ready for a change. After extensive research, they opted to change their name to Komen

for the Cure (in part because the cure provided the link that reinforces the past and the future). They felt that "cure" allowed them to explore more brand touchpoints. It was the one word that had the greatest pull across the broadest base of audiences.

So how did they get this message out? "With the new overall logo, and the new logo for affiliates, we felt that this spoke to our heritage and to our future," Callahan says. Komen added a new race logo that is similar to the Komen signature as well as a T-shirt design. They created a new branding guideline to direct the rebranding effort. It was important to get internal buy-in, so they held an event at the Frontiers of Flight museum in Dallas and held a one and one-half day training session on the changes. Once the internal communication was handled, the organization turned its attention to external communication. This included webcasts, e-mail blasts, a move to a common URL for all affiliates, and online brand management tool called Komen Brand Central, which was an interactive way to access guidelines and assets. All collateral material was uploaded into this system. Several news outlets ran an AP-exclusive story about the rebranding efforts. Local affiliates were also able to generate coverage in their communities. The organization used tools such as online wallpaper and business cards, a new Web site, and a new microsite about the 25th anniversary, which was used for just that time period. The new microsite included a viral e-mail component and video messages. The organization ran traditional and online advertising, garnered major press attention, and conducted a satellite media tour. "The effort for rebranding was led through PR, and we examine the share of voice metric quite a bit," says Callahan. "We feel that now there is an emotional connection and greater engagement with the Komen brand." To date, one of the most important ways to engage stakeholders is through social media, namely Facebook and other social-networking sites. "Social media has been one of the most cost-effective things we do," Callahan says. "We are learning as we go."

LESSONS LEARNED

- Regardless of the use of digital technology, public relations is still and always will be about the importance of relationships with relevant stakeholders.
- Internal and external audiences are both important; however, internal audiences can be taken for granted. Try to use technology to continue to reach out to internal audiences and build relationships.
- There are several ways to gain insights into stakeholders using social media. Developing a good PR audit is a good way to understand the perceptions of your stakeholders.

- Social media can be especially effective for media relations. It is important to develop a system that works with traditional media outlets as well as social-media outlets. Consider reaching out to bloggers using social-media releases and Twitter, develop an organizational blog to tell your story, consider developing podcasts and vodcasts, develop a strategy to reach out to stakeholders via social networks like LinkedIn and Facebook.

FURTHER READING

PR 2.0: New Media, New Tools, New Audiences by Deirdre Breakenridge
New Rules of Marketing and PR by David Meerman Scott
The New Influencers by Paul Gillin
Mobilizing Generation 2.0: A Practical Guide to Using Web 2.0 by Ben Rigby

NOTES

1. Deirdre Breakenridge, *PR 2.0: New Media, New Tools, New Audiences* (Upper Saddle River, NJ: Pearson, 2008).
2. Interview with Todd Mellow, Director of Marketing, Samaritan's Feet, July 9, 2009.
3. Dan Lattimore, Otis Baskin, Suzette T. Heiman and Elizabeth L. Toth, *Public Relations: The Profession and the Practice, 2nd Ed.* (New York: McGraw Hill, 2007).
4. Ibid.
5. Brian Solis, "Unveiling the New Influencers," (PR 2.0, June 29, 2009), www.briansolis.com.
6. Ed Keller and Jon Berry, *The Influentials: One American in Ten Tells the Other Nine How to Vote, Where to Eat and What to Buy* (New York: The Free Press, 2003).
7. Rob Brown, *Public Relations and the Social Web: How to Use Social Media and Web 2.0 in Communications* (London: Kogan Page, 2009).
8. David Meerman Scott, *The New Rules of Marketing and PR: How to Use News Releases, Blogs, Podcasting, Viral Marketing and Online Media to Reach Buyers Directly* (Hoboken, NJ: Wiley, 2007).
9. Brown, *Public Relations and the Social Web*.
10. Ibid.
11. Ibid.
12. Lattimore, Baskin, Heiman, and Toth, *Public Relations*.
13. Ibid.

CHAPTER 10

Digital Insights and Research

"If you want to succeed, it's critical to gain insights about what consumers want, what they talk about when you're not in the room, and how they really behave. It's a judgment that needs no algorithm."
—Allen Adamson, author of *Brand Digital: Simple Ways Top Brands Succeed in the Digital World* and Managing Director, Landor Associates New York[1]

CHAPTER OVERVIEW

Research and evaluation is pervasive in the world of branding, but oftentimes, the nonprofit sector has trouble justifying the expense of market research to donors. Yet, it is still valuable for these organizations. The purpose of this chapter is to understand the importance of a research process and to understand ways to use online conversations to gain insights on stakeholders. Using existing conversations in social media not only drastically reduces the cost of research, but some say these conversations are more valid, given that they are naturally occurring rather than contrived. This chapter also teaches nonprofits to develop a comprehensive listening system and examine common metrics for evaluating digital efforts and their relation to strategic objectives.

RED CROSS LISTENS AFTER HURRICANE KATRINA

After Hurricane Katrina hit the Louisiana and Mississippi Gulf Coast in August 2005, the outrage of the world was expressed using social media. Many of the platforms used (e.g., Flickr and YouTube) were only months old. By December, there were more than two million blog posts about Katrina. Eventually, video and photography became part of the collective memory of Hurricane Katrina and its aftermath for Gulf Coast citizens.[2] In order to express their desire to help where the government did not, millions of people donated money to the American Red Cross. However, there was a general perception that the organization did not perform adequately in this crisis. A scathing report about the American Red Cross's response to Hurricane Katrina said it was poorly planned, relied too heavily on inexperienced managers, and often failed to meet the needs of victims.[3]

The American Red Cross knew there were negative comments on blogs and social networks about its disaster relief efforts, but it had no capacity to track it or respond to them. Wendy Harman, the social media manager with the American Red Cross, had to first identify and follow existing conversations. "There were hundreds of mentions across social media platforms each day. I had to set up a listening post to monitor and analyze them, as well as figure out how or if to respond," she says. So they started a listening program with some key goals: to correct misinformation, to become more informed about public opinion, to track conversation trends, to identify important influencers, and to build relationships. They started listening to bloggers and then moved to Twitter and other sources. What was most surprising is that most of the comments were positive; people blogged about positive experiences like giving blood, for example. Harman believes that developing a listening system has helped to drive an internal adoption and interest in social media whereby people at American Red Cross are no longer scared about negative comments because now there is a forum for engagement. Negative comments are viewed as an opportunity for education. The American Red Cross has also established a response policy for Twitter and blogs. Harman uses Technorati to help determine which blogs to comment on. While this is one way to examine it, it is not the only input to determine who gets a comment. Harman spends about ten hours weekly monitoring social media, and then compiles a one-page update that is disseminated to staff and affiliates. "It is not rocket science, just keyword searches across social media platforms," she says.

THE IMPORTANCE OF RESEARCH AND EVALUATION

Research is one of the most important tools that an organization can use to gain information about their stakeholders. However, marketing research is quite expensive, primarily due to the technical aspects of it. Some marketing research does require advanced statistical methods, which most people cannot tackle. In addition, collecting the actual data (e.g., calling up people on the phone or sending out surveys in the mail) can be incredibly expensive and time-consuming. So many nonprofits have simply gone without good research and instead just made a decision based on their gut feelings. Sometimes that works; sometimes it doesn't.

However, now that much of marketing research has moved online, there are plenty of opportunities for simple and inexpensive research. Indeed, online research is one of the fastest growing areas for marketing research due to the lower costs and shorter time requirements. Furthermore, there are free ways to listen in on people's natural conversations online by monitoring social media. This chapter will first explain the traditional research process. This is important because there is a tendency for organizations to jump into an online survey or monitor a blog because it is cheap or free. But research needs an objective. Within the context of the research process, we also discuss online ways to collect traditional research—namely online focus groups and online surveys. Next, we discuss a whole new way to research by monitoring social media. In order to do that effectively, we develop some considerations for designing a comprehensive listening system. The other topic covered in this chapter is that of evaluation. We discuss why evaluation is important and its relation to good objectives. We then present a brief overview of search (including search-engine optimization) and Web analytics, including several metrics with a particular focus on social-media metrics since they provide more depth into the issue of engagement.

THE RESEARCH PROCESS

Regardless of whether the nonprofit organization decides to use online or offline marketing research techniques, it is important to understand that in order to be valid and reliable, it must follow a process. The first issue to be considered is the purpose of the research. Why is the organization engaging in research in the first place? In order to answer this question, managers need to develop a set of specific marketing research objectives. For example, if an organization needed to understand donor behavior, an objective would be to develop a demographic and psychographic profile of current donors. This is the most important step of the research process. In order to achieve any usable results, the objectives must be clear and concise.

Once the objectives are determined, the next phase is to determine the research design. Generally, there are two types of research. Secondary research is research that has been conducted for a purpose other than the one being investigated. This can include existing databases, existing reports (from associations, consultants, universities, and government sources), library research (including academic research), Internet research, and so forth. Mining insights from social media such as blogs, microblogs (like Twitter), Facebook, discussion boards, and the like are great secondary research arenas. Primary research is research that has been conducted to answer a specific question, usually one tied to the research objective. Typically, these include surveys, focus groups, interviews, and observation. While there are ways to conduct these online, we will spend more time discussing digital insights.[4]

One important issue to consider when developing the research methodology is your audience. If you are seeking opinions from so called "digital natives" (those younger than thirty years old), it makes sense to use technology, since that is the primary way that they interact with brands and with each other. If the audience is older, proceed with caution; perhaps use something simple, such as e-mail (although much of the growth of social networks is from women older than fifty).

While determining the most effective manner of collecting the information is important, it is also important to determine who to speak to—in other words, the sample. This often dictates what type of research technique will be most effective. For example, considering the original objective to develop a demographic and psychographic profile of current donors, and assuming that there are

> **Chapter Insight: Online Surveys and Focus Groups**
>
> There are several great tools to use for online surveys and focus groups. Some are really cheap, and some are actually free. Here are a few:
>
> *Online surveys* are Web-based survey tools that allow organizations to develop surveys and then send to an existing e-mail list or to a list that is purchased as part of an online consumer panel. Most of the software provides some analysis of the data. A few popular ones include WebSurveyor, Survey Monkey, Zoomerang, Survey gizmo, and Polldaddy. All have a basic version that is typically free; expanded response requirements typically run less than $500 per year.
>
> *Online focus groups* are group interviews of six to ten people who are communicating online, typically at their own computers, in locations around the world; newer technology allows for face-to-face virtual communication (such as through Skype). A moderator asks questions of participants, who then provide feedback similar to a traditional focus group. Some of this can be accomplished with screen-capturing technology, webcams, online bulletin and discussion boards, instant message, videos, online interactive photo journals, social networks, and online communities. Many of these tools are used together and there are several research firms that can facilitate online focus groups; otherwise, organizations can use anything from chat rooms to virtual meeting technology (such as WebEx, Enunciate, or Go2Meeting) to talk with stakeholders.
>
> *Online interviews* are individual discussions (or in some instances small-group discussion, such as husband/wife or parent/child) that are facilitated online in much the same way as online focus groups. Consider using many of the technologies discussed above and consider using multiple platforms (such as blogs and photo sharing). E-mail and chat programs also work well for online interviews.

hundreds of donors, it makes sense to develop an online survey and then send the survey out using donors' e-mail addresses (assuming the organization has them and the permission to send information to them). If e-mail addresses are not available, this changes the game—perhaps traditional mail surveys or telephone surveys are required. Managers must think through the objectives of the research to determine *who* to talk to and *how* to talk with them. Indeed, this also goes into the planning for capturing donor information in databases.

However, if the objective is to gain more information about a specific issue—for example, having a child who was diagnosed with cancer—monitoring online forums or blogs, especially those written or posted by caregivers, will yield very useful information for a cancer organization. So understanding who you want to talk to and how you want to talk with them to meet specific objectives is a key step.

Chapter Insight: The Research Process Checklist

Here is a typical research process. There may be some changes, but generally, if you follow these areas, you will conduct a valid and reliable research project.

Define problem and set research objectives

- Why is the research needed? What problem should it solve?
- What information is needed in order to solve the problem?

Determine the research design

- What type of research will be best to answer the research objectives (e.g., exploratory, descriptive, or causal)?
- What secondary research is available and relevant? Are there digital insights available (blogs, discussion boards, microblogs, social media) to answer the questions? Does it answer the research objectives?
- What primary research should be collected (survey [mail, telephone, online], focus groups [in person, online], interviews [in person, online], observation or other ethnographic research)?

Design the data collection forms

- What specific questions should be included?
- Have you included the survey questions? Discussion guides?

Determine the sample plan and sample size

- Who should you talk to?
- What is the best way to reach them?
- How many do you need to talk to?

Collect data

- What is the best way to collect the data? If you are dealing with internal stakeholders, do you have the proper contact information?
- If you are talking to external stakeholders, do you have a sample frame?
- Where can you get the best sources for samples?

Analyze data

- What techniques do you need to use?
- Do you need outside assistance for sophisticated techniques?

Prepare and present final report

- What format is needed for the report?[5]

After determining the objectives and setting out the plan, the next step is to collect the data. Again, this will be determined by the objective. If the objective is to determine the awareness levels of a San Diego–based organization's brand image, that organization can purchase a sample containing e-mail addresses in the San Diego area and can either develop the survey on their own and send it out or allow one of several organizations to collect that data (usually within a few days, depending on the size and the parameters of the sample). Then the data must be analyzed. The level of sophistication of the survey and objectives will determine whether outside assistance will be required. For example, if the organization is interested in simple analysis—such as frequencies or descriptive information—many times the software calculates that. Survey Monkey, for example, calculates the total number of people who answered the question and includes the percentage and the count for each question. If you have issues or questions that require more rigorous testing or more sophisticated analysis techniques, then outside assistance may be required; a local business school may be able to help. After the analysis is completed, then a report is generally prepared and disseminated.

DIGITAL INSIGHTS: SOCIAL-MEDIA MONITORING

What are digital insights? Digital insights are the naturally occurring conversations that take place online, primarily in social media, about an organization or company. This is part of a growing field called social-media monitoring. One of the biggest impacts of the explosion of social media is the ability to listen to real conversations in real time. Up until now, if organizations wanted to get research on what their stakeholders were thinking and saying, they had to actually ask them using traditional research tactics like those discussed above. However, now organizations can simply engage stakeholders in a variety of social-media platforms, such as blogs, microblogs, discussion boards, social networks, video and photo sites, review sites, and even proprietary online communities. Technology allows nonprofit managers to listen in on literally millions of relevant conversations taking place every minute of every day. It has magnified not only how people think online but also how they behave online—that holy grail of research is capturing behavioral data. Indeed, Fortune 100 marketers have said that using technology to capture consumer insights is the primary focus of using technology.[6] Given the speed with which technology changes—and with it stakeholder behavior—research and planning becomes an ongoing effort as opposed to a one-time or annual event.

One area of digital insights that is particularly useful is that of search behavior. As a branding tool, search functionality plays a huge role in magnifying online conversations. Search behavior allows organizations to hear what matters most to stakeholders and then determine whether their mission and how they are communicating that mission matches up with expectations. It also allows organizations to optimize their insights to meet strategic objectives. Think about it. Online search behavior is one of the first ways that people engage with your organization. Some will remember your domain name; many will simply use Google or another search engine to find what they need.

When organizations pay for a search, they choose search terms, or key words, and place ads relating to these terms. An organic search is a function of search-engine algorithms and "spiders" which travel the Web looking for key terms, which then determines where a Web site comes up on the search page, based typically on relevancy. Organic searching includes everything—Web sites are only one part of the results, which can include videos, images, social media, and blogs. Indeed, Google can now show real-time conversations.

PUT ON YOUR LISTENING EARS: DEVELOPING A LISTENING SYSTEM

The second area of importance for understanding digital insights is monitoring social media. Listening is an important step in a digital and social-media strategy. Sounds simple, but what does this mean? Listening means understanding what is being said about the organization, competitor organizations, the cause sector, and your community. It means using monitoring tools to be able to analyze the billions of pieces of information out on the Web. There are several reasons why listening is important. First, listening allows the organization to be able to serve stakeholders by knowing what they're saying to others and to you. Second, listening allows the organization to be able to respond to and/or engage critics. Last, listening allows organizations to stay abreast of the latest development in the cause area.

You *must* listen before you speak to your stakeholders online. For example, before developing a Facebook page, make sure that you develop a personal profile first and see how it works. Each social medium has its own culture. For example, one of biggest issues for bloggers is attribution. Give credit where credit is due since that is the currency of reputation. In order not to make mistakes, get familiar with the tools out there and, once the organization is comfortable, choose one or two to experiment with. However, as discussed previously, make sure that clear objectives have been developed for each endeavor.

But listening to social media is more than just free market research. It can be used to improve programs and identify any misconceptions. It can allow an organization to stay responsive and relevant. For example, a nonprofit that helps patients who have trouble affording their healthcare expenses after being diagnosed with cancer would benefit from listening to what people are saying about healthcare reform in order to know how to dispel faulty information and know what services need to be developed.

There are some steps that an organization should take in order to develop a comprehensive listening system. While it does not take a lot of monetary resources, it will take some time to educate the organization about the technology and the culture of social media. Beth Kanter, author of Beth's Blog,[7] which covers social media and nonprofit organizations, outlines a few issues to consider.

Get the organization ready to listen. Before embarking on developing a listening system, it is important to lay the proper groundwork, especially given that many nonprofits are underfunded and understaffed. Compile a list of the organization's current digital touchpoints. A digital touchpoint is any way that stakeholders can "touch" or access an organization online. For example, most nonprofits have a Web site, so determine what functions it includes. Is there a newsletter? Is there a volunteer database? If the organization has a Twitter account, how is it being used? Once this audit has been determined, there are a few additional steps that must be completed. Consider who will be listening and responding. Someone should take the reins of this project or it will go underutilized. Kanter identifies several approaches, depending on the size of the organization and the skills of the staff.

- First, one person can incorporate listening into their job and then prepare a report.
- Second, a team of people (e.g., the development team or a multifunctional team) can work together to listen and respond.
- Third, everyone at the organization can make listening to social media a part of their job.[8]

That is not to say that this takes a lot of extra time—it really doesn't—but it does take some time and energy, which should be considered. So consider how much time will be allocated.

Once the conversation is identified, it is important to consider how to respond to comments, especially the negative ones. Actually, responding provides a unique opportunity to really engage stakeholders. This seems to be especially important for blogs and Twitter. Be sure to analyze the results and share that insight with the rest of the organization. For example, if the organization employs case workers to help people who need financial assistance, and there have been positive comments about the case worker, that should be shared.

Identify the key skills for listening. Keywords are the most important tool for listening because search terms are the most primary input. So it is important to choose the right key words and begin to refine those words once the results are completed. It is also important to figure out what you want to search for: organization name, cause sector, competitive causes, events, programs, and so on. These are called "ego searches" and are basic in nature. Keep a spreadsheet of the terms used and the quality of results they yielded. Organizations can also run a search-engine referral report—words that people use as search terms in Google to find the organization's Web site—and then analyze the keywords that people are using in other systems like Delicious or StumbleUpon. "You may not know what it is worth searching until you try searching on it and revise it based on what you see. Don't assume that you'll get it right on the first try, either. It takes fine-tuning of those key words before you get it right," says Wendy Harman, social media strategist for the Red Cross.[9] There are several tools that you can use (see table 10.1 for a complete list).

Digital Insights and Research 199

Table 10.1: Listening and Evaluation Tools

Blog Search Tools	
Technorati	The largest blog search engine in the world; tracks blog reactions or blog links; subscribe through RSS
Google Blog Search	Google's index of blogs; there are ways to utilize advance search
IceRocket	Blog search; includes graphics files
Blog Pulse	Blog search by Nielsen Buzzmetrics
Bloglines	Web-based news and blog aggregator
Google Alerts	E-mail updates of the latest relevant Google results based on a query or search terms; subscribe through RSS; useful for tracking PR campaigns
Social Mention	A free comprehensive social search engine that searches for keywords on many different social media sites, including blogs, podcasts, video, social-media network sites, online discussion boards, microblogs, etc.
Buzz Tracking Tools	
Serph	Allows you to track buzz on topics in real time
Trendrr	Tracks trends on virtually anything
Google Trends	Google's trending tool; also shows news stories
Trendpedia	Creates charts showing the volume of discussion around multiple topics
BlogPulse Trends	Allows comparison of the mentions of specific keywords in blog posts
Omgili charts	Allows you to measure and compare the buzz of any term; mostly from review sites and forums
eKstreme	Trend data from Technorati (blogs) and Delicious (social bookmarks)
Message Board Tracking Tools	
Board Tracker	Word tracking in forums
Board Reader	Finds and displays information posted on the online discussion forums and message boards
Omgili	Search engine that focus on "many to many" user-generated content, such as forums, discussion groups, mailing lists, answer boards, etc.
Google Groups	Searches usenet groups on Google
Yahoo! Groups	Searches all Yahoo groups
Twitter Search Tools	
Twitter Search	Allows you to search and listen to what people are "tweeting" about related to the organization. Twitter can be considered a big online focus group
Tweetscan	Allows word searches on Twitter
Twitt(url)y	Search for what people are talking about on Twitter
Hashtags	Realtime tracking of Twitter hashtags
TweetBeep	Track mentions of brands on Twitter
TweetMeme	View the most popular Twitter threads
Website Traffic Tools	
Compete	Competitor site traffic reports (monthly visitor estimates)
Quantcast	Compare multiple websites in one chart (monthly visitor estimates)

Table 10.1: Listening and Evaluation Tools—*(Continued)*

Alexa	Comparative site traffic repots (estimated reach, rank, and page views)
Search Data Tools	
Google Trends	Search trends and see volume by region and country
Back Type	A search engine that searches through blog comments, social networks and Twitter to identify; can track conversations on a specific blog post
Google Insights	Compare search volume patterns across specific regions, categories, and time frame
Wordtracker Keywords	Average daily search volume of a given keyword or phrase
Yahoo! Keyword Tool	Displays search volume for keywords and phrases for previous month's search data
Facebook LEXICON	Displays volume of wall postings for specific terms; similar to Google Trends
Google Keyword Tool	Generates keyword ideas for related keywords and search volumes
Multimedia Search Tools	
YouTube	Search for videos and video channels; post videos
Metacafe	Video search engine
Google Advanced Video Search	Video search engine
Flickr	Photo search engine; post photos
Truvideo	Aggregate video search tool
Viral Video Chart	Displays top 20 most viewed videos
SociafyQ	Provides a free data analytic tracking services, including Facebook, YouTube, Twitter, etc.—which is accessible through a web dashboard, XML, and Dashboard and Yahoo! Widgets
Social Bookmarking Tools	
Digg	Social bookmarking
StumbleUpon	Social bookmarking
Delicious	Social bookmarking
Feed Aggregator Tools	
Yahoo! Pipes	Feed aggregator and manipulator; set up pipes for news alerts and overviews
Other Tools	
Page Rank Checker	Shows Google page ranking
Adonomics	Facebook analytics and developer application tracking and graphing
SiteVolume	Reports on how often keywords or phrases appear on Digg, Twitter, MySpace, YouTube, Flickr
Socialcast	Offers real-time analytics on microblogging and other social activities and identifies individual users' levels of activity
Competitious	A free beta tool that lets you track and organize news and data about other companies and organizations

Free Social Media Monitoring Tools, http://takemetoyourleader.com.

The Essential Tool: RSS Reader. The first tool you need is a RSS reader. This is software that grabs content from the Web, including blogs, videos, Twitter and other material. There are several types of readers: Bloglines allows you to keep information in folders; Google Reader makes it easy to use on a Google dashboard (or e-mail) and NetVibes has a visual interface and is used for executive listening. Whatever you choose, make time to read it but don't feel like you have to read everything. Remember, you will need to set up search terms for all of these tools, and it is worth the time to decide which are going to be the most effective search terms without overloading your results.

Pattern Analysis, Trends, and Reporting. Develop a place to combine the results. A good spreadsheet that includes the blog type or social media type is helpful. It is also effective to review the overall trends. Most of the tools that are available are free. If the organization finds that it needs more sophisticated analysis, there are several additional companies, such as Omniture, Buzz Metrics, Radian6, or Buzzlogic, that can help analyze and understand the magnitude and tone of conversations. These typically can come with a hefty price tag, but some have discounts for nonprofit organizations. This could be a good tool to consider if you have the budget and if you monitor a great deal of varied social media. In addition, check out Google Trends and Trendrr that provide trending information on pretty much anything. This helps track the conversation relating to a topic on blogs, Twitter, and other social and traditional media outlets. There are also ways to use Twitter to track trends (check out chapter 5 for more information on Twitter).

To give you an idea of what has been done and what works, we have highlighted several nonprofits that have utilized digital insights.

- The Smithsonian Museum used Twitter to find out how visitors feel about the institution as well as how they plan their museum visit. This translated into ways to reinvent the museum experience through audience-specific online navigation, personalized entry points for trip planning, modular content for deeper exploration, and behind-the-scenes content.[10]
- The American Heart Association decided to use a Twitter search to follow caregiver conversations about stroke. They used this information to determine which support and resources to provide to those in need.[11]
- Bay Area Discovery Museum uses RSS to track reviews on Yelp and Trip Advisor. The also use Delicious and tweetscan to track mentions. They use this to engage visitors posting positive and negative comments.[12]
- The Lumina Foundation for Education worked with the Ad Council to develop a campaign to convince low-income students to attend college. But before they started the campaign, the Council and the Foundation conducted a national survey of low-income families and found out that,

much to their surprise, most low-income students were planning to attend college, but their families didn't know how the process worked. Their new message strategy dealt with *how* to go to college instead of *whether* to go to college. This saved the Lumina Foundation about $2 million dollars on a campaign that could have sent the wrong message.[13]

Research plays an important role in decision-making in all organizations, whether or not they are nonprofits. There is no substitute for a well-developed research plan to answer important questions. While we have focused on digital research, remember that how research is conducted depends on who you want to talk to and how you want to talk to them.

Chapter Insight: Listen, Learn, Adapt to Revolutionize ROI (Return on Insight)[14]

David Armano, vice president of Experience Design at Critical Mass and a blogger at Logic + Emotion (http://darmano.typepad.com), recently released a white paper examining ROI—the return on insight. He argues that the current model of conducting a focus group with potential audiences before launching a new product or marketing campaign is becoming increasingly less relevant in a fast-paced digital world. In this world, a mass audience doesn't really exist. Focusing on a strict and traditional definition of ROI (return on investment) tends to limit the quality of insights that can be gained by launching in a real environment—the Internet. This is where Armano says that the collective is the focus group. Rather, he advocates that organizations simply launch on a smaller scale in a real environment and allow user feedback to dictate changes and modifications (and ultimately acceptance). He developed a three-prong process: listen, learn, and adapt.

Listen: Use the technology that is available to listen to the millions of real conversations out in cyberspace. Find out what is being said about the brand, competitors, programs, and related stories and passion points. It is easy to apply technology (Radian6, Buzzmetrics, Collective Intellect) or more rudimentary techniques (see the trend sites and blog search sites). In fact, Twitter searches can, in fact, be one of the most valuable search tools. This process of finding out what people are saying in real conversations is called "social sniffing." This must be an ongoing process as opposed to a one-time activity.

Learn: Launch the campaign, program, or product on a small scale. Pilot initiatives can be quickly launched using prototype methodologies. Learning is not a singular phase but rather should occur continually throughout the life of the initiative. The goal is to keep the momentum going in order to maximize engagement with audiences.

Adapt: Find out what works and what does not work and make the changes. Be nimble enough to do that. Analytics will play a huge role in evaluation, but it is important to understand both the quantitative side of analytics and the qualitative side of "digital anthropology."

Armando developed ten ways to maximize return on insight:

1. Are you actively listening to customers in the places they frequent online, such as communities?
2. Are you launching initiatives that can be easily updated? Are you enabling a "culture of rapid response"?
3. Are you evaluating current processes and updating them as needed?
4. Are you building a culture where "failure" is acceptable?
5. Are you allowing your teams to create "pilots" prior to scrutinizing them through traditional ROI exercises?
6. Are you planning initiatives that will help your organization learn prior to backing major marketing campaigns?
7. Are you synthesizing qualitative insights in addition to analyzing the hard data points?
8. Are you tweaking your strategy along the way and adapting where change may be needed?
9. Are you empowering all members of your teams to think and act like "digital anthropologists"?
10. Are you evolving the tools and methods you use to measure success (i.e., going beyond clicks and impressions)?

THE IMPORTANCE OF A GOOD EVALUATION SYSTEM

A good strategic planning system is the foundation of developing a plan for your nonprofit organization's digital presence. Part of this planning process includes evaluation, but despite its importance, evaluation sometimes becomes an afterthought. There are several reasons why the evaluation phase is crucial. First, an organization needs to know whether its communication efforts are working. Given that so many organizations are cash-strapped and time-poor, most of the effort for a fund-raising event or program development is in the beginning and middle and not at the end. Once it is completed, many organizations forget to complete the evaluation portion. But this step is necessary in order to fine-tune areas for improvement. Second, believe it or not, evaluation helps an organization engage with stakeholders by encouraging an examination of their priorities. Finding out what is important to stakeholders will help fine-tune new programs, events, and fund-raising. Third, evaluation helps in times of crisis, something all organizations go through at one point or another. Evaluation allows the organization to investigate how the crisis unfolds and how the organization adapts. Last, evaluation allows the organization to allocate resources wisely. Find out what is working and, more importantly, find out what is not working so that money and time is not wasted.[15]

Before adding anything to the Web site or adding any new social-media tactics, your team should answer two questions. First, what do we hope to accomplish by adding this tool or new area to the Web site (e.g., Twitter, Facebook, blog, widget)? Second, how will we know if we are successful? This gets into the concepts of goals, objectives, and measurement.

Goals are the long-term aspirations for the organizations. These are connected to the mission and theory of change for the organization. Typically these are five- to ten-year plans. For example, if an organization wishes to become an expert in children's neuroblastoma cancer, it is obvious that this will take some time. Goals can fall into several categories: awareness, support/advocacy, community building, policy change, and so forth. Most importantly, these are broad-based and do not necessarily have quantifiable terms.

Objectives are an outcome of goals. Objectives are different—these are used as a roadmap to achieve the goal. Objectives need to be SMART. That is, objectives need to be specific, measurable, action-oriented, realistic, and time-specific. Essentially, objectives need numbers. For example, if the goal is to become an expert in neuroblastoma cancer in five years, a related objective could be to produce a report on the state of neuroblastoma cancer research being conducted in the U.S. that will serve as a resource for the medical community and donors by the end of 2011. Objectives are important because they set up the evaluation process to be more effective. When choosing your objective, start with the end results. What do you want to achieve? Once you have determined that, then work backward to develop appropriate SMART objectives. Also, remember your stakeholders. When developing your objectives, include whom you are dealing with—donors, constituents, policy makers, and so on. Try to be as narrow as possible but also think about how you will measure the results. For example if you choose "community" as the relevant stakeholder, how will you know if you succeeded? You will need to conduct research with the community, which, depending on your budget and resources, could be costly.

After you have determined the goals and objectives, it is important to develop the *metrics* for final evaluation. Understand that a metric without a goal really is meaningless. Consider developing a baseline. There needs to be a consideration of where you are right now before you measure progress. For example, if increasing awareness of a policy issue is the intended goal, what is the current level of awareness? This is the baseline. If the objective is long-term, consider including milestones, using a metric to assess progress at various time intervals. For example, if the objective has a two-year timeframe, consider six-month milestones to assess progress. Once you have developed an idea of a baseline and what you want to evaluate, consider how you will conduct the evaluation. This goes back to what we discussed earlier in the chapter—what research techniques are most applicable in this situation. Is it focus groups? Online surveys? All of the same caveats apply here. We have included some considerations for evaluation in table 10.2.

Table 10.2: Evaluation Considerations

Issue	Assessment
Define your goals • Are they mission-based? • Broadbased?	
Define your objectives • SMART? • Consider how to evaluate? • Consider audience?	
Evaluation • Include baseline? • Include milestones? • Consider how to evaluate? • Determined method of research? (focus group, online survey, traditional survey, observation, social-media monitoring—specific platforms, other)	
Metrics • Use of traditional communication metrics? • Use of social media metrics? • Draft of additional metrics?	

GETTING PEOPLE TO YOUR WEB SITE

There are billions of pages on the Web, and getting people to your site is not only difficult but crucial. Luckily, there are tools that can be used in order to get people to your organization's Web site. Search-engine optimization (SEO) is the process of improving the volume and quality of traffic to a Web site via search engines. The idea is to get the highest possible position on the results page after a visitor conducts a search in a search engine. For example, Google may show twelve million search results, but most people don't go beyond the first or second pages. So, ideally, most organizations want to be included on the first page. SEO considers how search engines work and what people search by using Web analytics. Optimizing a Web site means using the results from Web analytics to decide what pages and even areas to improve upon. Optimization is achieved by modifying HTML code and/or editing java script (depending on what type of analytics program is being used).

Many people want to understand how the search results are created. The biggest three search engines—Google, Yahoo, and Microsoft's Bing—all use different algorithms and don't publish that information. Generally, page rank is a function of the quantity and strength of inbound links. Search engines use "crawlers" or "spiders" to find pages for their algorithms' search results. Yahoo has a paid submission service that guarantees crawling for a fee. This guarantees inclusion into a directory but not the search results' placement. Two large directories to include in your directory search are Yahoo Directory and the Open Directory Project, and there are several other specific directories for inclusion.

There are several sites that make the job of optimizing Web sites easier and thereby increase Web traffic to your site. Some of the major ones are Google Web Optimizer, Web Page Analyzer, Web Site Maestro, Omniture Site Catalyst, and Atlas Site Optimizer. Take a look at these, as many of them are free and are quite useful at maximizing the effect of the brand online.

Web analytics is the measurement, collection, analysis, and reporting of Internet data for purposes of understanding and optimizing Web usage.[16] Primarily, Web analytics measure a visitor's journey on Web sites. Typically, the results of Web analytics are compared with key performance indicators and then allow organizations to improve a Web site or campaign accordingly. One of the best (free) tools out there is Google Analytics. There are several great books and online guides that can get your organization started with Google Analytics. Regardless, analytics (the output of the information) should always be linked to key performance indicators.

A key performance indicator (KPI) is essentially a "measurement of performance based on your most important Web goals."[17] In their book *Defining Site Goals, KPIs and Key Metrics*, Jason Burby and Shane Atchison argue that KPIs should be tied to organizational goals and objectives, measured over time, and agreed upon by the organization. Usually they are expressed as a number, typically a ratio or count. Many will be based on financial measures (e.g., conversion rate, increased donation) but it is important to also include other goals based on communication outcomes, as well.

One of the best things about the Web is that almost everything is measurable. The explosion of social media has only increased the number of metrics that are available for organizations. Recently, Rachel Happe of The Social Organization[18] devised a list (with collaborators online) of social-media metrics. Table 10.3 outlines many of these metrics. A few things to consider. First, choose wisely. Don't feel the need to choose all of these metrics. In fact, start with a few and build from there. Second, link your metrics with your objectives so that you are ensuring that you can actually evaluate progress. Third, be creative. Things move fast on the Web, and this list may be expanded quickly. Last, this is an area where there will be much development in the future.

As stated, Web analytics are great because organizations can use them to really find what works and what does not work on the Web site. This allows organizations make adjustments and allows for the identification of return on investment.

LESSONS LEARNED

- Despite the fact that there are more and more cheap or free online tools for research and insight discovery, it is important to have good objectives and a research process. Start with a keen understanding of what you want to find out, who you want to talk to, and how you want to talk to them. This will be important regardless of research technique.

Table 10.3: Social Media Metrics

Hits	A request for a file from a Web server. This number is misleading due to the way it counts files and estimates popularity
Page Views	A request for a file that is defined as a page in log analysis. In log analysis, a single page view may generate multiple hits
Visit or Session	A series of requests from the same uniquely identified person with a set timeout (usually 30 minutes)
Number of Unique Visitors	The uniquely identified visitor generating requests on the Web server (log analysis) or viewing pages (page tagging) within a defined period of time (such as day, week, or month)
Repeat Visitors	A visitor who has made at least one previous visit. The period between the last and current visit is called visitor recency and is measured in days
Number of Members and Friends	The number of people classified as friends on social networks or members within online communities. These people have requested membership
Click Path	The sequence of hyperlinks one or more Web site visitors follows on a given site
Number of Posts (Ideas and Threads)	The number of comments that are posted to a blog
Comments and Trackbacks	The number of comments per post and the number of trackbacks per post
Number of Contributors	The number of people who contribute in some way usually via social media (e.g., blog posts, user-generated content)
Number of Active Contributors	The number of people who contribute in some way usually via social media on a regular basis
Number of Referrals	The number of people referred in social network sites like Facebook and LinkedIn
Number of Completed Profiles	The number of profiles that are completed in a social network site
Connections (between Members)	The number of people belonging to the same network in social network sites (e.g., mutual friends in Facebook)
Ratios: Member to Contributor, Posts to Comments	
Periods: by Day, Week, Month, Year	
Frequency: Visits, Posts, Comments	
Donations (Number, Amount, Frequency)	
Net Promoter Score	A measure to assess word-of-mouth
Impressions	Each time an ad loads on a user's screen (e.g., banner ads)
Visibility Time	The amount of time a single page (or blog) is viewed
Session Duration	Average amount of time that visitors spend on the site each time they visit
Page View Duration/Time on Page	Average amount of time that visitors spend on each page of the site
Page Depth/Page per Session	Average number of page views a visitor consumes before ending a session. It is calculated by dividing total number of page views by total number of sessions and is called page views per session

Social Media Metrics, The Social Organization, http://rhappe.typepad.com/thesocialorganization/social-media-metrics.html.

Chapter Insight: Experiments and Digital Media

Digital technology makes it easier to test messages and programs much more easily and inexpensively than traditional means. One easy way to do this (and there are many other companies out there that do this) is to use Google Web Optimizer. This free tool allows you to choose content from the Web site to test which is better at conversion. First, choose what you want to test. The top five are title, image, layout, selling proposition, and conversion incentives. For example, you may want to test two different images; or test three different donation messages. Second, choose the conversation metric—this could be something like a thank you page, a click button, or a submit button. Third, add the java script to the source code (Google helps with this). Fourth, Google Web Optimizer routes traffic to each of the site options and then measures which were the most successful at conversion. For more information, see www.google.com/analytics. They include webinars and articles that are easy to understand and simple to use.

Additionally, you never thought you would actually need experimental design from your school days, but there are some very effective experiments that can be conducted using a host of tools (Google Analytics, Omniture). Here are some terms from Google Web site Optimizer:

The American Cancer Society has been using Google Analytics for several years with amazing success. Started in 1913, the American Cancer Society is one of the top ten nonprofit brands and the second largest funders of cancer research after the U.S. government. Its Web site, www.cancer.org, is designed as a warehouse of information on all types of cancer. This online presence includes an array of content pages, wikis, social networks, open-source projects, and rich Internet applications, all of which are evaluated for performance. As an early adopter of Google Analytics in 2005, they decided to use it to optimize their AdWords key words and content to maximize their fund-raising efforts. They also used tools from Google Analytics to track their e-commerce activities, including product performance, seasonal purchasing trends, and the impact of traditional marketing campaigns. As a result, they were able to show increases in click-through rates and ROI. The ACS has also used Google Analytics for its mobile search-engine marketing campaign to measure each step of the process from clicking on the mobile AdWords link through contacting the call center. As Google Analytics reports, the ACS says, "It helps us use our dollars more wisely for our mission. . . . Google Analytics is literally helping in the fight against cancer."[19]

Table 10.4: Experiment Types

Test Type	Summary
Before and After	Track performance on a page, make a change, see if performance improved
A/B Tests	Splitting the traffic between two or more published pages and tracking which one gets the most conversions
Multivariate	Carving up a page into a few sections, then trying different content in each section to create different versions of the page—usually a handful of versions, occasionally a few dozen or a few hundred
Segmented, Personalized, and/or Experiential Testing	Multivariate plus cross-tabbing results based on visitor characteristics and modification of the entire user experience across pages

Conversation with the Pros: Steve Cleff, Senior Strategist, Razorfish

Steve Cleff is a senior strategist at Razorfish, a leading digital agency, in Philadelphia. The job of a senior strategist is to identify the business objective and the customer insight and then develop a clear plan that finds the balance between the two. The key is to understand how people experience Web sites and social media. Cleff finds that social media is a good insight-generating tool. The first thing he does when getting a new project is to go to Twitter, YouTube, and Flickr. He feels this is a good start to find out what people are saying and doing, and he uses it before starting more formal research tactics like interviews and focus groups. Social-media monitoring is useful. "People are very willing to talk about themselves in very personal ways," Cleff says. He also says that, while social-media monitoring is no substitute for formal research (Cleff likes qualitative research), it is better than nothing and is great for nonprofits on a budget.

As someone who has lived with the Internet day in and day out since 1995, he sees many trends. Since he first started working with digital media, he feels that there is a pattern to the Web; there is excitement, which turns to curiosity, which turns to adoption. Then, inevitably, there is a backlash and, finally, standardization. He says that right now, we are in a standardization mode as there are now best practices and rules for social media (like blogs, for example). Just looking back on the past few years, he says, you can see the excitement surrounding user-generated content in 2006—remember the Doritos Super Bowl television ads, which were made by consumers?—and then more companies started experimenting in 2007, when the specifics on budgeting and measurement were still major questions of interest. In 2008, companies started to find out what worked and what did

> not work, and then, in 2009, "rules" emerged. And that is where we currently are in 2010—experimenting with social media like Twitter, which allows people to communicate easier than with blogs because it consists of short bursts. Cleff believes that companies will get back to the essence of their brands. People want to participate with brands. Cleff says people are telling brands, "I want to tell you more about me in order to have a better relationship because I like your brand," and companies are listening.

- Monitoring social media allows organizations to see real conversations with its stakeholders, which yield better information. This is a growing area that nonprofit organizations should learn about, given the reduced costs involved.
- Evaluation is an important step; organizations should include goals, objectives, and relevant metrics. Choose metrics wisely; don't feel the need to include them all.

FURTHER READING

Multichannel Marketing: Metrics and Methods for On and Offline Success by Akin Arikin
Actionable Web Analytics: Using Data to Make Smart Business Decisions by Jason Burby and Shane Atchison
Google Analytics by Mary E. Tyler and Jerri L. Ledford
Advanced Web Metrics with Google Analytics by Brian Clifton
Web Analytics: An Hour a Day by Avinash Kaushik
Web Analytics Demystified: A Marketer's Guide to Understanding How Your Web Site Affects Your Business by Eric Peterson
www.seomoz.org

NOTES

1. Allen P. Adamson, *Brand Digital: Simple Ways Top Brands Succeed in a Digital World* (New York, NY: Palgrave Macmillian, 2008).
2. Tom Watson, *Causewired: Plugging In, Getting Involved, Changing the World* (New York, NY: John Wiley and Sons, 2009).
3. Stephanie Strom, "Foreign Experts Critique U. S. Red Cross on Katrina," (April 5, 2006), www.nytimes.com.
4. Alvin C. Burns and Ronald F. Bush. *Marketing Research: Online Research Applications, 4th Ed.* (Upper Saddle River, NJ: Prentice Hall, 2003).
5. Ibid.
6. Adamson, *Brand Digital*.
7. "Social Media Listening For Nonprofits," (Beth's Blog), http://beth.typepad.com/beths_blog.

8. Listening Primer Part 1: Why, What and How to Organize It, http://socialmedia-listening.wikispace.com/Primer+Part+1.
9. Listening Primer Part 2: Listening Skills, http://socialmedia-listening.wikispace.com/Primer+Part+2.
10. Listening Primer Part 3: Listening Skills, http://socialmedia-listening.wikispace.com/Primer+Part+3.
11. Tactical Track Module 1: Listening, www.wearemedia.org.
12. Ibid.
13. Edith Asibey, Toni Parras and Justin van Fleet, "Are We There Yet? A Communications Evaluation Guide," (The Communications Network), www.wearemedia.org.
14. David Armano, "The Collective is the Focus Group: Revolutionizing ROI Through Return on Investment," http://darmano.typepad.com.
15. Ibid.
16. Web Analytics Association, www.webanalyticsassociation.org.
17. Jason Burby and Shane Atchison, "Defining Site Goals, KPIs and Key Metrics," *Actionable Web Analysis* (Indianapolis, IN: Wiley, 2007), 75.
18. Social Media Metrics, The Social Organization, http://rhappe.typepad.com/thesocialorganization/social-media-metrics.html.
19. "The American Cancer Society Uses Google Analytics to Boost Roi on the Web and Help Treat Patients around the World," www.google.com/analytics/case_study_acs.html.

Appendix: Social Media Glossary of Terms[1]

Badge: An image, usually squared and displayed on a blog, which signifies the blogger's participation in an event, contest, or social movement
Blog post/entry: Content published on a blog. Entries may include pictures or embedded videos and links URLs for online sources used
Blogroll: An assembly of blog URLs—blogs that the blogger reads regularly—displayed at the sidebar of the blog
Blogs: A Web site where individual(s) provide entries of any type of content from video and podcasts to traditional text and photos in order to inform or create discussions; presented in reverse chronological order
Boardreader: An aggregator of message boards and forum discussions
Comments: Replies or opinions in reference to the topic at hand, usually left on blog posts
Compete: Provides Web analytics (i.e., unique monthly visitors to the site) and enables people to compare and contrast up to five different sites at a time
"Do-good" networks: Online communities aimed at making the world a better place
Facebook: An online community for people to connect or re-connect with others. Enables people to share videos, pictures, and information about themselves. One of the fastest-growing social networks of the past two years.
Flickr: An online site for storing, sharing, and commenting on photos
Friendfeed: enables you to keep up-to-date on the Web pages, photos, videos, and music that your friends and family are sharing. It offers a unique way to discover and discuss information among friends
Groundswell: A social trend in which people use technologies to get the things they need from each other, rather than from traditional institutions like corporations
Hashtag: Similar to regular tags, these are keywords associated and assigned to an item of content with a hash mark (#) attached to the front of the word. Hashtags make it easier to follow a topic of interest discussed on Twitter
Hyper-local community: A group of people from a specific location who interact in online communities and use social media tools
Influencer: A person specialized in a specific subject matter and highly recognized in an online community that has the ability to sway others' thoughts; key influencers are seen as references or for assistance on specific subject matters

LinkedIn: A professional online community used to network with fellow professionals; an online résumé-sharing site

Message boards/forums: An online discussion site; people looking to discuss particular issues or needing support post threads (a message) on the forum or message board in hopes to gain more information or start a conversation

Microblogging: A form of blogging where the entries/posts are limited to a certain amount of characters or words

Micro-philanthropy: Donating in small amounts ($1, $5, $10, $20)

Multimedia: Media and content in different forms such as videos, pictures, etc.

MySpace: A site where people can meet others with similar interests, creating online communities by sharing videos, photos, and personal information

Online community: A group of people using social media tools and sites on the Internet

Platform: The framework or system within which tools work; the platform may be as broad as mobile telephony, or as narrow as a piece of software that has different modules like blogs, forums, and wikis in a suite of tools. As more and more tools operate "out there" on the Web, rather than on your desktop, people refer to "the Internet as the platform." That has advantages, but presents challenges in learning lots of different tools, and getting them to join up

Podcasts: Online audio or visual recordings syndicated on the Internet and available to download to portable media players

Quantcast: Used to measure the amount of traffic a URL receives, as well as data about the readership (demographics, psychographics, etc.)

RSS feed: Really Simple Syndication; a system that generates frequently updated information from a site (i.e. blog posts, online articles)

RSS reader: Aggregates information from RSS feed into one site

Search engine marketing (SEM): Is a form of Internet marketing that seeks to promote Web sites by increasing their visibility in search engine result pages (SERPs). According to the Search Engine Marketing Professional Organization, SEM methods include: search-engine optimization (or SEO), paid placement, contextual advertising, and paid inclusion (Wikipedia, Search Engine Marketing)

Search-engine optimization (SEO): Is the process of improving the volume and quality of traffic to a Web site from search engines via "natural" ("organic" or "algorithmic") search results

Sentiment: A level of assessment that determines the tone of an article, blog post, a company, etc.; usually positive, negative, or neutral

Social bookmarking: A method for people to search, organize, store, and share items (i.e., blog posts, online articles, pictures, etc.) of interest using the item's URL

Social media: A term used to describe tools and platforms people use to produce, publish, and share online content and to interact with one another.

Social-networking sites: Large sites that host multiple communities comprised of people with profiles who have with similar interests. These sites offer a place where people engage with one another online and share content

Tags: a keyword or term associated and assigned to an item of content (i.e. blog post, video, photo, etc.). Usually added to an item of content to enhance search engine optimization and make it content easier to organize and find

Technorati authority: Used to determine the number of times a keyword or URL are mentioned and linked in blogs

Tweet: The post/entry made on Twitter
Twitter Search: A search engine that filters out real-time tweets
Twitter: A microblogging community where posts and links are 140 characters or less
Web 2.0: The business revolution in the computer industry caused by the move to the Internet as a platform, and an attempt to understand the rules for success on that new platform
Webinar: An online seminar
Widget: A mini application that performs a specific function and connects to the Internet
Wiki: Webpage(s) used to collect content about a topic. Anyone with access to the page(s) can edit or modify the information
YouTube: An online site for uploading and discussing videos; videos can also be embedded from YouTube onto other social media sites such as blogs or social networks

NOTES

1. The Buzz Bin Social Media Terms, www.livingstonbuzz.com/2009/02/24/social-media-glossary.

Index

Note: Page numbers followed by "f" or "t" refer to figures or tables respectively.

Accountability information, 61–63
Acteva, 117
Action alerts, 168–169
ActiveEvents, 137
Activism. *See* Online activism
Adamson, Allen, 191
Addresses, Web site, selecting, 69
Advertising
   banners, 135–136
   contextual, 136
   interruptive, 135
   online, 135–136
Advocacy. *See* Online activism
Advocate visitors, 44–45, 44f
Aggregators, 117–118
Alignment, defined, 53
American Cancer Society (ACS), 112, 113, 208
American Civil Liberties Union (ACLU), 168
American Heart Association (AHA), 14–15, 29–30, 113–114, 180, 201
American Red Cross, 94–96, 191–192
American Society for Prevention to Cruelty to Animals (ASPCA), 182
Anderton, John, 111
Angelou, Maya, 176
Angie's List, 118
Animal Enterprise Terrorism Act (AETA), 166–167
Animation, for online activism, 171–172
Applications, 113–115
Armano, David, 202
Armstrong, Lance, 77
Ashoka, 158
Attribution (CC-BY) license, 119
Attribution No Derivatives (CC-BY-ND) license, 119
Attribution Noncommercial (CC-BY-NC) license, 119
Attribution Noncommercial No Derivatives (CC-By-NC-ND) license, 119
Attribution Noncommercial Share Alike (CC-BY-NC-SA) license, 119
Attribution Share Alike (CC-BY-SA) license, 119
Audiences
   of social media, 82–83
   types of, 177
Audio Sharing. *See* Podcasts
Audits
   brand, 27–32
   communication, 29–30, 30t
   public relations, 179
Austin Tweet Up Blood Drive, 98–99

Badges, 114
Banners advertising, 93, 135–136
Basecamp, 117
Bay Area Discovery Museum, 201
Beachy, Elizabeth, 80
Bebo, 101
Bedbury, Scot, 17
Bernoff, Josh, 77
Best of the Left Podcast, 68, 127
Bhagat, Vinay, 5
Biden, Joe, 172
Bit Torrent, 117
Blogger, 41
Blogging tools, 41
Blogs, 11, 56t. *See also* Microblogs
   about, 92–93
   costs for, 94
   measurement interaction for, 94
   objectives of, 94
   for online activism, 169
   organization policies for, 95
   for public relations, 183–185

217

tools for, 94, 122t
top, 184t
Blog search, tools for, 122t
Bookmarks, social, 117–118
   tools for, 122t
Boys and Girls Clubs of Newark, 5
Brand audits, 27–32
   communication, 29–30
   external, 30–32
   internal, 28–29
Brand awareness, 9
Brand development, levels of, 9
Brand identity, 18
Brand image, determining mission and, 16–17
Branding
   defined, 17–18
   nonprofit organizations and, 18–19
   Obama campaign as example of, 32–38, 36t
Brand insistence, 9
Brand preference, 9
Brands
   communicating, 24–27
   requirements for stong, 19–24
Breast Cancer Fund (BCF), 125–126
Brown, Danny, 98
Browser capability, 50–51
Burchell, Denise, 71–73

Callahan, Emily, 188–189
Call to action, Web sites and, 52
Campaign Edge, 113
Campaign Edge program, 114–115
Campaign promotions, fund-raising, 138–139
Campfire USA First Texas Council, 29
Capsules, 114
Catholic Charities, 20
Causes, Facebook, 103f, 104
Celebrity endorses, 140
Center for American Progress, 65
Centers for Disease Control (CDC), 111–112
Citro, Sue, 104
Cleff, Steve, 209–210
Clinton, Bill, 42
Clinton, Hillary, 32
Clutter, Web sites and, 54
Collaboration, online activism and, 166–168
Color, use of, on Web sites, 54
Communication pathways, 3–4
Communication plans, types of media for, 81
Communications audits, 29–30
   elements of, 30t
Community-building, 66–67

Community in Schools (CIS), 24
Community in Schools (CIS) Dallas, 24
Community relations, 186–187
Community Storehouse, 180
Concentric circles recruitment, 151–152
Consumer-generated content (CGC), 56
Contact information
   staff, 64
   on Web sites, 52
Content section, of Web Site Assessment Tool, 55–56, 56t
Content strategy
   defined, 87
   making successful, 87–89
Contextual advertising, 136
Contrast, defined, 54
Conversation Prism, 85
Corcoran, Sean, 81
Cravens, Jayne, 1, 7
Creative Commons (CC), 118
Creative Commons (CC) License
   conditions of, 118–119
   types of, 119
Credibility, 187–188
Crisis communication, 185–186

Dean, Howard, 126, 164
   presidential campaign of, 5
Deitz, Peter, 114–116
Design, Web site. *See* Web sites
Diggs, David, 92
Digital engagement, 26–27, 27f
Digital insights, 196–197
   listening and, 197–203
Digital natives, 193
Digital storytelling, 24–26
Digital touchpoints, 26–27, 27f
Direct-marketing fund-raising, traditional, 6
Dollars for Darfur, 101–104, 102f
"Donate Now" buttons, on Web sites, 3, 52, 116, 131
Donations
   major, 128–129
   micro, 128
   online, 58–60
   security and, 60
DonorPerfect, 137
Do Something, 40–41
Double opt-in process, 59

Earned media, 81
E-books, 56t

80/20 rule, 45
E-mail, 3
  for fund-raising campaign promotions, 137–138
  for online fund-raising, 132
E-mail addresses, collecting, 57–58
E-mail campaigns, for online fund-raising, 132–134
E-mail newsletters, 56t
Energy Outreach Colorado (EOC), 62
E-newsletters, for online fund-raising, 139
Engagement, digital, 26–27, 27f
Epic Change, 25–26, 99
Episodic volunteering, 146
Ethics
  in online activism, 162–163
  of online fund-raising, 140–141
Evaluation, 11
  considerations for, 205t
  importance of, 191–192, 203–205
Every Human Has Rights, 115, 115f
Experiments
  digital media and, 208
  types of, 209t
External audiences, 177, 180
External brand audits, 30–32

Facebook, 78, 99–100, 101. *See also* Social media; Social networks
  best practices for nonprofits on, 101t
  Causes feature of, 104
  online activists in Egypt and, 170
  pages and groups in, 100t
Family volunteering, 146
Fan pages, Facebook, 100, 100t
Firstgiving, 134
First-time visitors, 43–45, 44f
Flakes, 114
Flanner, Jessica, 42
Flannery, Matt, 42
Flickr, 11, 79, 105. *See also* Photo sharing sites
Focal points, on Web sites, 54
Focus groups, 69
Forms, on Web sites, 52
$40 for 40 Years Fair Housing, 116, 116f
Fox, Michael J., 140
Fund-raising. *See* Online fund-raising; Online fund-raising campaign promotions; Viral fund-raising
Fund-raising events
  decentralized, 137
  online, 136–138
  peer-to-peer, 137–138

Gadgets, 114
Gallagher, Kris, 95
Gather, 101
GIFs, 54
Godin, Seth, 24
Google Ad Sense, 93
Google Alerts, 117
Google Analytics, 208
Google Docs, 117
Google Web Optimizer, 208
Go Red BetterU program, 15
Go Red for Women, 15, 15f
Go Red Heart CheckUp, 15, 16f
Grassroots activism, 163–165
Great Recession, impact of, on nonprofit organizations, 4–6
Greenpeace, 9, 20, 113
GreenSpeak.tv, 172
Groups, Facebook, 100, 100t
Grunig, James E., 167

Haiti earthquake, responses to, 91–92
Halvorson, Kristina, 87, 89
Harman, Wendy, 192, 198
Hartman, Jalali, 35
Hastags, 96
Haydon, John, 79
Heath, Chip, 25
Heath, Dan, 25
Henderson, Scott, 37
Hoffman, Donna, 22
Home page, of Web sites, 50
  must-haves for, 51f
Hon, Linda Childers, 167
Horvath, Mark, 166
Hughes, Chris, 36
Hunter, Ron, 176

Ice Rocket, 93
I Love Mountains campaign, 1–2, 7
Indexhibit, 41
Influencers, 79, 85, 188, 192
Instructions, Web sites and, 55
Intelligence gathering, 11
Interactivity section, of Web Site Assessment Tool, 56–57
Internal audiences, 177
Internal brand audits, 28–29
Interns, 147
Interruptive advertising, 135
InvisiblePeople.tv, 166, 172

Jolie, Angelina, 140
Joomla, 41
JPEGs, 54

Kanter, Beth, 80, 87, 89, 95, 116–117, 120, 121, 170, 197, 198
KaTREEna Plantometer, 115, 115f
Keep A Child Alive, 113
Keep Indianapolis Beautiful (KIB), 20–22
Keller, Kevin Lane, 17
Kerry, John, 126
Keywords, 197, 198
Kiva, 42
Komen for the Cure, 130, 188–189
Krug, Steve, 42, 69, 71

Lance Armstrong Foundation, 77–78
Li, Charlene, 77
LinkedIn, 78, 101
Links, on Web sites, 51
Listening
 defined, 197
 stakeholders and, 179
Listening systems, developing, 197–203
 tools for, 199–200t, 201–202
Livestrong, 77–78, 78f
Livingston, Geoff, 187
Loading times, Web sites and, 51–52
Lord, Meredith, 167
Lumina Foundation for Education, 201–202

Major donations, 128–129
Make-A-Wish Foundation, 129
Marlow, Cameron, 86
McCain, John, 32
McLachlan, Sarah, 140
Measurement. *See* Evaluation
Media, types of, 81
Media alerts, 166
Media kits, 181
Media relations, 180–185. *See also* Public relations
 news releases and, 181–183
Media rooms, 181
Meerman, David Scott, 184
Melloh, Todd, 175–176
Message development, for effective Web site use, 156–157, 157t
Metropolitan Museum of Art, 68–69
M4Girls, 23
Microblogs, 96–99. *See also* Blogs; Twitter
 for online activism, 169
 tools for, 122t
Micro-donations, 128
Millennials, 41–42

Miller, Kivi Leroux, 87
Miller Creative Edge, 113
Mission, determining, brand image and, 16
Mobile Active, 23
Mobile Giving Foundation, 112–113
Mobile technology, 112–113
Modest Needs, 22
Moli, 101
Monterey Bay Aquarium Seafood Guide, 113, 114f
Morawski, Terry, 186–187
Morrison, 187
MoveOn.org, 162
Multimedia elements, 56
Multimedia news releases, 181–182
 elements of, 183t
MySpace, 99, 101. *See also* Social networks
My Tree and Me, 20–21, 20f, 21f, 22f

National Public Radio (NPR), 110–111
Navigation, Web sites and, 51
Nelson, Jeffrey, 91
Network for Good, 116
Newsome, Vernon, 187
News releases
 elements of multimedia, 183t
 media relations and, 181–183
 video, 181–182
New York City Coalition Against Hunger, 19, 183
Nielsen, Jakob, 40
Nike brand, 18
Ning, 99, 101
Nonpersonal recruitment, 152
Nonprofit branding, 8–9
Nonprofit Commons, 112
Nonprofit organizations
 branding and, 18–19
 digital storytelling and, 24–26
 digital touchpoints and, 26–27
 functionality of Web sites of, 57–69
 impact of Great Recession on, 4–6
 impact of multiple communication channels of, 4
 importance of online marketing for, 2–3
 online tools and, 7–8
 public relations and, 176
 social media and, 79–80
 top ten brands, 18–19, 19t
 Web sites of, 7–8
Non-targeted recruitment, 151

Obama, Barack, 126, 164, 172
 campaign of, as example of branding, 32–38, 36t

Obama, Michelle, 19, 92
Ohonme, Emmanuel "Manny," 175–176
Ongoing volunteering, 146
Online activism, 11, 65–66
    collaboration and, 166–168
    developing relationships and, 153–160
    ethics in, 162–163
    growth of, 161
    integrated strategy for, 162
    tools for, 168–173
    vignette of, 160
    YouTube for, 171
Online advertising, 135–136
Online advocacy. *See* Online activism
Online auctions, 140
Online communities, 129–130
Online donations, 58–60
Online events, 136–138
Online focus groups, 194
Online fund-raising, 10
    advantages of, 126–127
    attracting new donors for, 130–131
    disadvantages of, 127–128
    e-mail campaigns for, 132–134
    major donations and, 128–129
    micro-donations and, 128
    monitoring organizations image and reputation and, 141–142
    online communities for, 129–130
    privacy and ethical issues of, 140–141
    reasons for increasing importance of, 6
    tips for writing e-mail messages for, 132
    tools for, 139–140
    traditional direct-marketing fund-raising *vs.*, 6
    vignette of, 125–126
Online fund-raising campaign promotions, 138–139
Online interviews, 194
Online micro-lending service, 42
Online nonprofit marketing, 1
    defined, 2
    importance of, 2–3
Online press releases, 166
Online press rooms, 64–65, 182
    best practices for, 184
Online public relations, 11
    vignette of, 175–176
Online purchases, 68–69
Online resource attraction pathways, 5
Online surveys, 194
Online tools, nonprofit community and, 7–8
Online volunteer recruitment, 10
Operation Smile, 23, 131
Organic searching, 197

Orkut, 101
Ortiz, Deborah, 145
Owned media, 81
Oxfam, 105–106, 105f, 106f

Paid media, 81
Palin, Sarah, 35, 172
Patrick, Jeff, 125
PayPal, 60
Peer-to-peer fund-raising, 137–138
Penn, Christopher, 5–6
People Against a Violent Environment (PAVE), 113
People for Puget Sound, 158
Personal recruitment, 152
Philabundance, 158
Photo sharing sites, 104–106. *See also* Flickr
    costs of, 105–106
    measuring, 105
    objectives of, 105
    tools for, 105, 122t
Planned giving, 60–61
Podcasts, 109–111
    costs of, 110
    developing, 110
    measuring, 110
    objectives of, 110
    in practice, 110–111
    tools for, 110, 122t
Posts, 92
Press releases, online, 166
Press rooms, online, 64–65
Privacy policies, 67–68
    online fund-raising and, 140–141
Productivity tools, 117–118
Profiles, Facebook, 100
Proximity, defined, 53
Public relations. *See also* Media relations; Stakeholders
    blogs for, 183–185
    relationships and, 176
    role of stakeholders and, 177–178
Public relations measurement, 121
Public relations (PR) audits, 179
Purchases, online, 68–69

Raghavan, Ramyan, 106, 107
Rainforest Action Network, 182
Rattray, Ben, 44
Really Simple Syndication (RSS) feeds, 52–53
Really Simple Syndication (RSS) readers, 52–53
Recruitment
    concentric circles, 151–152
    improving Web sites for, 153–155

nonpersonal, 152
non-targeted, 151
personal, 152
targeted, 151
Recruitment, volunteer, 66
RED campaign, 24
Red Cross. *See* American Red Cross
Regular visitors, 43–45, 44f
Repetition, defined, 54
Research, 11
  importance of, 191–192
  process of, 193–196
  purpose of, 193
Research reports, 56t
Retention, volunteer, 66–67
Return on insight (ROI), 202–203
Retweets, 96
Review sites, 117–118
Rigotti, Dave, 100
Room to Read, 24
RSS reader, 201

Samaritan House, 180
Samaritan's Feet, 175–176
Sanchez, Mike, 41
Scanability, Web sites and, 54
Schar, Molly, 127
Screen recording software, 70
Search behavior, 196–197
Search capability, Web sites and, 52
Second Life (SL), 111–112. *See also* Virtual worlds
Security, online donations and, 60
"Send to a friend" option, 61
Shah, Premal, 42
Shared Adventures, 63
Shue, Andrew, 40–41
Slideshare, 94
Smartphone technology, 112–113
SMART (specific, measurable, action-oriented, realistic, and time-based) objectives, 81–82, 204
Smile Train, 130
The Smile Train, 62
Smithsonian Museum, 201
Snippets, 114
Social bookmarks, 118
  tools for, 122t
Social media, 10. *See also* Facebook; Flickr; Social networking; Twitter; YouTube
  audiences of, 82–83
  content strategy and, 87–89
  defined, 78–80

  internal buy in for, 83–85
  low-risk experiment for successful strategy of, 85
  measurement of, 86–87, 119–121
  metrics, 207t
  nonprofit organizations and, 79–80
  objectives of, 81–82
  for online activism, 171
  planning for, 80–81
  strategy for, 80
  tools for, 85–86
  training for, 84–85
  use of, by Obama campaign, 33–35
  vignette of, 77–78, 91–92
Social Media Club, 98
Social-media monitoring, 121, 196–197
Social-media releases (SMRs), 182
Social network analysis, 86
Social networking
  defined, 10
  for online activism, 169–171
Social networks, 99–104. *See also* Facebook; MySpace
  costs of, 101
  measuring, 101
  objectives of, 101
  for online activism, 169–171
  in practice, 101–102
  tools for, 101, 122t
Social web design, 42
Society for the Prevention of Cruelty to animals (SPCA), 140
Solis, Brian, 85, 175, 182
Special events, 63
Staff contact information, 64
Stakeholders. *See also* Public relations
  determining important, 179
  determining issues of concern of, 180
  developing insights of, 178–179
  organization's reputation with, 180
  power of, 180
  role of, public relations and, 177–178, 178f
Stand Now, 102f, 104
Stewardship information, 61–63
Storytelling, digital, 24–26
  tips, 25t
Student volunteers, 146
Survey reports, 56t

Targeted recruitment, 151
Team in Training (Leukemia and Lymphoma), 130, 134

Technorati authority, 93, 192
Telemarketing, 3
Testimonials, on Web sites, 158
Text messaging, for online activism, 172–173
Thomas, Scott, 33
360 degree review, 30
TicketOps, 63
Tollett, John, 53
Tools
  for blogs, 41, 94, 122t
  for developing listening systems, 199–200t, 201–202
  for microblogs, 122t
  online, for nonprofit organizations, 7–8
  for online activism, 168–173
  for online fund-raising, 139–140
  for photo sharing sites, 105, 122t
  for podcasts, 110, 122t
  productivity, 117–118
  for social bookmarks, 122t
  for social media, 85–86
  for social networks, 101, 122t
  for Twitter, 97t, 98
  for video creation and sharing, 108, 122t
  Web Site Assessment Tool, 48–50f, 48–57
  for wikis, 122t
Touchpoints, digital, 26–27, 27f
Training, for social media, 84–85
Tweeting, 96
Tweets, 96
Tweetsgiving, 99
12for12K, 98
Twestival, 98
Twitter, 11, 78, 96–99
  costs of, 98
  measuring popularity for, 98
  objectives, 98
  in practice, 98–99
  tools for, 97t, 98
Typography, on Web sites, 54

Unaware public, 43, 44f
UNICEF, 113
Uniform resource locator (URL), selecting, 69
The United Way, 65
United Way of King County, 67
United Way of Tarrant County, 186
Usability section, of Web Site Assessment Tool, 48–49f, 50–52
Usability tests, 69–71
  for Web sites, 41–42

Vendantam, Shankar, 158
Video creation and sharing, 106–109. *See also* YouTube
  costs of, 109
  measurement and, 109
  objectives of, 108
  for online activism, 171–172
  tools for, 108, 122t
Video news releases, 181–182
Viral fund-raising, 134–135
Viral marketing, 94
Viral videos, making, 109
Virtual volunteering, 147
Virtual worlds, 111–112
Visitor engagement cycle, 43–45, 44f
Visitors, types of, 43–45
Visual design, Web sites and, 41–42
Visual design section, of Web Site Assessment Tool, 53–55
Volunteer matching sites, 152
Volunteer position descriptions, 153, 154t
Volunteer programs, developing, 148
Volunteer recruitment, 66
  vignette of, 145–146
Volunteer retention, 66–67
Volunteer roles, 147–148
Volunteers/volunteering
  attitudes and, 150
  benefits of, 150–151
  diversity and, 157
  facilitation, 150
  importance of, 146
  improving Web sites for, 153–155
  increasing diversity among, 157
  motivations for, 149–150
  recruitment tactics, 151–152
  tips for effective Web use for recruiting, 155–157
  types of, 146–147
Volunteers with disabilities, 147

Waters, Richard, 167
Watson, Tom, 44
We Are Media, 85, 94
Web 2.0, 10, 42. *See also* Social media
Webinars, 56t
Web of Trust (WOT), 60
Web queries, responding to, 155
Web Site Analysis Worksheet, 73–74
Web Site Assessment Tool, 27, 48–50f, 48–57
  content section of, 49–50f
  interactivity section of, 50f

224 Index

usability section of, 48–49f, 50–52
visual design section of, 49f
Web sites
  attracting people to, 205–206
  design and functionality of, 9–10
  designing, 41–43
  functionality of nonprofit organization, 57–69
  fundamental questions for, 45–46
  importance of design, 41–43
  improving, for recruiting volunteers, 153–155
  nonprofit, functionality of, 57–69
  nonprofit organizations and, 7–8
  planning, 46–48
  selecting addresses of, 69
  tips for effective use of, 155–158
  usability review of, 41–42
  visitor engagement design and, 43–45
  visual design and, 41–43
Web video, 139

Westen, Drew, 23
WhenToHelp, 67
White papers, 56t
Widgets, 114–117, 116f
Wikis, 56t, 92–94
  tools for, 122t
Williams, Robin, 53
Wood, Andrea, 132
Wood, John, 24
Wooley, Dan, 113
Word Press, 41
Wrench, Charlie, 14

Yazd Forum Software, 67
YMCA of the USA, 18–19
Young, Kim, 88
YouTube, 11, 78–79, 80, 106–108. *See also* Video creation and sharing
  for online activism, 171
YouTube Nonprofit Program, 107